C000147967

# Chinese Investment in Australia

# Chinese Investment in Australia

## Unique Insights from the Mining Industry

Xueli Huang

and

Ian Austin

© Xueli Huang and Ian Austin 2011
Foreword © Peter Drysdale 2011

All rights reserved. No reproduction, copy or transmission of this
publication may be made without written permission.

No portion of this publication may be reproduced, copied or transmitted
save with written permission or in accordance with the provisions of the
Copyright, Designs and Patents Act 1988, or under the terms of any licence
permitting limited copying issued by the Copyright Licensing Agency,
Saffron House, 6-10 Kirby Street, London EC1N 8TS.

Any person who does any unauthorized act in relation to this publication
may be liable to criminal prosecution and civil claims for damages.

The authors have asserted their rights to be identified
as the authors of this work in accordance with the Copyright,
Designs and Patents Act 1988.

First published 2011 by
PALGRAVE MACMILLAN

Palgrave Macmillan in the UK is an imprint of Macmillan Publishers Limited,
registered in England, company number 785998, of Houndmills, Basingstoke,
Hampshire RG21 6XS.

Palgrave Macmillan in the US is a division of St Martin's Press LLC,
175 Fifth Avenue, New York, NY 10010.

Palgrave Macmillan is the global academic imprint of the above companies
and has companies and representatives throughout the world.

Palgrave® and Macmillan® are registered trademarks in the United States,
the United Kingdom, Europe and other countries.

ISBN 978–0–230–29849–1 hardback

This book is printed on paper suitable for recycling and made from fully
managed and sustained forest sources. Logging, pulping and manufacturing
processes are expected to conform to the environmental regulations of the
country of origin.

A catalogue record for this book is available from the British Library.

Library of Congress Cataloging-in-Publication Data
Huang, Xueli.
   Chinese investment in Australia : unique insights
   from the mining industry / Xueli Huang and Ian Austin.
      p.   cm.
   Includes index.
   ISBN 978–0–230–29849–1 (hardback)
   1. Mineral industries—Australia.   2. Investments, Chinese—Australia.
   I. Austin, Ian.   II. Title.
   HD9506.A72H83 2011
   332.67′351094—dc22                                          2011011827

10   9   8   7   6   5   4   3   2   1
20   19   18   17   16   15   14   13   12   11

Printed and bound in Great Britain by
CPI Antony Rowe, Chippenham and Eastbourne

# Contents

# List of Tables

# List of Figures

# Foreword

The growth of Chinese outward direct investment (ODI) is a relatively recent and somewhat controversial phenomenon. So recently has it become important that, not unexpectedly, there are very few studies that provide reasoned analysis of the context in which Chinese ODI had grown so rapidly, what the pattern of investment has been, what the response has been in countries that have hosted it and what the effect of investment has been – economically, politically and socially – in those countries.

This book helps to redress that deficiency.

In 2009, China's ODI was running at US$48 billion, and ranked sixth, behind only the United States, the United Kingdom, France, Japan and Germany, with more than 5 per cent of global foreign direct investment (FDI) in that year. By the end of 2009, the stock of Chinese ODI in Australian amounted to almost A$6 billion, a 70 per cent increase on 2008. Between 2007 and 2009, the Australian government had given approval to 110 projects and around A$39 billion worth of Chinese investment, largely in the mining sector.

As China has opened up to engagement in the global market economy, Australia, it turns out, has been an important destination for Chinese outward foreign direct investment (OFDI). In the 1980s, when the first large-scale Chinese investments were undertaken abroad, in Rio's Channar iron ore mine in Western Australia (WA) and in the Portland aluminium smelter in Victoria, Australia was the largest destination for Chinese investment abroad. With the remarkable growth and industrialisation of China over the subsequent 30 years, the focus on resource procurement as Chinese demand for raw materials drove international commodity prices spirally upwards, and the recent policy of "going out" (or encouraging investment abroad) by large, Chinese state-owned enterprises, which was adopted by the Chinese authorities, Australia has again become a major centre for Chinese OFDI activity, mainly but not only in the minerals and energy sector. Indeed, tax-haven investments excluded, Australia can properly be regarded as China's largest overseas investment destination once again.

The experience of Chinese ODI in Australia, therefore, is of major interest both because of what it reveals about China as a major new player in international direct foreign investment and because of what it reveals about the policy, business and public response to Chinese investment in a major developed-country recipient of FDI.

Australia has perhaps the most efficient mining sector in the world. This is, importantly, due to its openness to foreign investor competition and participation, because that brings with it, and fosters, the technology, management know-how and market links that are essential ingredients in the development of a world class, internationally competitive industry. Australia has a long record of global competitiveness, and a strong policy regime, characterised by openness towards foreign investment in its resource industries. Yet Australia's foreign investment policies and foreign investment review process (through the Foreign Investment Review Board (FIRB)) – put in place to cushion the political impact as well as to capture the economic benefits of FDI – was buffeted by the surge of Chinese FDI and created some initial uncertainty about how the regime would deal with it.

The rise of Chinese investment in Australia, of course, caught many by surprise. This alone does not explain the elevation of policy and public interest in Chinese investment in the Australian mining sector or the discomfort of various Australian governments in dealing with the issue. The nature of Chinese ODI, dominantly from state-owned enterprise, the inexperience of Chinese investors in investing abroad and dealing in unfamiliar policy and political settings and a series of particular events and circumstances in the early stages of investment in Australia also contributed, all of which are reviewed in some detail in this book.

Xueli Huang and Ian Austin have done a splendid job in assembling information about Chinese ODI experience thus far in the Australian mining sector. The volume provides an excellent compendium of Chinese investments in the sector, the experience of Chinese investors in the sector and how investment has been managed by the Australian policy authorities. It is an essential handbook on the subject for those in business, those concerned with policy-making and for the interested public.

The book is not only an invaluable primer on Chinese ODI in the Australian mining sector. It also offers useful comment on the challenges that Chinese investors face in operating abroad, with illustration from the important Australian case. The context is one of the rapid growth and evolution of Chinese corporations, as state-owned enterprise finds its way in the global marketplace. A key issue is the practice and expectations of corporate governance in mature market economies such as Australia. Chinese firms lack experience in corporate governance as the concept of corporate governance in China is relatively new. Many Chinese companies are not familiar with standard corporate governance practice. Huge differences exist between the corporate governance system in China and that in countries like Australia. Although China has been gradually developing its market-based corporate governance system (the European or Japanese "insider" system of corporate governance with concentrated shareholders rather than the Anglo-Saxon system), it finds it a challenge to comply with the Australian system. The Australian government puts much (appropriate) emphasis on corporate governance of foreign investors. The authors provide anecdotal evidence that success in investment in Australia may be dependent, importantly, on whether Chinese investors can absorb local management know-how and practices and, through endogenizing learning about all aspects of corporate behaviour in that way, establish a foundation for both profitable and welcome business abroad.

The book also touches upon the huge learning process of government in managing the surge of Chinese investment abroad: for the Australian government in managing Chinese investment and the questions it raises, in the case of state-owned enterprise, about the relationship between the state and economic enterprise; and for the Chinese government and its strategies for encouraging and approving investment abroad. Here there is much research to be done, not only on the dynamic of national policy development and political economy, but also on the interaction between the two governments and between the Chinese government and its growing international enterprise abroad.

This book will whet the readers' appetite for continuing updates on developments in the Australian mining sector and very much more.

Peter Drysdale
The Australian National University
Canberra
January 2011

# Acknowledgements

This book would not have been completed without the contribution of many executives working in either Australian or Chinese firms, policy-makers from both Australian and Chinese governments and those in academia who shared the authors' view that this was a study of worth. For various reasons we do not name them here, but the authors are indebted to them. We hope they find the finished manuscript of value. We sincerely thank the generous financial support from Edith Cowan University for conducting this research project, and our research assistant Thang Cao Pham for many hours of research and review. We would also like to thank the professional staff of Palgrave Macmillan for their efforts throughout the process of bringing this book to fruition.

# 1
# Introduction

China's economy has been growing rapidly over the past three decades. Since it implemented its "open-door and economic reform" policy in 1979, its gross domestic product (GDP) has increased rapidly from $175.6 billion in 1979 to 4.91 trillion in 2009 (National Bureau of Statistics of China, 2010), which trailed only the US ($14.256 trillion) and Japan ($5.07 trillion) in the world (International Monetary Fund, 2010). China's average GDP growth rate over the past three decades is about 9.5 per cent. It is expected that the Chinese economy will grow by 9.5 per cent in 2010 based on the forecast by the World Bank in June 2010 (The World Bank, 2010) and will, for first time, become the world's second largest economy, surpassing Japan.

The rapid economic growth in China over the past three decades has been propelled by three drivers: domestic consumption, investment and export. With the rapid economic development, the GDP per capita has been increased to $3677 by 2009 (International Monetary Fund, 2010). Although this was just about 8 per cent of Australia's GDP ($45,586), China has become the largest market – owing to its huge population of 1.3 billion – for many products, including luxury goods. For example, new car sales in China reached more than 13 million in 2009, which exceeded those sold in the US in the same period. In fact, the average growth rate of China's domestic consumption was 13 per cent between 2000 and 2009, reaching $1.838 trillion in 2009 (National Bureau of Statistics of China, 2010).

China's urbanisation and industrialisation over the past three decades have driven its investment. Over the past decade, China's urbanisation rate has increased from 35.8 per cent in 2000 to 46.1 per cent in 2009 (United Nations, 2010), which means that more than 10 million people moved from the rural areas to the cities every year. This trend is expected to continue in the next decade as China's urbanisation rate in 2009 was lower than those in many developing countries, not to mention those in developed countries, such as Europe (80%) and Japan (67%) (Liu & McDonald, 2010). Such a huge number of migrants from rural to urban areas has substantially increased Chinese demand for infrastructure such as housing, transportation and electricity. The United Nation predicts China's urbanisation rate will reach 55 per cent by 2020 and 73.2 per cent by 2050 (United Nations, 2010).

Many foreign multinational corporations (MNCs) have considered China to be their key market, so are investing heavily. FDI inflow into China has increased from \$57 million in 1980 to \$95 billion in 2009, a 1500-fold increase over the three decades (UNCTAD, 2010a). China is therefore one of the largest destinations for FDI in the world.

China is also one of the largest export countries owing to its strong manufacturing sector, surpassing Germany for the first time in 2009 to become the world largest export country (Department of Foreign Affairs and Trade, 2010). The Chinese manufacturing industry accounted for 46.8 per cent of its national GDP in 2009 (National Bureau of Statistics of China, 2010). This, coupled with its cheap labour, has been the driving force for its exports, which have been growing at double-digit figures since 2002, with the exception of 2009 when the world economy was hit by the global financial crisis. Many Chinese manufacturing firms now compete with their foreign counterparts in both Chinese and global markets.

China has increasingly been committed to integrating its national economy into the world. China gained access to the World Trade Organisation (WTO) in November 2001, and was consequently obliged to open more of its industries and markets to the world. At the same time, WTO membership provides many opportunities for Chinese firms to integrate their business activities into the global economy.

At the organisational level, the "open door and economic reform" policies implemented since 1979 have changed not only China's national economic structure, but also various enterprises' ownership. As China's planned economy has been gradually transformed into a market-oriented economy, the ownership structure of Chinese firms has been changed. With the privatisation of state-owned enterprises (SOEs) and the deregulation of many domestic industries, an overwhelming majority of Chinese firms are now privately owned. By the end of 2008, the number of private firms was over 3.5 million, increasing from 1.98 million at the end of 2004 and accounting for 72.5 per cent of the total number of enterprises in China. At the same time, SOEs decreased from 179,000 to 143,000, only accounting for 2.88 per cent of firms (National Bureau of Statistics of China, 2009). However, these SOEs, although less than 3 per cent of firms, held 23 per cent of the total assets of all enterprises in China, while the private firms only held 12.7 per cent.

Chinese firms, both state-owned and privately owned enterprises, have improved their competitiveness over the past three decades as they have acquired and developed a huge amount of modern technology, learnt a large range of new managerial competences, gained a deeper understanding of international financial markets and mastered a great deal of knowledge and experience in competing in markets (Nolan, 2002). Moreover, they have accumulated many financial resources and gained a great deal of experience in competing with foreign firms, particularly in their domestic markets. However, they still face a critical challenge in global business as there are still big gaps in competitiveness between the Chinese firms and the world's leading firms.

China's emergence as an important source of investment is a new phenomenon, as underpinned by rapid development in the national economy, significant improvement of competitiveness of its domestic firms and a huge accumulation of foreign currency reserves ($2.45 trillion by the end of June 2010) (Zhang, 2010). In 2009, China's ODI reached $56.5 billion (Ministry of Commerce, 2010), and was ranked fifth in the world. It only trailed the US ($248 billion), France ($147 billion), Japan ($75 billion) and Germany ($63 billion), and accounted for over 5 per cent of the global ODI in that year (UNCTAD, 2010b). This is a significant achievement for China, considering its relatively short history of ODI, which started first in 1979 with a three-stage process: introduction and experiment between 1979 and 1997; development and fluctuation from 1997 to 2002; and rapid growth since 2002 (Huang, Austin, Zhang, & Grainger, 2009). China's ODI has touched many industries including car manufacturing, services and minerals and energy, and many countries (Ministry of Commerce, 2010).

Australia has become one of the largest destinations for Chinese ODI (Ministry of Commerce, 2010) because of its abundance of natural resources, geographical proximity to China, favourable economic environment and stable political institutions. On the one hand, China's rapid economic development, underpinned by its urbanisation, export and investment, has substantially increased its demand for natural resources. For example, China produced 567.8 million tonnes of steel in 2009, accounting for 46.5 per cent of the world's production (World Steel Association, 2010). But, on the other hand, China is relatively low in natural resources, for example, it has only 8.3, 6.6 and 5.4 per cent of the world's iron ore, cooper and nickel resources, respectively (US Geological Survey, 2004). By the end of 2009, Chinese ODI stock in Australia amounted to $5.863 billion, representing a 70 per cent increase from 2008 (Ministry of Commerce, 2010). In total, 85.9 per cent of these investments in 2009 were in the mining industries. The following section briefly examines FDI in Australia and its natural resources sector.

## Australia and its minerals industry

Australia is one of the most favoured countries in the world for FDI in the natural resources sector. FDI has been a driving force for the Australian economy. Since the mid-1800s, foreign companies from different countries have invested in Australia (Meredith & Dyster, 1999). The areas for foreign investment have also changed, corresponding with the development of the Australian economy and its industry deregulations. Early investors were the British who invested heavily in the pastoral and mining industries. After World War II (post-1945), Americans contributed much of the investment in the Australian manufacturing industries and resources sectors. Japanese firms started investing in Australia in the 1960s – mainly in the Australian mining industry – to secure commodity supplies for its industrialisation after the Australian government lifted its iron ore embargo on Japan in 1961. The 1980s to 1990s have witnessed many American and British multinational corporations (MNCs) acquire Australian companies in the services industry, partly due to the deregulation pursued by the Australian government in services industries, such as banking and financial services, and the floatation of the Australian currency in 1983.

Specifically, FDI has played a significant role in the development of the Australian *mineral* industry. This can be traced back to the 1880s when the British invested in the mining industries, and could be regarded as the first wave of FDI in the Australian minerals industry. The second wave of FDI was driven largely by Japanese in the 1960s to 1970s. The recent wave of Chinese investment in the Australian mining industries is the third wave in this regard. In fact, since 2005, all of Australia's export growth has been delivered by its resources sector, which has been driven by FDI. Moreover, major mining companies operating in Australia now are mainly owned by non-Australians, such as

BHP Billiton (BHPB) (76% owned by foreigners), Rio Tinto (84%), Anglo America (100%) and Xstrata (100%).

Besides its favourable investment environment, Australia has an abundance of minerals resources with world-class deposits. Australia's economic demonstrated resources (EDR) that were ranked the world's largest in 2008 included brown coal, mineral sands (rutile and zircon), nickel, silver, uranium, zinc and lead; and in the top six of the world for antimony, bauxite, black coal, copper, gold, industrial diamond, iron ore, ilmenite, lithium, manganese ore, niobium, tantalum and vanadium (Geoscience Australia, 2009). The resources and world ranking of some of Australia's EDR are listed in Table 1.1. In terms of export, Australia is the largest exporter of iron ore, black coal and gold (Geoscience Australia, 2009). For example, Australia exported 262 million tonnes of coal in 2009, accounting for 31.3 per cent of the world's coal exports (International Energy Agency, 2010).

The table shows that key Australian minerals are distributed widely across the country. However, some minerals are concentrated in particular states; for example, New South Wales (NSW) and Queensland are dominant in black coal deposits, South Australia in copper and uranium, and WA in iron ore, gold, diamond, zircon and nickel.

WA is the most important state in Australia in terms of minerals and energy production. Its output of minerals and energy in the 2009–10 Australian financial year was A$70,906 million, accounting for 48 per cent of the national output (Department of Mines and Petroleum WA, 2010a). More specifically, its share of national minerals (excluding coal), energy (including coal) and petroleum in 2009–10 in terms of value were 63, 33 and 64 per cent, respectively. The resources sector accounted for about one quarter (24%) of the state's GDP in 2009 (Australian Bureau of Statistics [ABS], 2009a). With a territory of 2.5 million square kilometres, WA is very rich in natural resources, and has been leading the nation in the production of a number of minerals; for example, a total of 97 per cent of the iron ore produced in Australia is from WA. The production of a number of selected minerals in WA in relation to the world production in 2008 is depicted in Figure 1.1.

## The trade relations between Australia and China

The recent rise of China's importance to Australia as a buyer of exports and a supplier of imports can be seen from the changes to its share of Australia's trade composition. China's share of Australia's merchandise

*Table 1.1* The EDR for some of Australia's minerals and their world ranking

| Minerals | EDR (Mt) | % of the world EDR | World ranking | Major location |
|---|---|---|---|---|
| Bauxite | 6.2k | 23 | 2 | Vast resources of bauxite in Queensland (QLD) in western Cape York, and in WA in the Darling Range |
| Black coal | 39.2k | 6 | 6 | The Sydney Basin in New South Wales (NSW) contains 35%; the Bowen Basin in QLD contains 34% |
| Brown coal | 37.2k | 25 | 1 | All of Australia's brown coal EDR is in Victoria (Vic) |
| Copper | 77.8 | 12.9 | 2 | The Olympic Dam deposit in South Australia (SA). 73% in South Australia |
| Gold | 0.006255 | 12.9 | 2 | All states, but WA has 47% of the national total EDR |
| Iron ore | 24kt | 15 | 3 | WA has 98% of Australia's EDR with about 86% occurring in the Pilbara district |
| Manganese | 181 | 13 | 4 | The Groote Eylandt deposit in the Northern Territory (NT) had 70% of the total manganese ore EDR |
| Nickel | 26.4 | 37.7 | 1 | WA holds 90.4% of the national total EDR |
| Uranium | 1.163 | 38.2 | 1 | The Olympic Dam deposit in SA and increased resources at the Ranger 3 Deeps ore zone in the NT |
| Zinc | 53.1 | 27.5 | 1 | The Dugald River deposit in QLD; McArthur River in the NT |
| Lead | 26.8 | 32.7 | 1 | The McArthur River mine (NT 32%), |
| Silver | 0.0614 | 20.3 | 1 | QLD (64%), SA (16%) |
| Tantalum | 0.051 | 39.2 | 2 | The overwhelming majority of resources are in WA |

*Note*: EDR – economic demonstrated resources.

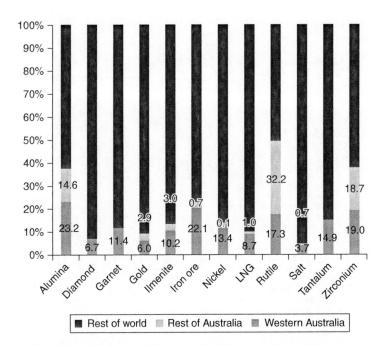

*Figure 1.1* Selected WA commodities related to the world production in 2009
*Source*: Department of Mines and Petroleum WA, 2010c.

trade over the past two decades is depicted in Figure 1.2. It shows that the total value of Australian trade with Chinese partners has increased 8 times, specifically 7.5 times in imports and 8.4 times in exports. Trade between the two countries grew steadily between 1989 and 1997, although it dipped slightly in 1997 and 1998 due to a variety of impacts from the financial crisis in Asia during that time. The overall trend then picked up with an even steeper growth rate. These trends clearly reflect China's rapid economic growth, thereby substantially increasing the importance of China as a trading partner throughout the world.

Although Japan remains Australia's most important export destination with values rising from A$13.7 billion in 1988–89 to A$55.5 billion in 2008–09 (ABS, 2009b), China has been Australia's largest trading partner since 2002. In 2008–09, the two-way trade between China and Australia reached A$76.4 billion with Australia's exports to China and imports from China being A$39.3 billion and A$37.05 billion, respectively (ABS, 2009b). China has also, for the first time in 2008–09, become Australia's largest importer.

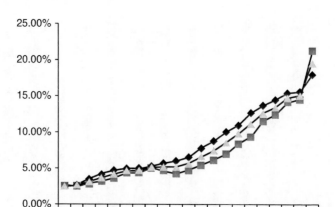

*Figure 1.2*   China's share of Australia's merchandise trade
*Source*: ABS, 2009b.

Historically, China has imported agricultural and pastoral products from Australia, including wool, wheat and dairy products. Mineral products, such as iron ore, emerged on China's import list in the early 1980s. Over the past several years, minerals have dominated China's imports from Australia, while the main products exported from China to Australia are garments, telecommunications equipment and parts, and computers. Table 1.2 shows the major trade items between Australia and China in the 2008–09 Australian financial year.

Table 1.2 also shows that Australia's exports to China are mainly minerals and agricultural products, while China's exports to Australia are primarily manufacturing goods. Iron ore exports from Australia to China accounted for more than a half of Australia's total exports to China in terms of value.

Trade relations between Australia and China have been largely driven by their complementarities and close geographical distance. Australia and China complement each other in many ways; for example, from a population and territory perspective, Australia has a territory of 7.6 million square kilometres with a population of 23 million, while China has a population of 1.3 billion and 9.6 million square kilometres of territory. Thus, Australia is a much bigger territory per capita (44.7 times) than China. China is rich in human resources, while Australia is

*Table 1.2*  Australian major trade items with China in 2008–09

| Major Australian exports 2008–09 | (A$ million) | Major Australian imports 2008–09 | (A$ million) |
|---|---|---|---|
| *Merchandises (total)* | *39,310* | | *37,046* |
| Iron ore & concentrates | 22,115 | Clothing | 4,281 |
| Coal | 3,157 | Telecom equipment & parts | 3,120 |
| Wool & other animal hair | 1,383 | Computers | 2,798 |
| Other ores & concentrates | 1,280 | Prams, toys & sporting goods | 2,197 |
| Copper ores & concentrates | 1,087 | Furniture, mattresses & cushions | 1,621 |
| Copper | 745 | Monitors, projectors & TVs | 1,329 |
| Machinery & transport equipment | 611 | Chemical & related products | 1,194 |

*Source*: Department of Foreign Affairs and Trade, 2009; Klinger, 2009.

abundant in natural resources both on a per capita basis and in absolute terms.

Additionally, Australia and China complement each other in industrial structure with China being very strong in its manufacturing industries. The complementarity in industry structure can be seen broadly from a perspective of industry's composition of national GDP. The manufacturing industries accounted for 46.8 per cent of China's GDP in 2009, but only for 9.4 per cent of Australia's. Although primary industries in China and Australia contributed 10.6 and 10.2 per cent to the national economy, respectively, about 70 per cent value of the Australian primary industry is from its resources sector. Hence, Australia's endowment with natural resources complements the fast-growing Chinese manufacturing industries. Such a complementarity is fundamental to the bilateral trade relationship between China and Australia as reflected in their major trade items (see Table 1.2).

The dominance of commodity exports from Australia to China is also underpinned by their geographical proximity. They are proximate partners relative to the other major minerals and resources export countries, such as Brazil, Canada and South Africa. Such geographical proximity creates economic value, particularly in the areas of commodity trading, as a close distance can substantially reduce transportation costs. For example, Australia's gains from its geographic proximity to

China can clearly be seen in the iron ore market. Brazil must sell iron ore at a reduced price into the China market to compensate for the higher transportations costs that the buyer must bear. In fact, Brazil is currently examining the feasibility of developing a new range of iron ore mega-ships to overcome this transportation-cost impediment.

## Chinese investment in the Australian mining industries

The significant increase in trade has lead to the growth of investment. Although Chinese firms have invested in 174 countries or regions, Australia is one of the top destinations for Chinese investment. By 2009, Chinese ODI stock in Australia amounted to $5.86 billion, ranking Australia fourth in terms of Chinese ODI stock, trailing only Hong Kong ($164.5 billion), the Virgin Islands ($15.1 billion) and the Cayman Islands ($13.6 billion) (Ministry of Commerce, 2010). In fact, Australia can be regarded as the largest foreign country for Chinese ODI, as Hong Kong is part of China, and the Cayman Islands and the Virgin Islands are tax havens that mainly attract FDI for tax reduction purposes.

Chinese ODI in Australia has touched many areas, including agriculture, finance and insurance, manufacturing, services, mineral exploration and development and resource processing (Foreign Investment Review Board (FIRB), 2010a). For example, Geely Automobile acquired Drivetrain Systems International (DSI) in 2008. However, the majority of Chinese investment has concentrated on minerals exploration and development (FIRB, 2009, 2010a). In 2009, 85.9 per cent of the Chinese ODI was in the mineral industry (Ministry of Commerce, 2010). Chinese firms only started investing in the Australian minerals industry from the mid-1980s when China's Metallurgical Import and Export Corporation (CMIEC, now Sinosteel) formed a joint venture (JV) with Rio Tinto – the Channar Project, which was established to supply 200 million tonnes of iron ore to China. However, most of the Chinese investment has been made in recent years. As an example, from November 2007 when the Australian Labor government came to office to November 2009, more than 110 Chinese investment proposals worth A$39 billion were approved. Chinese investment in the Australian mineral industry has been broadened from iron ore and coal, to base metals (such as copper, nickel and zinc), uranium and gold. These include CITIC Pacific's investment of $5.2 billion in WA for magnetite mining and processing, Yan Coal's $3.3 billion invested in NSW for coal, Minmetal's investment of $1.3 billion in base metals and Ansteel's $1.7 billion and Sinosteel's $1.2 billion in iron ore.

Despite the recent rapid increase of the Chinese investment in Australia, the total stock of Chinese investment in Australia is still relatively small compared with that of the US, UK, Japan and Singapore. Chinese ODI in Australia only accounted for 1.79 per cent of Australia's total FDI stock by the end of 2009 (Ministry of Commerce, 2010; UNCTAD, 2010a). This is very small compared with the China's share of Australia trade, which was about 20 per cent (see Figure 1.2) in 2009.

Chinese ODI, which has been growing very rapidly since 2003, is a relatively new phenomenon to Chinese firms and Australian politicians, businesses and public communities. Therefore, there are many challenges for the firms that have invested, or are considering investing in the Australian minerals industries. These challenges may come from two broad areas: (1) lack of internal resources, skills and knowledge concerning international investment and management, and (2) understanding the Australian regulatory framework on FDI, and the political system and public perceptions driving much of the government FDI policies and approval processes. In addition, Chinese firms need to learn how to govern and manage their investments in Australia, and what pitfalls they may encounter in making and managing their investments. Making investments in foreign countries, like Australia, is only the first step to "go abroad" (*zouchuqu*). How to manage these investments so as to achieve the organisation's long-term objectives, such as return on investment and the development of sustainable competitive advantage, is probably one of the biggest challenges facing many Chinese investors. Such after-investment challenges may include financing the project, getting state government approval, developing the project and managing its production and operation.

Understanding the Australian investment environment is also a challenge to many Chinese firms. Chinese firms have made substantial progress in understanding the nuances of investing in the Australian mineral industries, even though the pathway of China's investment in the Australian mineral industry has not always been smooth. For example, Rio Tinto terminated a deal worth of $19.5 billion proposed by the Aluminium Corporation of China (CHINALCO) on 5 June 2009. Australia's FIRB denied acquisition of the Prominent Hill copper and gold mine by Minmetals for "security reasons" as the mine was close to Woomera, a weapon-testing site of the Australian defence forces. China's Non-ferrous Metal Corporation (CNMC) withdrew its application for acquiring Lynas, a rare metals miner, as it was not allowed by FIRB to have a majority stake in Lynas due to a competition concern.

The recent rapid growth in ODI by Chinese firms has also brought challenges to Chinese policy makers. The Chinese government is committed to integrating its domestic economy into the world. It is widely recognised that Chinese governments play a significant role in directing, encouraging and facilitating its domestic firms to "go abroad". What policies and approaches should Chinese governments adopt for facilitating this role? Whatever is decided, it needs to be built on a good understanding of why and how Chinese domestic firms make their international investments and manage their international operations.

Investment is at the heart of economic growth. The mineral industry is the linchpin of the Australian economy. The development of the Australian minerals industry has relied heavily on FDI. China was the largest investing country for Australia in the mineral exploration and development in the period 2008–09, based on the investment approvals by the FIRB, and was the second-largest FDI country for Australia, only trailing the USA during the same period (FIRB, 2010a). Because there are huge differences in ideology, political systems and culture between Australia and China, Chinese ODI in Australia also presents a challenge to Australian governments at the federal and state levels for directing and controlling Chinese investments in Australia in light of its national interest.

Investment is a two-way concept. As China integrates more of its economy into the world, Chinese firms can be expected to invest more in Australia in the future. Many Australian firms have expanded their businesses directly into China or allied their business operations with their Chinese counterparts. A deep understanding of how Chinese firms invest and operate in the Australian minerals industry can equip Australian business executives with knowledge to better attract Chinese investment and conduct business with them.

## Book structure

This book consists of seven chapters. This chapter introduces readers to recent developments in the Chinese economy with its three driving forces: growth in domestic consumption, export and capital investment. It then briefly describes Australian minerals resources and the extent of Australia–China trade relations. This is followed by an outline of Chinese investment in Australia, particularly in the Australian minerals industry and the challenges for both business executives and policy makers.

Chapter 2 provides an overview of Chinese investment in the Australian minerals industry and examines the entry motives and approaches adopted by Chinese investors. Firstly, it offers a brief literature review of general FDI theory, particularly Dunning's OLI paradigm, and special theoretical perspectives on Chinese ODI, such as those proposed by Buckley and his colleagues (Buckley et al., 2008). Then it reviews literature on the historical development of Chinese ODI, its motives and entry approaches. Next, an overview of Chinese investment in the Australian minerals industry is presented. This covers several key characteristics of Chinese investments, including the Chinese investing organisations and the target organisations/projects, mode of entry, transactions, the major minerals invested and percentage of the ownership. Detailed analyses and discussion follow for the invested minerals distribution, ownership, the size of transaction, investment motives and entry approaches. Finally, the obligations and rights for Chinese investors as JV partners and minority equity participants in the Australian minerals industry are described.

Chapter 3 focuses on the Australian regulatory framework, its recent developments, the fundamental considerations behind the Australian government's approval process, the decision outcomes of the FIRB on FDI and the conditions imposed by the FIRB on the Chinese investments in the Australian minerals industry. Specifically, this chapter first introduces the importance of the mining industry to the Australian economy. It then provides a brief history of FDI in Australia and its mining industry. The Australian regulatory framework for FDI is then described and discussed. This framework primarily consists of the Foreign Acquisitions and Takeovers Act 1975 (FATA) and the Australian government's Foreign Investment Policy (Policy), which is administered by the FIRB and the federal treasurer. Their contents and role are described and explained.

Chapter 3 then elaborates and provides an analysis of Australia's national interest, a fundamental criterion that the Australian government applies in assessing FDI applications. This is followed by a description of and discussion on the recent development of the Australian regulatory framework. Next, the decision outcomes of the FIRB in assessing FDI applications between 2001 and 2009 are analysed. Finally, this chapter examines the concerns of the Australian public and politicians about Chinese investment in the Australian minerals industry, and analyses the conditions so far imposed by the FIRB on Chinese investments, therein exploring how the Australian government balanced the benefits of FDI and public concerns.

Chapter 4 discusses the impact of China's rising investments in the Australian minerals industry on the Australian political economy of China's rising investments in the Australian minerals industry. Australia and China have enjoyed 37 years of formal diplomatic relations, and for much of this time the two nations have enjoyed solid diplomatic and economic relations while China focused on its own internal economic reforms. More recently, particularly in the last five years, 2006 to 2010, the dynamics of the relationship have taken on a far more complex political nature, because China requires Australian natural resources for domestic consumption and to feed its massive export-oriented sectors, while Australia's political economy has increasingly come to see China's need for resources as essential to its future national prosperity. It is the political–economic nature of the relationship that is considered in this chapter. In particular, several hurdles including contentious foreign investment decisions, the arrest and sentencing of Rio Tinto executives and Australian citizen, Stern Hu, on corruption and stealing commercial secrets charges and changes to iron ore corporate structures and pricing, have together added a new dynamic to the Australia–China relationship.

This chapter also examines the Australia–China bilateral relationship over the past half decade (2006–10): the impact of the global financial crisis (GFC) on the Australia–China political economy; the political and commercial reverberations of the failed Rio Tinto–CHINALCO deal; the political and diplomatic tensions of the Stern Hu case; the politics of the rapid rise in Chinese investment into Australia's mining sector; and the impact of Chinese investment on the politics of WA, a state whose political economy is heavily dominated by natural resource extraction. It also elaborates on the difficulties arising from the different commercial and legal systems in each country, the resource super profit tax, which ultimately cost an Australian prime minister his position, and simmering tensions over the massive Rio–BHP joint iron ore deal, which could have impact on the long-term relationship between Australia and China. Finally, it explores how Australia–China political–economic relations sit within the broader picture of China's economic ascendancy and growing global investment reach in mineral resources. Collectively, these individual events and actions paint a picture in which the Australian prosperity story has become one of managing China's need for Australian mineral resources. As with any relationship, the capacity of the participants to manage it with minimal tension has been severely tested by events and international market activities. The chapter foreshadows the next decade as being unlikely to change in this regard, but a growing level of maturity within the relationship can be expected as experience informs and directs each party to move their objectives within increasingly established policy and corporate frameworks.

Chapter 5 focuses on the major activities conducted in the entry process by Chinese firms and the post-transaction issues in managing

Chinese subsidiaries or JVs. The three broad stages of the investment entry process are first noted and then explained: pre-transaction preparation, negotiation and transaction, each involving a different set of key activities. Pre-transaction preparation requires analyses of the macro environment in the host country and micro environment, such as the target project and company, and internal analysis of the investing firm itself. This can provide a solid foundation for the investment rationale and potential financial returns from such an investment. The negotiation stage is critical as the detailed information about the target project and company is gathered and the conditions for the proposed investment are set. The transaction stage usually covers the manner in which the financial payment is structured and the conditions under which the payment will be made. Understanding these activities can better prepare Chinese business executives to manage their investments in the Australian minerals industry.

Entering the Australian minerals industry is only the first step for ODI, particularly for those Chinese firms that have established subsidiaries in Australia. Managing these Chinese subsidiaries, including Chinese wholly owned subsidiaries (WOSs), controlling entities in which Chinese firms own over 50 per cent of the Australian company invested and JVs could present major challenges for Chinese managers in either their parent companies or Australian subsidiaries. This chapter also examines the corporate governance of the Chinese-controlled entities, their strategies and operational issues based on our in-depth interviews with Chinese executives in Australia and secondary data analysis. Issues investigated in this area include the composition and independence of the board, business strategy, financing, organisational culture, human resources management and project management.

Chapter 6 describes and discusses the key factors causing the failure of the proposed CHINALCO investment in Rio Tinto early in 2009. CHINALCO proposed a massive investment ($19.5 billion) in the Rio Tinto Group in February 2009; the largest Chinese ODI proposal so far. It was subsequently terminated by Rio's board on 5 June 2009, 114 days after its announcement.

The reason such a deal failed is the question asked by the business community, government and public worldwide, particularly those from Australia and China. This question is pertinent and complex as many players interacted and many factors influenced the deal's outcome. Ostensibly, Rio and CHINALCO were the key players or actors; however, others were also engaged, including BHPB, the Australian and Chinese governments, the media and the general public. The actions and interactions of these actors, all having complex connections, have brought many factors into consideration, including economic, competitive, political and cultural issues at the national, industrial, organisational and individual levels. This chapter examines these players, and their actions and influence on the fate of the CHINALCO–Rio deal after discussing background information about the proposed investment. Specifically, a comprehensive media search on three major Australian media (*The Australian, The Age* and ABC News) from 1 January to 31 October 2009 was conducted. Then the impact of several major events on the position of key stakeholders in this proposed deal was outlined. These included Rio Tinto, CHINALCO, BHPB, the Australian government and the Chinese government through their activities and dynamic interactions. Finally, the chapter summarises the key interaction pattern among the stakeholders and provides an in-depth analysis of the factors contributing to the failure of this proposed investment.

Chapter 7 summarises the key issues explicated in this book and discusses several policy issues for both Chinese and Australian governments to facilitate and/or guide Chinese investments in the Australian minerals industry. It also examines the potential challenges for Chinese firms in managing their investments in Australia in the future. In doing so, this chapter firstly provides concluding comments on the previous six chapters and outlines policy issues for both the Australian and Chinese governments on Chinese ODI in the Australian minerals industry. The concluding comments re-emphasise the key points presented in this book. China was Australia's largest trading partner in 2009 and the bilateral trade is still growing. On the one hand, China relies heavily on Australia for the natural resources that feed its economic growth; Australia was the fourth largest destination of Chinese ODI. On the other hand, FDI has been the driving force for growth and development of the Australian resources sector, which is a crucial part of the Australian economy. Therefore, Australia depends on China for its economic growth. As China becomes an important source of investment capital, coupled with its status of being Australia's largest trading partner, issues related to Chinese ODI in Australia need to be handled appropriately by both the Australian and Chinese governments with a comprehensive perspective of not only economic concerns, but also of political, social and regional security relations. This chapter points out several policy issues for the Australian government in dealing with Chinese ODI, such as FDI policies, minerals resources rent tax, infrastructure, the approval process of the state governments and immigration policy. These issues should be managed efficiently to attract, guide and facilitate future Chinese investments in Australia. For the Chinese government, streamlining the ODI approval process, the development of better ODI facilitating services and the improvement of its regulatory framework for FDI in China are important challenges.

Chinese firms face many challenges in investing in the Australian minerals industry and managing their subsidiaries. These challenges include corporate governance and strategic management to ensure their Australian subsidiaries can grow and develop in the Australian context. They also need to deal with operational challenges, such as leadership, human resources management, cross-cultural management and risk management.

# 2

# An Overview of China's Investment in the Australian Mineral Industry: Theoretical Perspective and Investment Characteristics

The huge increase in China's ODI has seen it expand as a major source of investment from $270 million in 2002 to $56.53 billion in 2009 (Ministry of Commerce, 2010). By 2009, China's total ODI stock had reached $245.75 billion, with more than 1200 Chinese enterprises having invested in over 13,000 firms abroad (Ministry of Commerce, 2009, 2010). China's ODI surged in 2008, as Chinese enterprises, both state-owned and privately owned, capitalised on the global financial crisis. Furthermore, this trend is expected to continue due to the increasing participation of state-owned enterprises (SOEs) and privately owned enterprises (POEs) in their international business activities, support from Chinese governments, better facilitation and services by Chinese financial institutes, such as banks and insurance companies, and China's vast foreign currency reserves. Although China started its "open door" policy in 1979, research efforts have been devoted overwhelmingly to FDI rather than ODI. In their review of the literature in 15 leading management journals between 1993 and 2006 on FDI, Lau and Bruton (2008) found only two articles on China's ODI, compared with 172 articles on FDI in China. Nevertheless considerable progress has been made on China's ODI recently, particularly for entry modes, motivation and location of Chinese ODI for SOEs (for example, Buckley, Clegg et al., 2008; Buckley, Cross, Tan, Xin, & Voss, 2008; Deng, 2009; He & Lyles, 2008).

This chapter provides an overview of China's ODI in the Australian minerals industry. It firstly reviews literature on China's ODI, including its theoretical perspectives and key characteristics, such as motives and entry approach. It then examines Chinese investments in the

Australian minerals industry, particularly entry modes, ownership, minerals invested and transaction size. Finally, obligations and rights for Chinese investors as JV partners or equity participants are examined.

## Existing theoretical perspectives on Chinese ODI

### General theoretical perspectives on FDI

Why do firms make ODI? Two general principles can explain this phenomenon (Buckley & Casson, 1976). First, firms can reap the benefits of internalising their missing and/or imperfect external activities in their value chains. Second, firms can make use of other locations (countries) as markets and suppliers of resources and technologies to improve their organisations' performance and capabilities. These two broad benefits comprise the value and location aspects of the mainstream FDI theory. For the value chains aspect, monopoly advantage and transaction cost are two theories frequently used to explain the underlying value of ODI. They are similar to the concepts of "strategising" and "economising" (Williamson, 1991) used in the area of strategic management to explain how "economic rent" can be generated by firms through market positioning and leverage of unique resources and competencies.

The new trade theory (NTT) proposed by Krugman (1980) helps explain further how different countries trade with each other, providing a basis for FDI. In essence, NTT explains that the existence of a variety of customer preferences for different products, economies of scale in production and technology difference result in an increase of world trade, even between countries where endowment is similar (Krugman, 2009). The NTT is more powerful in explaining trade relationships between China and other Asian countries than between China and Australia.

Probably the most widely used theory for explaining international business activity and behaviour is Dunning's eclectic theory or paradigm (Dunning, 2001). This theory states that:

1. MNCs can possess some assets that can be leveraged to other countries, that is, the ownership advantage;
2. Different countries can offer different opportunities for MNCs, be they markets, efficiencies, natural resources or strategic assets – this is the location consideration; and
3. MNCs select means, such as the market entry model, which are most appropriate for *internalising* its international business activities based on their ownership and location considerations. This is the Ownership-Location-Internalisation (OLI) model.

In summary, while internationalisation principles (Buckley & Casson, 1976) help explain why firms go international and Krugman's new trade theory explains the fundamental basis on which trade occurs between countries and intra-industries, Dunning's eclectic paradigm (2001) offers detailed explanations of why firms invest abroad. These theories and models provide a general theoretical framework to understand why firms invest in other countries.

## Special theoretical perspective on China's ODI

Several researchers including Buckley, Clegg et al. (2008) and Sauvant (2005) have argued that a special theory for a better understanding of ODI from emerging economies, such as China, is needed. For example, Buckley et al. (2007) pointed out that three factors are both unique in China and powerful in explaining the motives and behaviours of Chinese ODI; these three factors are:

1. capital market imperfections;
2. special ownership advantages of Chinese firms; and
3. institutional factors.

There are substantial differences in the institutional environment and organisational resources between Chinese SOEs and POEs, which warrant elaboration (see below).

Capital market imperfections exist due to:

1. below-market rate available to Chinese SOEs, via soft budget constraints;
2. soft bank loans to potential outward investors;
3. inefficient internal capital markets in conglomerates; and
4. cheap capital from family members.

Ownership advantages cover the ability to operate in an uncertain environment or developing countries and in the network of Chinese diaspora. These can help Chinese firms conduct their businesses in developing countries or in those with good networks of overseas Chinese.

Institutional factors encompass national institutions, such as the level of government support or constraints and supranational institutions, and include bilateral investment treaties, membership of WTO and double tax treaties (Buckley, Clegg et al., 2008). Recent studies (Meyer,

Estrin, Bhaumik & Peng, 2009; Peng, Wang & Jiang, 2008) suggest that consideration of national institutions enhances our understanding of ODI activities and patterns, particularly for firms in emerging economies. This institutional perspective is also supported by several other studies (Cui & Jiang, 2009; Deng, 2009).

Chinese SOEs have been considered by Chinese governments as the pillars of the national economy, while POEs were only permitted to exist after 1978. Therefore, many Chinese government policies and regulations have been intentionally developed to support its SOEs. In contrast to the SOEs, Chinese POEs have been discriminated against in many aspects; for example, they were not permitted to operate in many industries, such as oil and gas, power supply and telecommunications. In fact, Chinese POEs were only allowed by the Chinese government to operate in about 40 industries in 2007, 20 fewer than for foreign firms operating in China, while SOEs could operate in more than 80 industries. The industries within which POEs now operate are usually very competitive, such as textiles, electronics and machinery. From a financing perspective, Chinese POEs have great difficulty getting their bank loan applications approved as they were often perceived by Chinese banks as being more risky than SOEs. This high risk perception is often caused by the size of their tangible assets and the difficulties Chinese banks face when evaluating these. Most of the Chinese POEs are small-and medium-sized enterprises (SMEs), while SOEs are large enterprises. Thus, many Chinese POEs go international with their own capital and/or profits (Liu & Tan, 2004). From an internationalisation viewpoint, they were permitted to import or export directly only after 1998 when the then Ministry of Foreign Trade and Economic Cooperation allowed Chinese privately owned manufacturing firms and research institutes to do so. Therefore, most Chinese POEs lack experience in international business operations.

Chinese POEs' ODIs only commenced after the Chinese government eased its restrictions on their investing in foreign countries in 2002; however, ODI for Chinese firms still requires approval from Chinese government authorities, particularly the National Development and Reform Commission (NDRC), the Ministry of Commerce (MOC) and State Administration of Foreign Exchange (SAFE) (Yuan, 2010); these are often more restrictive for POEs than SOEs.

Such differences in institutional environment not only affect the ODI motives and behaviour of Chinese POEs, but also influence their resources and competencies in conducting international activities. As Chinese POEs generally lack international experience, their value chains are less internally integrated, especially those involving international value networks. They also have limited financing capacity and face a greater degree of uncertainty than SOEs in obtaining finance from Chinese banks. However, operationally, they are usually experienced and skilful in managing their business within competitive industries. All of these differences in resources and competencies could make Chinese POEs' ODI motives and behaviour differ from SOEs. The relationships between institutional environment, organisational resources and competences, and ODI are depicted in Figure 2.1.

Several Chinese researchers (Chen & Wang, 2010) have pointed out that the sheer size of Chinese domestic market is another unique factor that influences Chinese firms' ODI motives and behaviour. Many Chinese firms have made their ODI decisions primarily based on the huge size of Chinese markets for their products or commodities acquired through their ODI.

The theories used to explain Chinese ODI have focused primarily on the reasons for Chinese firms making cross-border investments. Several studies have investigated the manner in which Chinese firms enter into international markets and other important characteristics of Chinese ODI, such as its developmental process, patterns, motives and entry mode (Cui & Jiang, 2009; Deng, 2009; He & Lyles, 2008). The following section discusses these characteristics.

## Chinese ODI: The developmental process, patterns and characteristics

### The development stage of Chinese ODI

China opened its doors to the world in 1979 through its first ODI when a state-owned trading company established its JV in Japan. Since then, Chinese ODI grew quite slowly as it passed through several stages of

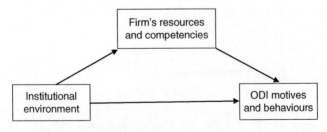

*Figure 2.1* The effect of institutional environment and firms' resources on Chinese firms' ODI motives and behaviour

development, culminating in exponential growth in the five years to 2008 (see Figure 2.2). Because of the dominant role of the Chinese government, researchers focused on its ODI policy development and its influence on ODI. For example, Buckley, Clegg et al. (2008) divided Chinese ODI policy since 1979 into five stages:

1. cautious internationalisation (1979–85);
2. government encouragement (1986–91);
3. expansion and regulation (1992–98);
4. the "go global" period (1999–2001); and
5. the post-WTO period.

Similarly, Zhang (2009) focused on the development of Chinese government ODI policies and services, identifying several important changes in administrative procedures, foreign currency exchange control and services or facilities provided by Chinese banks and insurers. First, the Chinese fundamental ODI policy was changed from limiting ODI before 1997 to encouraging it, notably by the announcement made to the 15th Congress of the Communist Party of China in 1997. Second, the ODI approval process has been gradually simplified and formalised since 1991, particularly after 1997, as demonstrated by a number of important policy changes. These included: changes to the level of approval authority depending on the amount of ODI, types of documents submitted for approval and number of parties consulted, such as the Chinese Embassy

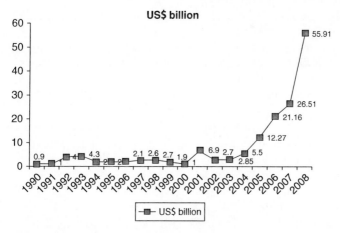

*Figure 2.2*   Chinese ODI between 1990 and 2008
*Source*: Ministry of Commerce, 2008, 2009.

in the host country; the number of host countries controlled; and the approval process. Third, the government control of foreign currency exchange was gradually loosened, particularly after October 2002, when SAFE delegated its control of less than $3 million ODI to the corresponding provincial authority. Fourth, a number of new ODI-facilitation policies in the areas of lending, issuance and taxation were launched after 2003, such as increasing the cap of bank loans to Chinese firms, extending loan terms, setting up special funds, providing low-interest loans, speeding up loan approval processes and providing warranty services for ODI project bids and international settlement. Finally, new services were launched after 2002 by the Chinese government to support ODI. These policy developments also show that ODI is a complex phenomenon and that its growth requires systematic policy support and facilitation from government departments, banks and insurers.

Based on Zhang's (2009) findings above, the role played by the Chinese government in ODI can be considered as being:

1. cautious control and restriction (before 1997);
2. encouragement (1997–2002); and
3. facilitation and support (after 2002).

These three stages are in line with the patterns of Chinese ODI between 1990 and 2008 (see Figure 2.2), which show three stages of development:

1. introduction (before 1997);
2. development (1997–2002) as indicated by the incremental, albeit fluctuating, ODI due to the Chinese government's supportive policy, the improvement and development of ODI-facilitating services, and the negative impact of Asia's financial crisis in 1997; and
3. growth after 2002. It should be pointed out that the year 2003 also marked the start of ODI by Chinese POEs.

Figure 2.2 also shows that the amount of Chinese ODI during 2005–08 accounted for nearly two-thirds (62.97%) of the total Chinese ODI between 1979 and 2008, with the ODI in 2008 exceeding the sum of the first 15 years (1979–93).

### The motives behind Chinese ODI

The early objectives of Chinese ODI were to integrate China's economy into the world and improve access for domestic firms to natural resources, the lack of which were limiting China's development. The primary motivations for Chinese ODI before 2001 were mainly market-seeking and resource-seeking, particularly in the area of natural resources (Buckley et al., 2007). Market-seeking was a trade-oriented stance aiming to generate foreign currency for the Chinese government, while resource-seeking ODI attempted to supplement China's domestic supplies of critical mineral resources, such as iron ore and oil. Since the late 1990s, particularly after 2002, other objectives were identified in the literature, including securing strategic assets, such as technology and brand names, and enhancing the overall competitive advantage of Chinese firms through integrating their businesses in the global value networks.

Based on a recent survey conducted by the China Council for the Promotion of International Trade (2009), the motivations for Chinese firms (mostly POEs) to invest abroad include: market expansion (39%), acquisition of foreign advanced technology and management (30%), cost reduction (24%) and acquisition of natural resources (19%). Other key motivations include acquiring international brands (19%) and bypassing trade barriers (16%). It is surprising to learn that acquisition of advanced technology and managerial knowledge has become more important than natural resource acquisition, reflecting the importance of obtaining strategic assets in the recent wave of Chinese ODI, particularly by POEs.

Focusing on Chinese strategic asset behaviour, Deng (2007) explored why Chinese firms, such as Haier, Huawei and TCL, now POEs, acquired such assets, particularly in the developed countries. These strategic assets covered resource and development (R&D) capability, brand names, technology and marketing expertise and channels. Merger and acquisition (M&A) was the major approach used by Chinese MNCs entering a foreign market to acquire these strategic assets and capture the externalities offered by host country technology clusters and innovation centres. Deng (2007) argued that such behaviour is motivated by strategic needs, which were to improve Chinese firms' vulnerable strategic position or to fulfil their strategic aspirations to become world leading enterprises. Both drives should enhance their competitive advantages in the global marketplace.

The motives of Chinese SOEs and POEs seem different. While Chinese SOEs are engaged more in natural resource-seeking and market expansion, Chinese POEs seem more likely to invest for strategic asset-seeking and market expansion. As China has deregulated most of its competitive industries and privatised many SOEs operating in these industries, the market-seeking objectives for Chinese SOEs have become less dominant in recent years.

### Entry approach of Chinese ODI

Child and Rodrigues (2005) outlined three broad routes to internationalisation used by Chinese firms: the acquisition route, the organic expansion route and the partnership route through being an original equipment manufacturer (OEM) or joint venturing. They considered the final route as "inward internationalisation", and the first two routes as "outward internationalisation", which can be undertaken through "Greenfield" and "Brownfield" investment approaches (Globerman & Shapiro, 2009).

Cui and Jiang (2009) investigated the adoption of two dominant entry modes by Chinese firms: JV and WOS through either organic development or acquisition. They found that Chinese firms preferred the WOS mode when pursuing assets, adopting a global strategy and operating in the host country. However, the JV mode was preferred if they invested for market expansion in host countries with a high growth market. This may reflect the difficulties in acquiring distribution channels in host countries.

Organic growth may be preferred by Chinese POEs, particularly SMEs, possibly due to the dominant objective of market-seeking in their ODI. The survey conducted by China Council for the Promotion of International Trade (2009) also showed that more than half (53%) of the respondents indicated that they would like to initiate their ODI by establishing their own sales office abroad. This preference was followed by the setting up of retailing outlets or marketing networks (24%), or a brand-new subsidiary (20%). Only 26 per cent and 8 per cent indicated that they would like to use JV with local firms and M&A for their international expansion, respectively. These figures differed from those reported in the media for Chinese SOEs, such as CHINALCO, China National Offshore Oil Corporation (CNOOC) and Minmetals, where acquisition has been the dominant approach adopted in their ODI. These differences could be attributed to a number of factors, including the investment motives and size, and the industry within which the target company operated.

Focusing on ODI by Chinese SMEs, Hilmersson and Jansson (2009) observed that many Chinese SMEs go international in clusters, particularly in the retailing industry. Examples include those operating in DragonMart, Dubai (UAE), The Wolka Kosowska Centre, Warsaw

(Poland) and The AsiaCenter, Budapest (Hungary). Those investing Chinese SMEs can be either producers, wholesalers or retailers. Some made use of the export platform, often a market for wholesalers and retailers built by the proprietor – a firm built for managing the export platform. These authors termed this a "clustering internationalisation process", their dominant motive in these cases being market-seeking. However, the researchers did not explain why these Chinese SMEs went international by cluster.

In summary, the approaches used by Chinese POEs are quite different from those used by SEOs. While acquisition has been observed as a dominant mode for Chinese SOEs in their ODI, often for accessing natural resources, Chinese POEs are more likely to use organic development in their international expansion and acquisition when securing strategic assets. Their investment motives are mainly strategic assets-seeking and market-seeking. These differences in making ODI can be attributed to the institutional environment faced, various international experiences, the firm's resources and the industries in which they invest.

## Chinese ODI in the Australian minerals industry: An overview and key characteristics

### An overview

Australia was the fourth-largest destination for Chinese ODI by the end of 2009, with its ODI stock reaching $5.863 billion (Ministry of Commerce, 2010). China's ODI in Australia started from a very low base but has grown rapidly since 2007. In 2006, China's ODI stock in Australia was only $908 million but Chinese firms invested $532 million in 2007 (Ministry of Commerce, 2008), and $1.892 and $2.436 billion in 2008 and 2009, respectively (Ministry of Commerce, 2009, 2010). The year 2009 witnessed the largest Chinese ODI in Australia with several major Chinese acquisitions, including Yanzhou Coal's acquisition of Felix Resources for $3.3 billion Minmetals' acquisition of OZ Minerals for $1.3 billion and Valin's investment of A$1.28 billion in the Fortescue Metals Groups (FMG).

Compared with ODI from the US, UK and Japan, China's ODI in Australia is still very small. By the end of 2009, the stock of China's ODI in Australia was less than 1.8 per cent of the Australia's total FDI stock (UNCTAD, 2010), even after the rapid increase of Chinese ODI in Australia in 2009. At this time in the Australia–China investment relationship, policy decision-making and public perception seem to be driven more by the likely rapid growth of China's investments in the resource and agricultural sectors over the coming decade rather than by current investment levels.

Most Chinese investment in Australia has been in the resource sector. Despite this rapid growth, Chinese ODI accounted for a relatively small share of the global resources sector. For example, it is estimated that China only had control over 51 million tonnes of iron ore through its ODI by the end of 2008, accounting for less than 12 per cent of its total iron ore imports into China (444 million tonnes), whereas the equivalent figure for Japan in 2008 through its ODI was 67 million tonnes, 45 per cent of its total iron ore import. Table 2.1 outlines the major Chinese investments in the Australian minerals industry and their key characteristics.

## Characteristics of Chinese investment in the Australian mining industry

This section examines the characteristics of Chinese investment in the Australian minerals industry, including the distribution of minerals invested, the ownership by the Chinese investors and the size of their transactions.

### Mineral distribution and the developmental stage of investment

Table 2.1 outlines 38 major investments above the A$10 million made by Chinese companies in Australia. Among them, 20 investments have been primarily made in the iron ore industry, three in coal, 13 in base metals and two in uranium, although some investments have been made in Australian companies with more than one major mineral.

Among 20 investments in the Australian iron ore industry, the majority (11) of the iron ore investments are in magnetite; all being made after 2006. The remainder were in the higher grade iron ore: hematite or so-called "direct shipping ore" (DSO). Five of the hematite investments were made before 2005 in mining companies at the development or production stage. Three of these Chinese investments were with two super iron ore producers, Rio Tinto and BHPB, when the global iron ore demand was relatively low; two other Chinese investments were made during the period of the recent GFC, by Valin in FMG and in Mt Gibson by Capital Iron and Steel Corporation (Shougang). This suggests the importance of timing when investing in established iron ore mines at the development or production stage. Four other Chinese investments in hematite were made in three other junior iron ore mines: Aquila Resources, Ferrus and Golden West Resources.

*Table 2.1* The entry mode, developmental stage, transaction and industry of the target companies and projects acquired by Chinese firms

| Chinese firm | Targeted Australian firm | Share (%) | Date announced and effective | Entry mode and developmental stage | Transaction | Major type of minerals | Ownership |
|---|---|---|---|---|---|---|---|
| **100% ownership** | | | | | | | |
| Yanzhou Coal | Southern Land Coal | 100 | 12/2004 02/2005 | Acquisition (Production) | A$32m | Coal | SOE |
| Yanzhou Coal | Felix Resources Ltd | 100 | 10/2009 12/2009 | Acquisition (Production) | A$3.54bn | Coal | SOE |
| CITIC Pacific (2007) | Mining right of 2bn tonnes | 100 | 03/2007 11/2007 | Acquisition (Exploration) | US$470m | Iron ore (M) | SOE |
| Minmetals | OZ Minerals | 100 | 02/2009 04/2009 | Acquisition (Production) | A$1.7bn | Precious and base metals | SOE |
| Sinosteel | Midwest | 100 | 12/2007 09/2008 | Acquisition (Development) | A$1.4bn | Iron ore (M) | SOE |
| MCC | Cape Lambert mine | 100 | 02/2008 N/A | Acquisition (Exploration) | A$400m | Iron ore (M) | SOE |
| CHINALCO | Aurukun Project | 100 | 03/2007 | Greenfield | N/A | Bauxite | SOE |
| Shenhua Energy | Watermark Project | 100 | 08/2008 | Greenfield | A$300m | Coal | SOE |

*Table 2.1* (Continued)

| Chinese firm | Targeted Australian firm | Share (%) | Date announced and effective | Entry mode and developmental stage | Transaction | Major type of minerals | Ownership |
|---|---|---|---|---|---|---|---|
| **Majority ownership (>50–90%)** | | | | | | | |
| Hunan Non-ferrous Metal Corp (now Minmetals) | Abra Mining Limited | 74.27 | 05/2008 09/2008 | Acquisition (Greenfield) | A$70m | Base metal, copper and gold | SOE |
| China Guangdong Nuclear Power Corporation | Energy Metals | 66 | 09/2009 12/2009 | Acquisition (Greenfield) | A$81.4m | Uranium | SOE |
| Hanlong | Moly Mines | 55 | 10/2009 04/2010 | Acquisition (Development) | US$140m (plus US$60m shareholder loan during 10 years) | MO and iron ore | POE |
| Zhongjin | Perilya | 50.1 | 09/12/08 09/02/09 | Acquisition (Production) | A$45.5m | Zinc, lead and silver | SOE |
| **EJVs (>50%)** | | | | | | | |
| WISCo | Centrex (project-based JV) | 60 | 21/7/09 26/113pt/09 | Exploration | A$186m A$9.7m for company | Iron ore (M) | SOE |

| | | | | | | | |
|---|---|---|---|---|---|---|---|
| Ansteel | Gindalbie (project-based JV) | 50 | 3/4/06 N/A | Exploration | A$372.06m | Iron ore (M) | SOE |
| Chonggang Minerals Dev. Inv. Ltd | Asia Iron (project-based JV) | 60 | 11/09 N/A | Exploration | A$280m | Iron ore (M) | SOE |
| Baotou Steel | Centrex (project-based JV) | 50 | 05/10 N/A | Exploration | A$40m | Iron ore (M) | SOE |
| Yunnan Tin Group | Metals X (project-based JV) | 50 | 03/10 N/A | Exploration | A$50m | Tin | SOE |
| **Marketing JV** | | | | | | | |
| CMIEC (now Sinosteel) | Rio Tinto (project-based JV) | 40 | 1987 | Development | N/A | Iron ore | SOE |
| Baosteel | Rio Tinto (project-based JV) | 46 | 12/2001 06/2002 | Development | A$57m (US$29.4m) | Iron ore | SOE |
| WISCo, Maanshan Steel, Shasteel and Tangsteel | BHPB (project-based JV) | 40 | 09/2004 | Development | A$12m | Iron ore | SOEs |
| **Minority ownership (5–49.9%)** | | | | | | | |
| Shasteel | Grange Resources | 46.71 | 06/2008 01/2009 | Merger Exploration | N/A | Iron ore (M) | POE |
| Ansteel | Gindalbie | 36.28 | 03/2006 | Greenfield | A$372m | Iron ore (M) | SOE |
| Shougang APAC | Mt Gibson | 2020 | 11/2008 | Production | A$162.5m | Iron ore | SOE |

*Table 2.1* (Continued)

| Chinese firm | Targeted Australian firm | Share (%) | Date announced and effective | Entry mode and developmental stage | Transaction | Major type of minerals | Ownership |
|---|---|---|---|---|---|---|---|
| Guangdong Foreign Trade | Kagara | 19.9 | 07/2009 08/2009 | Production | A\$88m | Base metals | SOE |
| Creat | Galaxy | 19.9 | 08/2009 04/2010 | Development | A\$27.3m | Lithium | POE |
| Sichuan Taifeng | IMX Resources | 19.9 | 11/2008 07/2010 | Exploration | A\$25.06m | Fe/Cu/Au | POE |
| Valin | FMG | 17.4 | 02/2009 04/2009 | Production | A\$1.2bn | Iron ore | SOE |
| Valin | Golden West Resources | 11.4 | 08/2008 | Exploration | A\$26.65m | Iron ore | SOE |
| Baosteel | Aquila | 14.99 | 10/2009 | Exploration | A\$286m | Iron ore | SOE |
| Shougang | Australasian Resources | 11 | 2007 | Exploration | A\$56m | Iron ore (M) | SOE |
| Western Mining Company | FerrAus | 10 | 05/2008 | Exploration | A\$15m | Iron ore | POE |
| CNMC Industry's Foreign Engineering & Construction Co., Ltd (NFC) | Terramin Australia | 9% | 06/2009 | Exploration | A\$10m | Zinc | SOE |

| Jinchuan | Metals X | 12.9 | 03/2007 | Exploration | A$50.4m | Tin and base metals | SOE |
| CRMC | FerrAus | 12 | 09/2009 12/2009 | Exploration | A$12m | Iron ore | SOE |
| Yizhao (Shanghai) | Cauldron Energy | N/A | 11/2009 02/2010 | Exploration | A$10m (A$3m placement and A$7m convertible note) | Uranium | POE |
| Jilin Tonghua Steel (now Shougang) | IMX Resources | 8.2 | 12/2007 02/2008 | Exploration | A$13.93m | Fe/Cu/Au | SOE |
| Yankuang | Bauxite Resources | N/a | 06/2009 11/2009 | Exploration | A$9.85m | Al | SOE |
| Rockcheck | Aurox | 14 | 07/2007 and on market | Exploration | N/A | Iron ore (M) | POE |
| WISCo | Centrex | 13.03 | 12/2008 11/2009 | Exploration | A$9.5m | Iron ore (M) | SOE |

*Notes:* M = Magnetite; H = Hematite; MO = Molybdenum; Fe = Iron ore; Cu = Copper; Au = Gold; Al = Aluminium; EJV = Equity joint venture.

The investments in magnetite have been the most substantial Chinese investments in the Australian minerals industry so far. All were in Australian miners at the exploration stage, except Shasteel's investment in Savage River, already a producer of 1 million tonnes per year of concentrated iron ore and pellets. Although the initial transactions ranged from A$56 million to A$470 million, the additional investment to move from exploration to production would be much larger. For example, CITIC Pacific has made an additional investment of over $5 billion to develop its magnetite project to an annual production capacity of 28 million tonnes of iron ore concentrate. Ansteel is expected to spend A$2 billion to move its Karara Project from exploration to annual production of 15 million tonnes of iron ore concentrate.

Chinese investments have been made in other minerals, such as base metals (copper, lead, zinc, tin), alumina, gold, lithium and molybdenum. These investments are widely spread across these metals without a concentration on a particular metal. Except in the case of Minmetals' acquisition of OZ Minerals, all other Chinese investments in the base and/or precious metals in Australia have been in Australian miners primarily at the exploration or development stage.

Two Chinese SOEs have acquired three coal mining companies or exploration tenements. Yan Coal had taken over Felix Resources in 2009 and acquired Southern Land Coal in 2004 after it was closed due to a fire disaster in 2003. Both targeted companies had already moved to the production stage. In another Chinese investment in coal, Shenhua Energy was the successful bidder for a coal exploration tenement in NSW in 2008. In addition, Aquila Resources, which is 15 per cent owned by Baosteel, also produces coal in Queensland.

Chinese firms have also invested in the mining of uranium – another important energy-producing mineral. China Guangdong Nuclear Power Corporation invested A$81.4 million in Energy Metals as a majority shareholder (66%) and a private Chinese company (Yizhao) spent A$10 million in Cauldron Energy (A$3 million share placement and A$7 million as convertible notes).

## The characteristics of acquiring Chinese organisations

*Ownership of the Chinese investors*

Most of the Chinese investors (23 out of 30) in the Australian minerals industry are large state-owned or controlled enterprises. In fact, 9 of them are on the list of 123 centrally controlled SOEs. All these are very large Chinese SOEs with large financial resources. Except for three companies, Guangdong Nuclear Power Corporation, Guangdong Foreign Trade Corporation and CRMC, all Chinese firms have been involved in mining and/or minerals processing activities.

Seven Chinese investors are from the private sector: Shasteel, Rockcheck, Hanlong, Creat, Taifeng, West Mining and Yizhao. Shasteel and Rockcheck are operating in the Chinese steel industry, while Hanlong, Taifeng and Yizhao are investment firms or conglomerates. Shasteel and Hanlong have a controlling stake in the companies in which they have invested and thus are actively involved in their corporate governance.

*Industry profile and method of strategic development*

The largest group (10 out of 30) of Chinese investors are from the Chinese steel industry, including Baosteel, Ansteel, Wuhan Iron and Steel Company (WISCo), Valin, Shasteel, Chongqing Steel and Maanshan Steel. Their investments have been made in the Australian iron ore industry, either in hematite or magnetite. The key motive for these investments is primarily to secure stable supply. Thus, these investments can be regarded as part of their strategy of backward integration. However, dual motives can also be observed for some Chinese companies in this group – securing supply and trading. These include Sinosteel, Shougang and the CITIC Group, which have not only secured minerals for their own production, but also for resale to other Chinese companies. China Guangdong Nuclear Power Corporation's investment in Energy Metals for securing a uranium supply can also be regarded as backward integration.

Another group of the Chinese SOEs have invested in the Australian minerals industry in the area of their existing operations. These include Yan Coal's acquisition of Felix Resources in coal mining and Minmetals' takeover of Oz Minerals' assets. These Chinese firms aim to leverage their expertise and technologies for achieving synergy effects, and to learn from the companies acquired, particularly in the areas of management and marketing.

*Size of transactions*

Transaction size varies significantly with the developmental stage of the companies invested in and the Chinese share of the target companies. The takeover of three established Australian companies, namely Felix Resources, OZ Minerals and Midwest Steel by Yan Coal, Minmetals and Sinosteel, respectively, represented the largest transactions so far for Chinese investments in the Australian minerals industry. Valin's investment in another established Australian company, FMG, is the largest transaction of a minority equity participant.

The transactions made by the Chinese POEs are relatively small compared with their SOE counterparts, most of them being less than A$30 million. This generally reflects their financing capability. Hanlong's transaction has been the largest so far, with $140 million invested in Moly Mines for a 55 per cent share.

## Motive and mode of entry by Chinese investors

### Entry motive

As discussed earlier, there are three major motivations for FDI: market-seeking, efficiency-seeking and strategic asset-seeking; the latter includes resource-seeking. Obviously, the most salient motive for Chinese firms to invest in the Australian mining industries is resource-seeking. By 2009, 85.9 per cent of Chinese investment into Australia was in mining and exploration (Ministry of Commerce, 2010), increasing from 45.5 per cent at the end of 2007 (Ministry of Commerce, 2008). This indicates that an overwhelming proportion of Chinese investments between 2008 and 2009 were in the Australian resources sector. The rapid development of the Chinese economy over the past 30 years, and particularly in this decade, has created a huge demand for natural resources, such as minerals and oil; however, its domestic supply of these resources is very limited. Therefore, many Chinese firms, encouraged by the Chinese government's "going out" policy, have invested in the international resources sector to secure their supply (Lawrence, 2002, cited in Buckley et al., 2007).

Strategic asset-seeking, such as learning from the target firms in the areas of mining technology and management, and acquiring distribution channels, could also play an important role in Chinese investment in the Australian minerals industry, although it may not be as important as resource-seeking. The Australian mineral industry is very advanced in technology and management (Drysdale & Findlay, 2008). An example of this is Minmetals' acquisition of OZ Minerals. OZ Minerals was formed through the merger in 2008 of Oxiana and Zenifix, two companies with a long operational history and accumulated knowledge in management and mining technology. Minmetals has appointed a former CEO of OZ Minerals as the CEO of its newly acquired company (Sainsbury, 2010f).

Nevertheless not all Chinese investments in the resources sector are made to secure supply, as demonstrated by the attempt by China's

CNMC to acquire Lynas, which is an explorer of rare earth metals in Australia. China has more than 90 per cent of the global reserve of rare earth metals (Doggett, 2010) and is a major exporter for these metals. This investment proposal was withdrawn because CNMC did not want to meet the conditions imposed by the Australian FIRB.

In summary, resource-seeking has been the salient strategic motive for many Chinese investments in the global resources sector, although strategic assets-seeking could also be a motive for Chinese investments in the Australian minerals industry. However, whether such a strategic motive of securing much-needed resources supply also makes economic sense could be the greatest challenge for Chinese firms. In other words, it is questionable if these investments can also generate satisfactory financial returns, particularly through the leveraging OLI advantages of Chinese firms.

For many Chinese SOEs, ownership can be to their competitive advantage. General ownership advantages as discussed by Dunning (2001) for Chinese firms may include technology, such as that used in magnetite mining and processing, distribution channels and project construction. A typical example of this is Yan Coal, the second largest coal mining company in China. Yan Coal, which has developed its technology in long-wall mining, set up its office in NSW for promoting this technology. It acquired Southern Land Coal in 2004, before it took over Felix Resources Limited – a large coal mine in NSW – for A$3.54 billion in 2009. Other similar ownership advantages include magnetite mining and processing by Ansteel, and the international project construction of the CITIC Group.

There are other special ownership advantages for Chinese firms in terms of financing and secured markets. As elaborated in Buckley et al. (2007), below-market-rate capital may be available to SOEs due to inefficient Chinese banking systems or an interest subsidy from the Chinese government. For example, the interest rate for the failed proposal of CHINALCO's investment in Rio Tinto in 2009 was only 90 points above the London Inter-Bank Offered Rates (LIBOR), which was substantially lower (by 255 points) than that obtained by BHPB on the open market at the same time. Chinese family firms may obtain cheap capital from family members. Securing markets is the most dominant motive for minority equity participation as many Chinese firms would like to secure their supply or leverage their distribution channels in China.

Other ownership advantages for Chinese firms are their expertise and operating networks in the huge Chinese market, which are crucial in industrial markets where buyer–seller relationships can be highly advantageous. The state ownership of SOEs, the extensive business networks of Chinese firms and their access to the sheer size of the Chinese market are their competitive advantages.

Location advantages refer to the contribution of country-specific factors to economic activities (Dunning, 2001). Australia is abundant in natural resources, geographically close to China, and has a stable political and economic environment. All these factors make Australia a favourite destination for Chinese firms, particularly in the resources sector, compared with other countries, such as Brazil, Canada and South Africa. Zhou Zhongshu, the president of Minmetals, clearly expressed this: "There are three main countries for iron ore deposits, Australia, Brazil and South Africa. The country I would definitely like to have an investment in is Australia. It has geographical advantages and favourable investment conditions" (Sainsbury, 2010f).

Some Chinese firms such as Ansteel, WISCo and China Guangdong Nuclear Power Corporation have also invested in the Australian resources sector for internalisation of value chain activities, particularly backward integration. The institutional factors at home and in host countries also encourage firms to invest abroad. Since 2003, the Chinese government has issued many policies to encourage and assist its firms to go international, with the development of many ODI-facilitating services such as those in the banking and insurance industries (G. Zhang, 2009; W. Zhang, 2010). This not only shapes Chinese firms' corporate strategies, but also helps them accelerate their international processes.

## Entry approach and the developmental stages of target companies acquired

With regard to the mode of entry, Greenfield and acquisition are two broad modes for entering the Australian minerals industry. Greenfield often refers to obtaining an exploration permit from state governments while acquisition is about acquiring a project or company in Australia.

The developmental stage of the project or company targeted is an important consideration for acquisition. From a mining company's perspective, a mineral project can be broadly classified into three stages: exploration, development and production. Major activities in the exploration stage include prospecting and drilling to identify and scope the project's resource. This stage also requires various regulatory and environment approvals, and pre-feasibility and bankable feasibility study reports. The development stage refers to project construction and development after the feasibility study is completed. Thus, it covers infrastructure construction, such as road, port, power and water supply, installation of major equipment and awarding of contracts. The production stage consists of mining, ore processing and transportation.

Chinese investment in the Australian mineral industry has been primarily through acquisition, except by CHINALCO and Shenhua Energy, who acquired their exploration permits in Queensland and NSW. The developmental stages of the Australian mining companies acquisitions by Chinese firms have displayed a pattern of production – exploration – production and exploration. This pattern can be attributed to the changes in the macroeconomic environment. Early Chinese entries into the Australian mining industry since the mid-1980s were via acquisitions and were on a relatively small scale due to the stable supply and demand in minerals, and the lack of foreign currency in Chinese companies. For example, Sinosteel formed a JV, the Channar Project, with Rio Tinto in 1987. This was followed by a JV, Bao–Range, between Baosteel (46%) and Rio Tinto (54%) in 2001, and a JV (the Wheelarra Project) between four Chinese steel companies (A$120 million) and BHPB in 2005. The dominant motive for all these early Chinese ODIs was to secure a stable supply of iron ore, with the Channar, Bao–Range and the Wheelarra Projects supplying respectively 10, 10 and 12 million tonnes of iron ore annually to their Chinese partners.

The global demand for resources, driven primarily by Chinese demand, increased rapidly during 2005–07. This propelled the establishment of many junior miners in Australia and saw increased investment in exploration activities. For example, there were more than 80 iron ore mines in Australia by the end of 2009, most of which were either newly established or transformed from other commercial activities to iron ore exploration. These junior miners are usually small, thus needing strong financial support for their exploration activities. They are relatively easy to acquire. Therefore, Chinese investments during this period were mainly in the miners at the exploration stage. Nevertheless the global financial crisis in 2008 caused a slump in demand for minerals and a shortage of financing. Many mining companies, even at the production stage, desperately needed cash to survive or pay their debts. This created many opportunities for Chinese firms to acquire Australian assets at a relatively low price, particularly established Australian miners at the production stage. Now that the capital restrictions of the GFC have eased, it has become more difficult and expensive to acquire large established Australian miners. It is also unclear as to whether the same opportunities exist for acquiring Australian small-cap miners, or if these Australian miners can source capital from traditional partners in the US, Britain and Japan.

Entry mode has been another important strategic consideration in FDI. Four major entry modes were observed for Chinese investment in the Australian resources sector: WOS, acquiring a controlling stake, JV and minority equity participation.

## WOS

Seven Chinese firms have acquired 100 per cent of an Australian entity and operated it as a WOS, or set up a new WOS due to their successful bid for a new minerals exploration permit in Australia. The Australian takeover laws require that an investor launches a compulsory purchase of 100 per cent of an Australian company if its share exceeds 19.9 per cent of the target company (unless agreed by its shareholders), and that its share should exceed 90 per cent if a launch bid is to succeed.

The most obvious advantage of a takeover is that the Chinese company will have 100 per cent control of the acquired company. It also offers the advantage of relatively easy coordination and communication between the parent company and its Australian subsidiary. Nevertheless a takeover of an Australian miner often involves a large capital expenditure and difficulties in managing cultural differences between Australian and Chinese employees.

There are only seven WOSs established by Chinese firms in eight acquisitions (see Table 2.1); these covered coal, iron ore, alumina, precious metals and base metals. The total initial transaction cost for these eight acquisitions was about A\$8 billion. This does not account for the further investment required of CITIC Pacific Mining and Sinosteel Midwest to develop their projects from exploration to production.

The WOS entry mode into the Australian minerals industry has been so far adopted by large state-owned Chinese companies such as: Yan Coal, a subsidiary of Yanzhou Coal Corporation; CITIC Pacific Corporation (CPC), a subsidiary of CITIC Group; Minmetals; Sinosteel; and CHINALCO. These companies are the first movers, exemplifying that large quantities of capital are required in acquiring a whole foreign company; thus it can be easily understood that only large companies can afford such investments. This may also reflect the level of international business experience of these companies; for example, Sinosteel was the former Chinese Metallurgical Import and Export Corporation, a flagship agency for importing and exporting steel materials and products, while Minmetals has been the largest import and export company in China for non-ferrous minerals and metals. Both have a relatively long history of international business operations. CITIC Pacific and Yanzhou Coal are listed on the Hong Kong Stock Exchange Market. CITIC Pacific is based in Hong Kong with its parent company, CITIC Group, established in 1984 for international trade and trust operations. Thus, these companies can be regarded as first movers of Chinese SOEs in international business.

Concerning the developmental stage of the target companies or projects, two Chinese MNCs have entered the Australian minerals industry through acquiring target companies in production; while three of their peers (CITIC Pacific, Metallurgical Corporation of China and CHINALCO) procured exploration projects. Sinosteel took over an Australian company in the developmental stage.

The method used by these Chinese investors was by friendly takeover, except in the case of Sinosteel's full acquisition of Midwest Corporation. Sinosteel launched a hostile acquisition of Midwest Corporation because of the strong opposition of the former Midwest's managing director who held more than a 10 per cent share of the target company.

### Acquiring a controlling stake

Four Chinese firms entered the Australian mining industry through taking a controlling stake in the target company. For example, Guangdong Nuclear Power Corporation took a 66 per cent share of Energy Metals Limited while Minmetals acquired 74 per cent of Abra Mining Limited. Hanlong's acquisition of a 55 per cent share in Moly Mines was the first case of a Chinese private firm taking a majority stake in an Australian listed company.

Compared with a takeover, acquiring a controlling stake in a listed company offers several advantages. First, it usually requires less capital for the initial transaction; second, it remains listed on the Australian Stock Exchange, retaining options for raising funds from the stock market through issuing shares; and third, it can keep senior managers and directors, thus stabilising the company's management and corporate governance after the acquisition. However, there are disadvantages, including compliance with the Australian Stock Exchange's rule for strict information disclosure and timely corporate reporting, and potential difficulties in internal communications and decision-making. Chapter 5 examines these issues in more detail.

### JV

Eight JVs have been established between Chinese and Australian companies, all of which are project-based. Among these eight JVs, three are marketing JVs established before 2005 and have now progressed to production. These are the Channar JV Project between Sinosteel and Rio Tinto, established in 1987; the Paraburdoo JV Project established in 2001 between Baosteel and Rio Tinto; and the Wheelarra JV Project between BHPB and four Chinese steel mills (WISCo, Maanshan Steel, Shasteel and Tangshan Steel) in 2004. These three early JVs are project-based and aimed at securing a Chinese market for two of the largest global iron ore mines, with the equity share of Chinese partners ranging from 40 per cent to 46 per cent. These three projects were signed before 2005 when iron ore was oversupplied and its price was relatively low. Thus, in retrospect, the terms and conditions specified in their JV agreements were very favourable to the Chinese steel mills. As a consequence, these three marketing JVs have financially outperformed other Chinese WOSs and JVs so far, partly due to the booming iron ore prices since 2005. Therefore, the timing for establishing a JV and the size of a JV partner may be crucial to the investment performance from the Chinese investors' perspective. The Chinese firms invested in these three JVs to secure iron ore supplies and gain financial returns from their investments.

The remaining five JVs were established after 2006; all were at the exploration stage when they were set up. The investment in these JVs varied substantially with four large Chinese steel companies investing most in their JV project: Karara Mining Limited (KML) (A\$372.06 million) between Ansteel and Gindalbie; Eyre Mining (up to A\$186 million) between WISCo and Centrex Metals; the Bungalow Project by Baotou Steel and Centrex (A\$40 million); and the Asia Iron Project (A\$280 million) between Chongqing Steel and SINOM Investment Limited, a Hong Kong-based company. All these four JVs are for magnetite iron ore. They differ from the Bluestone JV Project between the Yunnan Tin Group and Metals X, which explores for tin-bearing minerals. Metals X is the only tin producer in Australia.

The major benefits of forming a JV in the mining industry are to share risk and complementary resources, including financial, management, HR and technology. These are well-demonstrated in the recently established JVs, including Ansteel's JV (50:50) with Gindalbie Metals Limited, KML, and WISCo's partnership with Centrex Metals Limited at a project level (60:40). The fundamental consideration is to share the expertise and knowledge of the Australian partner, particularly in the areas of exploration, dealing with aboriginal communities and government approval processes, while reducing risks. These JVs are usually established at an early stage of the project; for example, Ansteel signed its JV agreement with Gindalbie in March 2006 to develop Gindalbie's Karara Iron Ore Project in Western Australia's Midwest region in two stages. Stage one was to conduct a feasibility study of magnetite and hematite deposits on a 50:50 basis of exploration cost, while stage two involved project financing terms. Ansteel has invested A$372 million from 2006 to 2008 to uncover an estimated 2 billion tonnes of magnetite. In stage two, Ansteel was required to provide 70 per cent of the equity funding component of this project and assist Gindalbie in securing its 30 per cent of equity funding, if requested to do so by the Australian partner. Gindalbie requested Ansteel to provide such a 30 per cent of project funding in November 2008 during the GFC; the whole JV project thus cost approximately A$1.8 billion.

Wuhan Iron and Steel Company (WISCo) formed a JV of 60:40 with Centrex Metals Limited in December 2008 for exploring and developing in South Australia two 5-million-tonne magnetite concentrate operations over the next five to seven years. The payment to Centrex Metals by WISCo was structured in six stages based on the reported inferred resources as specified by the Australasian Joint Ore Reserves Committee (JORC). The first instalment of A$52 million was made 15 days after government approval and the second payment of A$26 million was made on the first anniversary of the JV deal completion date. A further four instalments of $27 million each will be made when JORC-inferred resource reaches 1.25, 1.5, 1.75 and 2.0 billion tonnes, respectively. Such a payment arrangement can substantially reduce WISCo's risk in exploration. Moreover, WISCo and Centrex Metals have agreed to jointly develop a deep-water port at Sheep Hill for loading the iron ore produced. The JV terms used by WISCo are more complex than those by Ansteel, reflecting the increased knowledge and experience of Chinese steel mills when making entry decisions. Moreover, WISCo is required to solely fund the first A$75 million of work commitments into the JV to cover exploration and study costs. In addition to setting up a JV with their Australian partner, both Chinese steel mills have also acquired their equity in the Australian partners (Ansteel holds 36.28% of Gindalbie, and WISCo took up 13.04% of Centrex Metals through share replacement).

Several reasons have contributed to the adoption of this type of entry. First, the mining industry is risky, involving a high level of uncertainty in exploration, but a JV can spread the risks. Second, most Chinese firms have little experience in doing international business, lacking the managerial and technical competencies in operating a foreign miner; these include the Australian legal environment, business practices and networks. A JV could be a good platform for Chinese firms to learn from their Australian partners in these areas. Third, a JV can also spread demand for financial input from Chinese partners.

However, several disadvantages of JVs include the cost of coordination between partners, issues of control and agency costs and several problems related to corporate governance and management. These issues will be dealt with in Chapter 5.

## Minority equity participation

Many Chinese firms have invested in the Australian minerals industry in the form of minority equity participation (MEP) for different reasons. This is a more flexible and less committed entry mode, compared with WOS and JV. The three Chinese firms with a high percentage of shares are: Shasteel in Grange (46.7%), Shougang (and APAC) in Mt Gibson (40.4%) and Ansteel in Gindalbie (36.3%). In fact, Shasteel has *de facto* shareholding control of the target company after its controlling Australian company (Australian Bulk Minerals (ABM)) merged with Grange Resources in January 2009. ABM accounted for 76.3 per cent of the merged company.

For an overwhelming majority of Chinese investors, their share in the target company is less than 20 per cent. This reflects partly their intention to invest as a minority participant, rather than to take over the target company, and partly because of the legal limit placed by the Australia's corporate law on takeover, as discussed before. Other influencing factors include the Australian regulatory framework on FDI that deals with the status of foreign ownership, whereby if an Australian company has more than 15 per cent foreign ownership it would be considered by the Australian government to be a foreign entity. The proposed investment thus becomes exposed to a number of special approval processes and restrictions imposed by them. So far, most Chinese investors in this group have invested in Australian junior miners at the exploration stage. Several Chinese investments were made in Australian companies at the production stage, examples being Valin's huge investment in FMG, and Shougang's in Mt Gibson.

The disadvantages of Chinese minority equity participation include little participation in the company's strategic decision-making processes, which means no management representation and no board representation in many cases. This usually leaves the minority investors also having no say in the operations of the company.

Investment in the Australian minerals industry can have several rights and obligations. As JV partners or minority equity participants, Chinese investors can be entitled to various rights and are obliged to meet conditions as specified in their investment agreement with the company invested. The following section examines these obligations and rights.

## Obligations and rights for Chinese investors as JV partners or equity participants

As JV partners or minority equity participants, Chinese investors also have other obligations and rights, depending on the outcomes of their investment negotiations. The obligations borne by them can be grouped into three categories: financing, buying convertible bonds from the company invested and providing loans.

Project financing, such as helping secure bank loans for project development, has been one of the key obligations placed by the Australian companies on Chinese investors, for example, in the case of Ansteel with Gindalbie.

The several rights for JVs include: board representation, management representation, marketing rights, minority protection, veto power and an ability to dispose of their interest. The marketing rights usually cover off-take rights, long-term supply contracts and minority partners' share control. These are usually the rights demanded by Japanese firms in their JVs with Australian mining companies. These rights are not automatically granted to investors, but often result from investment negotiations.

There are two types of JV between Chinese investors and Australian mining companies: the marketing JV and the project-based JV. The marketing JVs concluded are: Sinosteel–Rio Tinto (Channar Project), Baosteel–Rio Tinto (Bao-Range) and BHPB four Chinese steel mills (Wheelarra Project). The rights of Chinese investors in these JVs depend on the nature of the JV they established.

The three marketing JVs between Chinese investors and Australian mining companies all provide marketing rights to Chinese investors in terms of a long-term supply contract for a specified amount of commodity – in the above cases, iron ore. Interestingly, this commodity amount is independent of how many tonnes the JV project produces and can be supplied by the Australian partner from the production of other mines. The Australian partners are solely responsible for the JV's management and operations, while the Chinese partners provide financial input to the JV operations, implement the off-take agreements and only participate in major decision-making. The partnership

*Table 2.2*   The rights of Chinese partners in their JV with Australian companies

| Marketing JVs | Annual production and supply | Duration of the sales contract | Investment and share of JV partners |
| --- | --- | --- | --- |
| Sinosteel–Hamersley Rio Tinto | 200mt (annual production 10mt) | 24 years (signed in 1987, produced in 1990) | A$420m for the project (40% for Chinese and 60% for Rio Tinto) |
| Baosteel–Rio Tinto | 200mt (annual supply of 10mt) | 20 years (signed in Dec 2001) | A$124m Baosteel (Chinese 46% and Rio Tinto 54%) |
| Four Chinese mills–HPB | 12mt/year | 25 years (signed in 2003, executed in 28 September 2004, commissioned in October 2005) | Four Chinese mills (10% each), BHPB (51%), and two Japanese trading houses (4.8% Mitsui and 4.2% Itochu) |

of these three marketing JVs and their key terms are presented in Table 2.2.

The project-based JV between Chinese investors and Australian mining companies include: KML, between Ansteel and Gindalbie Metals Limited, on a 50:50 basis established in April 2006; and the JV between WISCo and Centrex Metals Limited set up in July 2009 on a 60:40 basis. KML aims to produce 15 million tonnes of iron ore concentrate and 3 million tonnes of direct shipping ore annually, while WISCo's JV plans to produce 10 million tonnes of iron ore concentrate per annum. Both Chinese investors also hold a share in their Australian partner's parent company. The Chinese commitment to the JVs has been established in stages, primarily to reduce risks during exploration.

Ansteel has secured several JV rights, including board representation (two Chinese directors out of four for KML). More importantly, it also has management representation by sending several managers to be involved at infrastructure, project and finance levels. In March 2009, Ansteel signed a mine-life long-term supply contract with KML for all iron ore produced from the JV.

For minority equity participants, a possible right for Chinese investors is representation on the board. Board representation may be offered to Chinese investors, such as Guangdong Foreign Trade Corporation in

Kagara (19.9% of shareholding and one non-executive director). Several Chinese investors have also secured the rights for signing an off-take agreement, examples being the following investments: Valin in FMG, Jinchuan in Metals X and Rockcheck in Aurox (Aurox was acquired by Atlas in July 2010). Regarding obligations, Chinese investors may be requested to provide funds for project development, such as Creat's investment in Galaxy, in which it was asked to provide financial support of \$130 million for the development of Mt Cattlin Spodumene and Jiangsu Lithium Carbonate Projects.

# 3
# Australian Regulatory Framework on FDI and its Application to Chinese Investment

## Introduction

The Australian economic structure has changed significantly since the 1960s, becoming increasingly reliant upon the mining sector, including minerals, oil and gas. Before then, Australia was widely portrayed as a nation that "lives on the sheep's back", with its agricultural and pastoral activities accounting for more than 15–35 per cent of its GDP (Caves & Krause, 1984). However, these sectors have declined steadily, only accounting for 3.6 per cent of national GDP in 2009. The mining sector, conversely, has increased from about 2 per cent of the national GDP in 1921 (Caves & Krause, 1984) to 7 per cent in 1991, remaining relatively stable (6.51–7.5%) over the past two decades (ABS, 2010a). In fact, the Australian mining industry has been the driving force of its national economy since 2005. Mineral exports accounted for 44.8 per cent of total exports from Australia, reaching A$284.7 billion in the 2008–09 financial year (Australian Bureau of Agricultural and Resource Economics, 2010). Therefore, Australian mining industries are regarded as a crucial source for long-term national income and employment.

The importance of the Australian mining industry was described in an article in the *Year Book of Australia* in 2008:

> Overall, mining activity accounts for around 8% of Australia's gross domestic product and has contributed over A$500b directly to Australia's wealth during the past 20 years. There are around 320,000 Australians employed in the industry, either directly or indirectly in support industries. Many are in sparsely populated, remote and regional Australia. (Geoscience Australia, 2007)

The article also ranked the production and export characteristics of Australia's mining industries:

> Australia is the world's largest exporter of black coal, iron ore and gold. It also holds the status of being the leading producer of bauxite and alumina as well as the second largest producer of uranium, lead and zinc; the third largest producer of iron ore, nickel, manganese and gold; the fourth largest producer of black coal, silver and copper; and the fifth largest producer of aluminium.

FDI in the Australian mining industries has played a vital role in their exploration, development and production activities. Such a role was elaborated by the Federal Treasurer Wayne Swan, who stated that without foreign investment,

> based on the last few years of foreign investment levels, we could expect business investment to be initially about 25 per cent lower and output to be about 3 per cent lower, resulting in around 200,000 fewer jobs. There would also be very substantial costs to Australia's productive capacity, given the role of foreign direct investment in building our capital stock. (Swan, 2009a)

Therefore, it is easy to comprehend why Australian governments have now attached such a high importance to FDI in its resources sectors.

This chapter describes the Australian regulatory framework and its recent developments that have impacted upon Chinese investment in Australia. It also examines the approval procedure, the fundamental considerations behind the approval process, and the approval outcomes, particularly in relation to Chinese investment in the Australian resources sector.

## A brief description of FDI in Australia and its mining industries

Historically, foreign investment has been the driving force of the Australian economy. Before World War I (1914–18), the majority of international capital and investments flowing into Australia was from private British investors seeking higher return due to low interest rates within the UK (Meredith & Dyster, 1999). The bulk of these investments were used for financing infrastructure, such as port facilities, railways, road, power and gas projects. Although British investment and capital remained the major source for Australia until the early 1960s, it fluc-tuated as it was influenced by the return rate in 1880s and the global recession in 1930.

The second half of the twentieth century witnessed changes in the patterns and sources of FDI in Australia. American MNCs became dom-inant investors from the 1950s to the 1970s, specifically focusing on the Australian manufacturing sector and mining industries. Thus, for-eign ownership became a political issue. During this period, Japan also became an important trading partner because its industrialisation had rapidly increased demand for Australia's minerals and energy. The 22-year iron ore embargo on Japan was lifted in 1960 and that country commenced importing iron ore from Australia in the 1960s and invest-ing in Australian mining industries, particularly iron ore and coal. In the past two decades of the twentieth century, foreign investment came from a wider variety of sources and most investments were in the Australian services sector because the Australian government started deregulating its financial services industry in the 1980s (Meredith & Dyster, 1999).

## FDI in the Australian resources sector

Although foreign investment in the Australian resources sector started as early as the 1880s (Meredith & Dyster, 1999), major FDI in that sec-tor has been most evident since the 1960s when Japanese steel mills and trading companies invested in the Australian iron ore industry after the iron ore export embargo from Australia to Japan was lifted in 1960 (B. Smith, 1978). The early 1960s also witnessed a low period in the Australian mining industry's contribution to the national economy (see Figure 3.1).

Japanese trading companies, such as Mitsui and Itochu, and several steel companies like Nippon Steel, started investing in the Australian iron ore industry, particularly in the Pilbara iron ore region in WA in the mid-1960s. Japanese firms were a major source of investment in 1970s and 1980s in the Australian resources industries; this represented the second wave of FDI in the Australian mining industries after the British investment of the late nineteenth century. The recent surge since 2007 of Chinese investment in Australia can be regarded as the third wave of FDI in Australian mining industries. This Chinese investment only began in 1987 when a Chinese trading company and SOE, China Metallurgical Import and Export Corporation (now Sinosteel), invested A$168 million (40%) in Hamersley Iron to establish a JV, the Channar

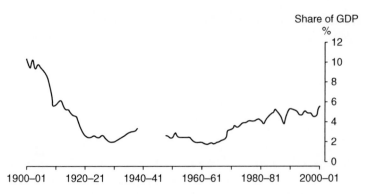

*Figure 3.1*  The contribution of the Australian mining industry to the national economy
*Source*: ABS, 2005; ABS data used with permission from the Australian Bureau of Statistics.

Project (see Table 2.1). However, China became the third-largest investment nation in the Australian economy at the close of 2008, trailing only the UK and US. Nevertheless the FDI stock of the US (A\$99.2 billion), UK (A\$63.2 billion) and Japan (A\$45 billion) in Australia was still far larger by 2009 than the A\$9.2 billion of China (ABS, 2010b).

Although investment from overseas has, historically, been a driving force in the growth of the Australian economy, the response from Australian politicians, business executives and the public towards foreign investment in Australia has varied widely, ranging from fear to support. Deep concerns, sometimes bordering on fear, of foreign control were high towards American investment in 1950s and 1960s, the Japanese in 1970s and 1980s, and, more recently, were directed towards the Chinese. The following section examines the Australian regulatory framework for FDI.

## Australian regulatory framework for FDI

### An overview

Australia's inward investment is primarily regulated by legislation including the FATA and guided by the Australian government's foreign investment policy (Policy). The FIRB is the government body administering the FATA; its primary function is to advise the federal treasurer on whether an inward FDI is contrary to Australia's national interest on a case-by-case basis. The federal treasurer has the authority to approve, conditionally approve or reject an investment proposal. The fundamental position for the Australian government over the past half century has been to welcome foreign investment, with the specific qualification that this foreign investment should be made by privately owned and operated investors without explicit links to any national government or entity.

## The FATA and the policy

Until the 1970s, a foreign exchange control mechanism was used by the Australian government primarily to regulate foreign investment flows to Australia, despite its intervention in other proposals from time to time (The Treasury of Australian Government, n.d).

The Foreign Acquisitions and Takeovers Act 1975 formalised such control and, by the end of 2009, has been amended 12 times. It provides guidance for an Australian government agency to screen FDI applications, including foreign investment in Australian real estate, lands and business. It also gives the Australian government, specifically the FIRB and the federal treasurer, power to block an investment proposal. The Foreign Acquisitions and Takeovers Regulations 1989 (the Regulations) established thresholds for the monetary size of an investment and share of an Australian business to be acquired.

The amendment of the Regulations in August 2009 set a single threshold of 15 per cent in a business worth $219 million and indexed it with inflation. This means that private foreign investment in Australian businesses below A$219 million (A$231 million in 2010) can proceed without submitting its investment application to the Australian government for approval, provided it does not exceed 15 per cent of the Australian company in which the investment is being made. However, investment by foreign governments and their agencies, such as SOEs and Sovereign Wealth Funds, requires review by FIRB and approval by the federal treasurer irrespective of the investment size (Foreign Investment Policy Division, 2009).

As in many OECD (Organisation for Economic Co-operation and Development) countries, the FATA *per se* is quite broad and applies to relevant inward FDI proposals regardless of investor nationality. The regulations have been written to deal with FDI from countries similar to Australia. The pattern for Australian governments has been to be as "non-intrusive...as possible" (Swan, 2009a), reflecting a consistent and positive Australian government policy on FDI.

Chinese investment, specifically by SOEs, has created a quite unique situation for the FIRB and the Australian federal treasurer, particularly in respect of Australia's political–economic-sensitive resources sector, due

to Chinese SOE's close links to their governments. The most fundamental criterion for the Australian federal government when screening
foreign investment is to examine if the proposed investment application is contrary to Australia's national interest. The following section
describes and analyses this key concept.

### The Australian national interest

What constitutes the national interest? The Policy defines national
interest as "the widely held community concerns of Australians" (FIRB,
2008, p. 72). This definition is widely regarded as too broad and open
to interpretation by different stakeholders. For example, an Australian
investment manager was quoted as saying, "The true national interest served by Australian iron ore producers is receiving the maximum
price for their maximum production volume" (Tasker, 2009g). This is
obviously very narrowly defined and only considers economic issues.
The issue of short-term gain and longer-term costs for Australia and its
industries has also to be considered in assessing foreign investment into
Australia. Other key aspects of the national interest cover political and
social interests.

These three important aspects of the national interest (political,
economic and social) are depicted in Figure 3.2.

The economic interest or benefit of FDI is pivotal. This includes job
creation, wealth generation and economic sovereignty as outlined by

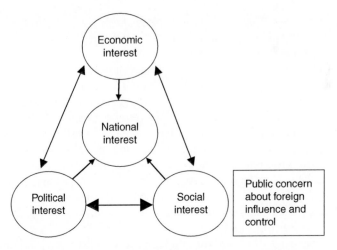

*Figure 3.2*   Key elements of Australia's national interest in assessing FDI

the federal treasurer (Swan, 2009a). The political interest often involves ideological issues between the Australian government and the investing nation, and the political doctrine of the incumbent Australian party and other politicians. National security naturally comes from this interest; it may be more accurately described as national concern. The social interest is often reflected by the Australian public's understanding and perception of FDI, media comments and the social ties between the two countries. While some of these interests are relatively stable, such as social ties and ideology, economic interest has been quite dynamic over the past three years as the Australian government has responded to rapid changes in the global economic environment. These three elements will be further analysed in the following sections.

### Recent developments on the Australian regulatory framework

Several factors have contributed to China's very rapid growth in OFDI, particularly in the Australian minerals industry since 2006. First, the rapid development of the Chinese economy, particularly after the Asian financial crisis in 1997, substantially increased its appetite for raw materials and energy supplies. This has resulted in the rapid increase of commodity prices over the past five years. For example, the annual contracted iron ore price has increased from $36 per tonnes in 2004 to $140 in 2008. Figure 3.3 shows China's iron ore import and its benchmark price between 1997 and 2010.

Second, since 2002, the Chinese government has launched a series of policies to encourage Chinese firms to invest overseas as part of the effort to implement its "going out" policy. Third, the massive accumulation of more than $2 trillion of foreign currency reserve in China by the end of 2008 drove Chinese firms to look for global investment opportunities. Australia is a favourite investment destination for Chinese investment, particularly in the resources sector as it has abundant natural resources, is geographically close to China and has a stable political and economic environment. Consequently, a slew of Chinese investment proposals have flooded into Australia since 2007. Given the importance of the resources sector to Australia's national economy, increasing Chinese investment caused a debate among the Australian public, politicians and business communities regarding how FDI should be guided and controlled.

In responding to the debate, the incumbent Australian government and its agency have made several changes in its regulatory framework,

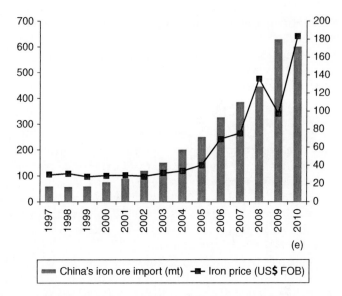

*Figure 3.3* China's iron ore import and its benchmark price between 1997 and 2010

notably the Six Principles announced in the February 2008, amendment of the FATA on the issue of convertible bonds and warranty in FDI in February 2009, the increase of the investment monetary screening threshold for FDI in August 2009 and the clarification of the terms of "national interest" and "foreign government and a related entity" in June 2010.

### The Six Principles, SOEs and "Sovereign Wealth Funds"

The Australian government issued a set of FDI guidelines, "The Six Principles", to further guide decisions on inward FDI to Australia. These specifically addressed concerns about government ownership (SOEs) and "Sovereign Wealth Funds" (FIRB, 2008). These Six Principles are:

1. An investor's operations are independent of the relevant foreign government.
2. An investor is subject to and adheres to the law and observes common standards of business behaviour.
3. An investment may hinder competition or lead to undue concentration or control in the industry or sectors concerned.

4. An investment may impact on Australian government revenue or other policies.
5. An investment may impact on Australia's national security.
6. An investment may impact on the operations and directions of an Australian business, as well as its contribution to the Australian economy and broader community.

The key issues emphasised in these principles are: independence, commerciality (including corporate governance and business behaviour) and national security. These touch three broad areas: economic, political and social areas (see Figure 3.2). Economic interest includes economic sovereignty (Principles 1 and 2), wealth generation (Principles 3, 4 and 6) and job creation (Principle 6); political interest covers national security; while contributions to the broader Australian community can be regarded as part of social interest.

These Principles were intended to "promote transparency" for making clear the factors evaluated when considering Australia's national interest; they are "non-discriminatory" as they apply equally to all investments by foreign governments and related entities (Swan, 2009b), although some believed Chinese investment was specially targeted to alleviate public concerns. Public debate is considered as being "healthy and positive" by the Australian government for policy making as explained by the then minister for foreign affairs, Mr Stephen Smith (2009). The issue of these Six Principles also raised concerns from Chinese governments and business communities about possible discrimination by the Australian government against Chinese investment.

Responding to the concern about transparency and how these "Six Principles" are used when reviewing investment proposals, the federal treasurer further explained, in his speech to the Australia–China Business Council in July 2008, that Australia aims to maintain "a market-based system" in which companies are responsive to their shareholders and strategic decisions, such as sales, production and investment, are driven by market forces instead of political considerations (Swan, 2008b). He further pointed to three specific issues related to investment from SOEs and Sovereignty Wealth Funds, particularly the concerns of: conflict of interest for an investor as both buyer and sellers; control over pricing and production in the acquired firms by investors; and size and developmental stage of the firms acquired. He added that this stresses the importance of the elements of wealth creation and economic sovereignty in national interest.

Nevertheless, the Six Principles are also very broad in their terms of being "independent of a foreign government". This and other commercially related issues are very complex and difficult to define and operate, thereby leaving much room for the federal treasurer to exercise discretionary powers. However, these Six Principles are only policy, rather than laws, and thus are not necessarily enforced. Veteran researchers regarded them as unnecessary (Drysdale & Findlay, 2008) because existing regulations were considered adequate to deal with the SOEs (Huang, Austin, Zhang & Grainger, 2009). In fact, the FIRB has not rejected any investment proposals by Chinese SOEs so far, and only imposed conditions on 5 out of 170 Chinese investment proposals from November 2007 to June 2010 (Crean, 2010).

### Convertible bonds, and lifting the threshold for foreign investment reviews

In early February 2009, just before Rio Tinto announced its proposal for strategic partnership with CHINALCO in a deal worth US$19.5 billion, the Australian government introduced new legislation that treated convertible notes and warranty as equity. Although it was explained that such complex investment instruments did not exist when the FATA was originally drafted, media and business communities have widely considered that it was amended to deal with the CHINALCO–Rio alliance proposal, as part of the deal involved $7.2 billion of convertible bonds from CHINALCO to Rio. It is noteworthy that the amendment was made during the GFC when foreign investment was desperately needed for both Australia and the Australian business community.

Further operational changes to Australia's foreign investment framework were made by the Australian government on 22 September 2009. One of these changes was the increase of the monetary screening threshold for privately owned foreign investors from A$100 million to A$219 million, which is to be adjusted with the annual consumer price index (CPI). The Australian government also abolished the screening requirement on setting up new, privately owned businesses by foreigners wanting to invest over A$10 million. Many business executives, particularly those from junior mining companies, expressed concern that this reform did not help with securing financing from Chinese companies because it did not loosen any restrictions for Chinese SOEs wishing to invest in Australia. As a consequence, a further relaxation of foreign ownership control for FDI was demanded.

A speech by Patrick Colmer, the general manager of the Australian Treasury's Foreign Investment and Trade Policy Division in 2009, further confused global investment communities. Colmer explicitly expressed a view about the Australian government's preferences for FDI at the China Investment Forum on 4 September 2009. He said: "Our Government has expressed a preference for projects that are joint projects in various forms,... In particular, we are much more comfortable when we see investments that are below 50 per cent for greenfield and around 15 per cent for major producers." Additionally, the Australian government preferred that Australian firms remain listed on the Australian Securities Exchange (ASX) after being acquired by foreign companies. It seems that the FIRB prefers to place a cap on foreign investment in Australian companies, particularly in the mining sector. It was also the first time that the ownership and the developmental stage and/or size of the company or project were explicitly mentioned as factors in the review process. Nevertheless such attitudes can be regarded as preferences only, rather than law, as Yanzhou successfully acquired 100 per cent of Felix Resources for A\$3.5 billion in November 2009 after Colmer's speech.

### Clarification of national interest

Responding to the wide criticism on the vagueness of the term "national interest", the treasurer has clarified the consideration of national interest in a further amendment to the Policy in June 2010 (FIRB, 2010b). The factors, considered in assessing a foreign investment proposal cover, include:

- National security – the degree to which an investment affects Australia's ability to protect its strategic interests;
- Competition – the extent to which an investment may result in an investor gaining control over market pricing and production of a good or service in Australia, and the potential impact an investment has on the make-up of the relevant global industry;
- Other Australian government policies (including tax) – the level of impact of an investment on Australian tax revenue, and its consistency with the Australian government's objectives in relation to matters such as environmental impact;
- Impact on the economy and the community – the impact of an investment on the general economy and its fair return for the Australian people; and

- Character of the investor – the extent to which the investor operates on a transparent commercial basis and is subject to adequate and transparent regulation and supervision.

This amendment to the Policy can be regarded as a further explanation and removal of the "Six Principles", with their formal incorporation into the Australian regulatory framework on FDI. Not surprisingly, three important aspects of the national interest (political, economic and social) have been highlighted in the amendment. It also explicitly states for the first time that the character of the investor is considered in assessing the investment proposal. In addition, the amended framework has also relaxed the requirement for foreign governments and their agencies, such as SOEs, to notify the FIRB prior to any investment in Australia only if their investment is less than 10 per cent of the company invested in and not used to influence and control it, for example, through the appointment of directors and off-take agreements (FIRB, 2010b).

## Summary of national interest

Based on the contents of FATA, and the Regulations and their recent developments, it is quite clear that the economic interest is a fundamental element of the national interest that the Australian government aims to regulate so as to guide foreign investment. The broad components of economic interest have been wealth creation, employment and economic sovereignty. The Australian government can emphasise different aspects in response to the changes in the global economic environment.

Public perception about inward FDI into Australia is another important element of national interest because the policy defines national interest as "the widely held community concerns of Australians" (FIRB, 2008, p. 72). This must be considered by the Australian government in assessing FDI into Australia as the government is democratically elected by its citizens. It could be an important trigger for the treasurer to reject an inward FDI proposal if public opinion towards a particular FDI is overwhelmingly negative. Public concern or perception is a "soft issue" as it is difficult to define and measure; however, even a subtle shift in public perception can result in the political and policy elite taking a highly conservative stance towards foreign investment issues.

In contrast, the national security interest is a more tangible issue that can be dealt with more openly and swiftly by the Australian government when assessing FDI applications. Other political issues, such as ideological differences and political debate between the Australian Labor Party and the coalition of conservative parties, are often subtle. These political issues, coupled with the public perception of FDI, have been deftly handled by the Australian government through amending regulations such as the Six Principles, communicating to the Australian general public and business community, initiating dialogue with foreign governments, and defending the incumbent party's position or attacking the opposition's viewpoints.

Despite the Australian government having made frequent changes and amendments to its regulatory framework on FDI, it has been pragmatic in assessing FDI proposals so far, including those from Chinese SOEs. The review outcomes over the past several years clearly demonstrate the Australian government's position on FDI and are analysed in the following section.

## The outcomes of FIRB decisions on FDI applications between 2001 and 2009

The FIRB is an advisory unit within the Commonwealth Department of Treasury. Before 10 December 2009 there were three members of the board; subsequently four members were appointed to the board.

A foreign investment application is reviewed by the board with a decision usually being made with in 30 days, but an additional 90 days can be added to the review process. The board can also ask the acquiring company to withdraw and resubmit its application. However, each withdrawal and resubmission involves 30 days for a review. The board's ultimate recommendation awaits the final decision of the federal treasurer. Potential investors are advised to discuss their investment proposal with the FIRB before it is formally signed and submitted for the review process.

The board usually classifies applications into different categories. For example, a large project application involves investment of more than A\$500 million (Swan, 2009b). At the application level, a case-by-case approach has been used by the FIRB when assessing each application. The review outcomes between 2001 and 2009 are presented in Table 3.1.

Table 3.1 shows that the Australian government approved most inward FDI applications with conditions (an average of 73.2%). The proportion of conditionally approved investment applications decreased to 57.6 per cent in 2008–09, reflecting the impact of the GFC on the conditions imposed by the Australian government on the inward investment proposals. From July 2001 to June 2009, the FIRB made decisions on 42,825 applications, with more than 99 per cent being approved.

Table 3.1 The number of proposals considered by FIRB between 2001–02 and 2008–09

| Outcome | 2001–02 n (%) | 2002–03 n (%) | 2003–04 n (%) | 2004–05 n (%) | 2005–06 n (%) | 2006–07 n (%) | 2007–08 n (%) | 2008–09 n (%) | Mean n (%) |
|---|---|---|---|---|---|---|---|---|---|
| Approved unconditionally | 1,041 (23.0) | 1,105 (23.3) | 995 (22.1) | 1,127 (25.5) | 1,386 (26.5) | 1,520 (24.5) | 1,656 (21.1) | 2,266 (42.3) | 1,387 (25.9) |
| Approved with conditions | 3,405 (75.3) | 3,562 (75.0) | 3,452 (76.5) | 3,233 (73.2) | 3,800 (72.8) | 4,637 (74.9) | 6,185 (78.7) | 3,086 (57.6) | 3,920 (73.2) |
| Rejected | 77 (1.7) | 80 (1.7) | 64 (1.4) | 55 (0.7) | 37 (0.7) | 39 (0.6) | 14 (0.2) | 3 (0.1) | 46 (0.9) |
| Total decided | 4,523 | 4,747 | 4,511 | 4,415 | 5,223 | 6,196 | 7,855 | 5,355 | 5,353 |
| Withdrawn | 402 | 365 | 319 | 287 | 373 | 629 | 521 | 341 | 405 |
| Exempt | 172 | 203 | 206 | 182 | 185 | 200 | 172 | 125 | 181 |
| Total considered | 5,097 | 5,315 | 5,036 | 4,884 | 5,781 | 7,025 | 8,548 | 5,821 | 5,938 |

*Source*: FIRB's annual report 2008–09 (FIRB, 2010a).

An overwhelming majority (over 90%) of these applications were in the real estate industry. Potentially, the range of imposed conditions in a conditionally approved application is unlimited. If they are appropriately selected, they can be an effective means for addressing three elements of the national interest. The Australian government is very experienced in imposing conditions on inward FDI, as the majority of FDI applications were approved with conditions. Additionally, these conditions have changed as the Australian government responds to the global economic environment and the rapid increase of FDI from Chinese firms. The following section describes concerns about Chinese investment before it examines the conditions imposed by FIRB on such investments.

## Concerns about Chinese investment and their review outcomes

### Concerns about Chinese investment in the Australian mining industries

The primary concern about Chinese ODI in the Australian resources sector is the ownership of the acquiring firms; in most cases this is by Chinese SOEs such as CHINALCO, Minmetals, Sinosteel and the Metallurgical Corporation of China (MCC). Foreign ownership has been an important issue in the Australian mining industry. It is widely recognised in the literature (Globerman & Shapiro, 2009) that these large Chinese SOEs have strong links with the Chinese government, leading to concerns that they might pursue non-commercial objectives and so potentially jeopardise the host country's national interest. Similarly, some Chinese investment funds, such as the China Investment Corporation's (CIC) so-called "Sovereign Wealth Funds", have also been actively engaged in pursuing foreign investment. Additionally, Chinese SOEs often secure their funding from state-owned banks for their acquisition of foreign firms at a very low, non-market-driven interest rate. For example, as previously stated, CHINALCO's bank loan for financing its equity injection into Rio Tinto was reported to be only 90 basis points over the LIBOR, far less than the 375 basis points required when compared with the normal commercial loan rate in the sector at that time. Some view this as anti-competitive behaviour.

The most serious concern for Australian politicians and policy makers is probably Chinese control of Australian resources, particularly in the minerals industry. Politically, China is dominated by the Chinese

Communist Party (CCP), which is ideologically different from Australia's major political parties. Such control, if realised, might put Australian's national interest at risk; for example, its defence system. Economically, the minerals industry has been the driving force in the Australian economy. Thus the prospect of potential Chinese control could undermine Australia's economic activities and national wealth, by pushing down commodity prices and thus reducing tax and related revenue for Australian and state governments.

Another widely held concern is the potential conflict of interest between Chinese SOEs acquiring Australian resources and Chinese investors or other SOEs buying the resources generated by their target firms. All Chinese SOEs are closely linked because of government ownership. Consequently, Chinese investors could exert their influence on the supply and price of such resources in response to Chinese government pressure. A hypothetical case in this instance could be Rio Tinto pushing less aggressively in iron ore and coal price negotiations with Chinese buyers, as suggested by some Australian politicians and investors (AFIC, 2009; Turnbull, 2009). Moreover, internal price transfer has been a tactic used by MNCs for tax reduction purposes (Fraedrich & Bateman, 1996), particularly when a MNC is also the buyer of the minerals extracted. Both could put Australia's economic interest, in terms of royalties and taxes, at risk.

**FIRB decisions on Chinese investment**

In considering investment proposals from Chinese firms, particularly SOEs, the Australian government assesses each application against the national interest, which covers economic, social and political issues as guided by the FATA, the Regulations and specifically by the Six Principles for SOEs which was replaced by Australia's amended foreign investment policy issued in June 2010. However, other factors may also be influential. Bilateral trade between Australia and China and the huge potential of the Chinese market for Australian services and products are economic factors that must be considered in the treasurer's decision on Chinese investment in Australia. Their bilateral trade reached A$76 billion in 2009 and China became Australia's largest trading partner in that year. Recognising the importance of bilateral trade and the investment relationship, the Australian and Chinese governments held 15 rounds of free trade agreement (FTA) negotiations before the end of June 2010. The Australian government has pressed China to open its markets for agricultural products and the services sector, such as banking and education, in the latest rounds of FTA negotiations.

Reciprocity is another crucial factor in developing a bilateral relationship, forming part of the social contract. While Chinese investments in Australia have increased recently, so have Australian investments in China, reaching approximately A\$7 billion by 2008, up from A\$1.35 billion in 2003 (Crean, 2010). Commenting on Australia's bilateral relationship with China, former Australian trade minister, Simon Crean, openly expressed his view: "Investment with China is a two-way street. This [Australian investment in China] is an area where Australian companies need to do more to seize the opportunities available" (Crean, 2010). Reciprocity is a crucial ideological factor in the whole debate as it underpins the concepts of free market competition between nations. This is a bipartisan approach to the Australian economy and should not be subject to a change of government in Australia.

The review outcomes for Chinese investment applications have so far reflected both the complexity of the relationship between China and Australia, and the variety and diversity of factors to be considered by the Australian government. So far, most of the Chinese investments have been approved without conditions, particularly those investing in junior mines such as MCC's 100 per cent acquisition of the Camp Lambert iron ore project for A\$400 million, and Sinosteel's hostile takeover of Midwest (see Figure 2.1).

Because many factors are considered by the Australian government in assessing a FDI application, a case-by-case approach has been used. Consequently, it not only produces three broad categories of results: reject, conditional approval and unconditional approval, but also imposes different conditions for different applications.

The three broad review outcomes by the FIRB are presented in Table 3.2: approved without conditions, rejection and conditional approval. Since the Labor government came to power in November 2007, it approved more than 170 Chinese investment applications by the end of June 2010, an investment totalling more than A\$60 billion, although the real capital flow into Australia has been much less than this approved investment amount. Only five applications have been required to consider further undertakings or amendments, or have had conditions imposed upon them (Crean, 2010). In addition, only two applications were withdrawn: CNMC's proposed investment in Lynas and WISCo's proposed establishing of a JV with Western Plains Resources. The details of these seven investment applications are presented in Table 3.2.

Concerning the two Chinese investment applications that were withdrawn after being signalled by the FIRB for amendment or rejection, the

*Table 3.2* The review outcomes for several major Chinese investments in the Australian resources sector

| Acquiring firm (year) | Target firms | Transaction and developmental stage | Value and main assets | Outcome |
|---|---|---|---|---|
| Yanzhou (2009) | Felix Resources | 100% takeover; major producer | A$3.5 billion; thermal coal | Approved with conditions |
| Minmetals (2009) | OZ Minerals | 100% takeover except Prominent Hills Project | A$1.700 million; base and precious metals | Resubmitted and approved with exclusion of Prominent Hills mine in Woomera Prohibited Area |
| Valin (2009) | FMG | 17.4% via issuing new shares and buying shares from Habinger; major producer | A$1.200 million; iron ore | Approved with conditions (granted for up to 17.55%) |
| Ansteel (2009 Q2) | Gingalbie Metals | 36.28% via issuing new shares | A$162.06 million; iron ore | Approved with conditions |
| Sinosteel | Murchison | Proposal only | A$1.36 billion; iron ore | Approved with conditions (granted for up to 49.9%) |
| China Non-ferrous Metal Corp. (2009) | Lynas | 51.6% via issuing new shares; junior explorer | A$252 million; rare earth metals | Withdrawal after FIRB signalled it would not approve a majority stake because China is the world's largest major producer of rare earth metals |
| WISCo (2009) | Western Plains Resources | 50%; junior explorer | A$271 million; iron ore | Withdrawal after FIRB flagged a national defence concern in the Woomera Prohibited Area |

WISCo case had involved a plan for Australian mines to be located close to one of the Australian Defence Force's weapon-testing areas, Woomera Prohibited Area in South Australia. WISCo proposed to institute a JV with Western Plain Resources, which has a mine in Hark Nest Mining Area, near the Woomera Prohibited Area. WISCo withdrew its application because the Australian Defence Force did not support such an application. Given the sensitivity of national security, the Australian government has been adamant that it will not approve foreign investment applications that could compromise national security. The WISCo case followed the case of Minmetals, which originally proposed acquiring all of OZ Minerals' assets, including the Prominent Hill mine, which is also located near Woomera. Minmetals was required by the FIRB to amend its proposal to exclude OZ Minerals' Prominent Hill assets before it was approved.

Competition is another important issue that the Australian government considers in approving FDI. Besides the conflict of buyer and seller, industry concentration is another concern as demonstrated by the proposed investment by CNMC in Lynas, Australia's largest miner of rare earth metals. The FIRB required CNMC to reduce its share of Lynas to less than 50 per cent from the originally proposed 51.66 per cent. China has more than half of the world resources of rare earth metals and is a globally dominant producer of rare earth metals. Its global market share was over 90 per cent in 2009. CNMC withdrew its investment application (see Box 3.1).

---

**Box 3.1   Why did CNMC withdraw its application?**

The proposed acquisition of Lynas (a rare earth metals explorer) by CNMC was scrutinised by the FIRB. Originally, CNMC proposed to acquire 51.66 per cent of Lynas for A$252 million on 1 May 2009. However, the FIRB had asked CNMC twice to *withdraw and resubmit* its application. The conditions sought by the FIRB included "reducing the proposed percentage ownership to be held by CNMC to below 50%, and reducing the number of Board director positions to be held by CNMC to less than half of the Board. These were in addition to already agreed undertakings between Lynas and CNMC aimed at ensuring independent Director control of all marketing of rare earths products" (Lynas Corporation, 2009). Subsequently, CNMC withdrew its investment application to the FIRB and terminated its proposed acquisition of Lynas on

> 24 September 2009. In this case, the FIRB was concerned about the competition in the rare earth metals market as China had more than 90 per cent market share. Thus, the FIRB was concerned about the potential monopoly by Chinese firms in the global earth metals market.

Conditions have been imposed on five Chinese investment proposals in the Australian minerals industry. In the case of Sinosteel's proposed acquisition of Murchison Metal Limited (Murchison), the sole condition imposed by the FIRB, announced on 28 September 2008, was that Sinosteel only be allowed to acquire up to 49.9 per cent of Murchison to "maintain ownership diversity in the Mid-West region" (Swan, 2008a). Sinosteel originally proposed 100 per cent, but withdrew from 100 per cent takeover after the FIRB flagged non-approval. In this case, ownership and control were an issue for the FIRB.

In May 2009, FIRB approved Ansteel's A$162 million additional acquisition of Gindalbie Metals Ltd to increase its share from 12.6 per cent to 36.28 per cent. Three conditions were imposed, namely: to support the development of the Oakajee Port and Rail Project, use the Oakajee Port when that port is available to ship Karara production to customers and not change the proposed 50:50 ownership of the pellet plant that Ansteel and Gindalbie intend to build in China without first seeking the prior approval of the Australian government. These conditions seem focused on job creation for Australians and were accepted by Ansteel.

The conditions imposed by the FIRB for major Chinese investments have become more sophisticated in recent times as they include corporate governance, information disclosure, management, ownership, business behaviours, employment and operations. These conditions have been imposed on a case-by-case basis. They may also reflect the size and the stage of the Australian companies for investment as the three other Australian companies targeted were large and well-established. The conditions imposed on the other three major Chinese investments are listed in Table 3.3.

Despite these varying and diverse ranges of conditions imposed on Chinese investment applications, several patterns are evident when outcomes and conditions imposed are reviewed.

First, national security is probably one of the core issues of national interest. The term "national interest" often implies national security

*Table 3.3*   Conditions imposed by FIRB on three major Chinese investments

| | Valin (approved on 31/3/09) | Minmetals (approved on 23/4/09) | Yanzhou Coal (approved on 23/10/09) |
|---|---|---|---|
| Corporate governance | • One director who will comply with the Director's Code of Conduct and submit a standing notice of his potential conflict of interest relating to Fortescue's operation<br>• The Chinese director will comply with information segregation | • At least two directors reside principally in Australia<br>• The majority of board meetings be held in Australia | • Two directors to reside principally in Australia and one of them to be independent from Yancoal Australia and its operating subsidiaries<br>• The majority of board meetings to be held in Australia |
| Information disclosure | • Valin will report to FIRB on its compliance | • Annual financial report will be lodged to the Australian Securities and Investments Commission (ASIC) and uploaded on the company's website | • Annual financial report to be lodged to ASIC and uploaded on the company's website<br>• CEO of Yancoal to provide an annual report to FIRB on compliance |
| Management | | • CEO and CFO of the Australian operations to reside primarily in Australia; a predominantly Australian management team should manage OZ Minerals' (OZM) assets acquired | • CEO and CFO to reside primarily in Australia |

| Ownership | Up to 17.55% can be acquired | • OZM's assets in Australia owned by companies incorporated, headquartered and managed in Australia | • Yancoal Australia to own all future Yanzhou Coal operations in Australia; list Yancoal in Australia by 2012; reduce existing Felix's assets ownership to no more than 50% and Yancoal to 70% |
|---|---|---|---|
| Business behaviour (production, pricing and marketing) | | • Operate the acquired mines as a separate business with commercial objectives | • Operate on a commercial basis |
| Mine operations and employment | | • Maintain or increase production and employment at several mines; pursue growth in several mines; reopen the Avebury mine, and develop it. | |
| Community employment | | • Maintain or increase the level of indigenous employment in its local operations | |

interest as discussed earlier in this chapter. An inward FDI application can be quickly rejected if it has the potential to put Australia's national security interest at risk. Therefore, national security assessment is probably the first test in assessing an FDI application. This is well-demonstrated in the cases of Minmetals' acquisition of OZM (100% takeover) or WISCo's proposed JV with West Plains Resources (50:50 JV).

The second pattern observed concerns the size and developmental stage of the Australian companies or projects acquired. Greenfield investment, particularly with a junior explorer, is more likely to get unconditional approval from the Australian government. Most of the

Chinese investments in the Australian mining industries that have received unconditional approval have been with junior mines, particularly in the exploration or development stages, and with a relatively small investment (less than A$100 million). It is clearly in Australia's national interest for FDI in Australian resources to expand the overall capacity of the mining and energy sector, as opposed to simply acquiring existing capacity.

The third observation is that ownership is another test. The Australian government prefers foreign investment to be less than 50 per cent and 15 per cent in Greenfield and established companies, respectively. An FDI meeting these criteria is more likely to get approved by the FIRB. However, such a preference is not part of the Australian government's policy; thus is not legally enforced.

The fourth general pattern of the conditions imposed on Chinese investment falls into several broad categories at the organisational level, which include corporate governance; information disclosure; management and business behaviour regarding production, pricing and marketing; ownership and employment. These concerns are centred on economic benefits. The key reasons behind these conditions are to maintain the market-based characteristics of the Australian company, whether acquired totally or partly by foreign firms, particularly Chinese SOEs, and to minimise potential harm to the Australian economy in general, and tax revenue and employment specifically.

Competition is another factor receiving serious scrutiny from the FIRB. This is clearly reflected in the FIRB's decision on the proposed 51.6 per cent investment in Lynas by CNMC. The Australian government is concerned with the undue concentration in a market by Chinese firms – rare earth metals in this case, as China is already the world's most dominant producer.

Finally, the conditions imposed by the Australian government change with the economic environment and seem to have become more restrictive as the GFC abates (see Table 3.3).

# 4
# The Impact on Australian Political Economy from Chinese Investment into Australia's Mining Industry

> The politics of the Australia–China economic partnership remain in their infancy...Australia–China ties are entering a far more complex era. A critical test is whether they become a divisive political issue. If bipartisanship breaks down, relations are guaranteed to be damaged.
>
> (Kelly, 2009)

> On the business side, no one except the parties involved are buying into the (Rio–Chinalco) debate. In part this is because, with a couple of rare exceptions, Australia's leading corporations lack, in their commanding heights, people with direct experience of operating in China or, even more broadly, in Asia.
>
> (Callick, 2009e)

## Introduction

For much of the 1970s to the beginning of the twenty-first century Australia and China have enjoyed solid diplomatic and economic relations as China focused on its own internal economic reforms. More recently (particularly the past five years, 2006 to 2010) the dynamics of the relationship have taken on a far more complex political nature. China increasingly requires natural resources, of which Australia is a major supplier, for domestic consumption and to feed its massive export-oriented sectors, and as a direct result Australia's own political economy has increasingly come to see China's need for resources as essential to its own future national prosperity. Despite the political difficulties that have arisen in the relationship during the recent past, the sheer scale and growth of China's investments, particularly in the resource sector, make it clear that pure mutual commercial interests are driving contemporary relations. In the first two years of the current Labor government (2007–09), over $40 billion worth of Chinese investment was approved (Hewett, 2009d). This was on the back of a resource investment boom under the John Howard coalition government (1996–2007), which enabled it to deliver ever-increasing budget surpluses throughout its time in office. Even so, while Chinese enterprises have significantly expanded their Australian resource investment, this must be kept in context as British, American, Japanese and South Korean enterprises today continue their historical dominance of Australian natural resource exploitation. Only Chinese investments, however, raise a level of political concerns that see them being an almost constant topic of exploration among the nation's policy-oriented media, think tanks and diplomatic and corporate analysts. The reason is that much of China's overseas resource investors have explicit links to the CCP government. This political dynamic is in direct opposition to the ideological and pragmatic considerations of contemporary Australia political economy.

It is the political–economic dynamic of the relationship that will be the consideration of this chapter, and the structure is as follows. The first section explores Australia–China bilateral political and diplomatic relations as they have gained new ascendancy between 2006 and 2010 as a direct result of China's vast need for Australian iron ore resources to develop its internal economy and maintain its export drive. It then examines the impact of the GFC on Australia–China political economy, as Australia found itself in the position of being a main beneficiary of the Chinese government's decision to unveil a massive stimulus package that was heavily dependent on securing a continuing supply of Australian resources. The process of expanding Australia–China resource relations, while unquestionably highly beneficial to both the nations, has been anything but politically and diplomatically smooth. The following sections examine the political implication of the Rio Tinto–CHINALCO deal collapse; the heightened tension between China's minerals regulators and steelmakers and Australia's major iron ore producers after the announced, and then derailed, BHPB–Rio Tinto merger of iron ore assets in the Pilbara region of Western Australia; the arrest and eventual sentencing of Australian citizen and Rio Tinto employee, Stern Hu; and an end to the traditional annual benchmark iron ore pricing system. Also examined is the domestic political impact of China's willingness to invest heavily in Australian minerals and resources. Political relations between

Western Australia and the federal government have once again raised their head over the minerals bounty found in Western Australia's northern regions. A prime minister's attempts to introduce a super mining tax raised the ire of the politically powerful mining lobby within Western Australia, and ultimately led to his removal from that office. His successor immediately called a political truce, and stitched up a modified deal with Australia's biggest mining groups (BHPB), Rio Tinto and Xstrata). None of this would have taken place without China's role as the largest Australian buyer of iron ore and its willingness to signal its long-term continuation in this role. Finally, the chapter examines how Australia–China political economy relations fit within the much broader landscape of China's rise as a global economic power, with particular reference to its need to secure international mining resources.

Collectively the individual political–corporate pronouncements and actions examined in this chapter paint a picture in which the Australian prosperity story of the past decade, and for the foreseeable future, has become one of managing China's need for Australian mineral resources. McCrann (2009) states:

> the complex bilateral, multilateral and multi-layered relationship with China is not just the single most important for Australia in the 21$^{st}$ century, its importance is only going to grow in both absolute terms and relative to all the others.

As with any relationship the capacity of the participants to manage expectations with minimal tension has been severely tested by events and international market activities. In the next decade little is likely to change in this regard, but a growing level of maturity within the relationship can be expected as practice and experience informs and directs each party about how to position their objectives and behaviour within increasingly established policy and corporate frameworks.

## Australia–China economic relations

China's emergence as a global power, particularly since the onset of the GFC in 2007, which has seen the economies of the United States of America and Europe beset with anaemic economic growth and bourgeoning private and public sector debt levels, has had an immediate impact on Australia (Wilkins, 2010). Although the trade relations between two countries have become increasingly important, other factors – defence, political and social – have also substantially shaped the overall relationships. In fact, no assessment of Australia's future security and prosperity can be undertaken without considering the policy framework being established in *both* Washington and Beijing (Kang, 2010). For example, a clear sign of the complex and growing nature of the Australia–China relationship is in Australia's current defence strategy. The Australian Defence White Paper of 2009, which sets out Australia's long-term strategic and security objectives in its region, was widely interpreted as viewing China's growing regional strategic influence as the primary challenge to Australia's position (Department of Defence, 2009). However, a new phase in the military relationship between the two countries was established when the Australian Royal Navy joined the People's Republic of China's Navy on joint "Live-Fire" exercise for the first time in September 2010 (Mercer, 2010). At the same time, while Australia–China relations are now extremely important, it is widely accepted among Australian policy makers that the health and future direction of US–China relations is the most important bilateral dynamic for Australia's future prosperity and security. In the policy realm Australia–China interaction at all levels of government, from local governance to federal portfolios across a wide breadth (from agriculture and mining to education and financial services), is now so much a part of the norm that it rarely rates a mention in national media outlets. Only leadership talks gain significant national press coverage. The same applies in the two nations' commercial life, with ever-increasing commercial aviation links highlighting the two-way migration of business leaders and tourists from one shore to the other. Australia's largest export sector, mining and energy, is being driven to new heights of exploration and productivity by China's demand to such an extent the national budget is underpinned by this increasing demand (Macdonald-Smith, 2010). In Perth, Australia's mining capital, Chinese resource enterprises are now a permanent fixture on the corporate landscape in the same way that other long-term investors, from the US, Japan and South Korea, are. The same can be said for the impact of Chinese culture upon Australian socio-cultural life, with record numbers of Australians travelling to the Chinese mainland and studying Mandarin, museums exhibiting new and old Chinese arts, library reviews of Chinese literature becoming common and new intellectual explorations of Chinese migration and integration with the broader community taking place. Collectively the picture is one in which Australia is meeting China's growing economic, strategic and cultural influence in the Asia-Pacific by embracing it, sometimes hesitantly and with awkwardness, and other times with relish.

In the fiscal year to 30 June 2009, Australian commodities exports amounted to A\$197.44 billion, and the Australian Bureau of Agriculture and Resource Economics–Bureau of Rural Sciences (ABARE–BRS) has forecasted that this will rise by 26.0 per cent in 2010–11 to around \$214.9 billion. Energy and minerals export earnings alone are forecast to increase by 29.9 per cent to around \$179.9 billion in 2010–11 (Department of Innovation, 2010; Tasker, 2009h). While the above figure may change due to changing economic conditions, the below quotation is now generally accepted among the nation's political and economic operators:

> China's economy pulls the Australian economy along. We are very exposed to Asia, and Asia itself is very exposed China, said Ian Harper of Access Economics. (Callick, 2010b, p. 28)

China–Australia two-way trade in 2008 stood at \$59.7 billion (Zhang, 2009). By end of 2008, 300 Chinese companies had invested in Australia, but this accounted for less than 1 per cent of the total foreign investment in Australia. While the trend is phenomenal, the underlying fact often forgotten within the Australian political debate on Chinese investment into Australia is that it is coming from an extremely low base. China is only ranked tenth in investment levels over 2008–09, well behind the United States of America, Britain and Japan, who form Australia's most significant origins of investments in the post-1945 era (Callick, 2010b). These investments from the traditional investment partners are not gaining the same attention for the very simple reason that, unlike their Chinese counterparts, they are fully private enterprise concerns and their countries of origin are long-term strategic security partners of Australia.

In stark contrast to China's growing inwards investment into Australia, Australian investment into China in the first half of 2009 was miniscule, but growing, amounting to \$250 million, or 33 per cent higher than 2008, but importantly 70 per cent below the record \$820 million of 2006 (Jury, 2009). At the beginning of the decade (2000) Australia's two-way trade with China was a mere \$8.45 billion compared to the amount of trade generated between these two nations in 2008, which, as stated above, had escalated to US\$59.7 billion, making China Australia's largest trading partner.

Australia has benefited from China's emergence as a global economic power and in all likelihood will continue to benefit, through highs and lows in the marketplace. Don Argus, recently retired long-term chairman of BHPB, Australia's largest company stated:

> A country which relies on mining, such as Australia, where the resource industry contributes 18 percent of gross domestic product – $202 billion – and comprises 42 percent of Australia's total exports, requires shareholder funding to explore and mine its mineral resources. It must of course compete with other countries for that investment.

It is not so long ago that the story with mining was very different. In 2003, mining comprised 21 per cent of total exports and in six years it has more than doubled:

> Why is that so? There were other regions in the world blessed by a rich resource endowment like Australia which did not develop as quickly, like Africa – but it was Australia who benefited. (Cornell, 2010)

The ongoing industrialisation and urbanisation in China have generated increasing demand for energy and resources, in both of which Australia plays a role as a major international supplier (Zhang, 2009). China has produced strong demand for Australian resources such as iron ore, aluminium and other raw materials, along with energy supplies in the form of coal and, increasingly, natural gas. Indeed, Australia has been a major beneficiary of the Chinese government's moves to counter the GFC as the government remains totally focused on ensuring economic growth of more than 8 per cent. China's initial 2008 stimulus package of 4 trillion yuan ($586 million), later backed up by another equally large injection to bring the total to nearly 8 trillion yuan ($1 trillion), ensured that China entered recovery mode in the second half of 2009 (Ryan, 2009). *Caijing*, China's leading business magazine, stated that, "a hefty chunk of China's huge economic stimulus package is being spent on bricks, asphalt and whatever else goes into major infrastructure construction projects" (Callick, 2009j). China's combined approach of government stimulus packages, a policy of encouraging aggressive bank lending, and direct state investment, has generated a number of gigantic infrastructure and new building projects. Collectively these projects are distorting the global market prices of all base resources required in their construction as the laws of supply and demand have taken effect.

These new buildings, roads, railways and construction projects, along with China's burgeoning car production (China has overtaken the US in car production), all rely on steel and other raw materials, and Australia as one of the world's largest iron ore and raw materials supplier is in a primary market position to supply these. China today consumes more than a third of the world's output of aluminium, a quarter of its copper and almost a tenth of its oil, and accounts for more than half of iron ore trading. According to the China government 2008 data the net worth of iron ore, refined copper, crude oil and alumina purchased by Chinese enterprises totalled US$211 billion (China Mining Association, 2009). With economic growth of 10.3 per cent in 2010 (National Bureau of Statistics of China, 2011) and 700 million poor farmers still to be brought into the growth equation, China's demand for mineral resources is only likely to expand. From an Australian perspective, China's hunger for resources has tended to focus on its iron ore demand, but natural gas, copper, aluminium and others have all increasingly come to be seen as essential to China's continued economic expansion.

Chinese investment into the Australian resource sector is, of course, not new, but the most significant indicator of its growing importance began with the purchase of 10 per cent of the Portland aluminium smelter in 1986 by CITIC, who is still considered to have the most diverse spread of Australian interests among Chinese companies (Earl, 2007). It was not until a decade later, however, that the significance of China's economic boom reached full maturation when Baosteel, China's largest steelmaker, attempted to take a lead negotiations role in pricing of iron ore in 2005. As China's 12th largest company, Australia's biggest China customer, a buyer in the Australia resource sector since 1985, and a 46 per cent owner of the Eastern Range JV with Rio's Hamersley unit, Baosteel saw itself as having a legitimate price-setting role. When the Japanese and South Koreans dismissed this move and went about setting the benchmark price completely independently of Baosteel consideration, Baosteel and other China investors moved their strategic approach away from seeking portfolio investments towards buying resource investments outright. It has been this shift in strategy towards outright ownership or control over resource enterprises that has transformed the role of China within the Australian political economy landscape. Xie Qihua, the former chairwoman of Baosteel, in 2007 made it clear that Chinese enterprise had the revenue required to secure Australian resource investments, but not at any price:

> This is a critical time for both countries. China has rapid demand and they need more iron ore. Later, it is hard to say because the situation may change. If they [Australian miners] can decrease [the price] a little bit but not too much, then both countries can feel good about each other and make a big deal... Our budget is open. As soon as we make a deal with our business partners we can make our investment straightaway. (Earl, 2007)

Within the Australian context any such "deal" on pricing would fall well outside of long-established corporate norms. Indeed, any Australian resource sector supplier that even infers that international pricing is not the *sole* consideration will find itself in regulatory and legal troubles with the FIRB under the auspices of the Australian federal government's Department of the Treasury.

Australian companies in an array of industries including energy, resources and services, on the other hand, have been investing in China for the past two decades. A total of 8954 Australian companies were permitted by China to invest in the region by the end of 2008 with a paid-in amount of $5.82 billion. In the time since then, a further 337 Australian companies have penetrated the Chinese market with investment worth $400 million. This includes Telstra obtaining a 51 per cent share in China's primary real-estate website runner SouFun Holdings. BlueScope investing $430 million to establish its steel business in the region and ANZ's investment of A$1 billion in China's commercial banks, Tianjin City and Shanghai Rural (Zhang, 2009).

Ultimately, Australia, currently and in the coming decades, is going to benefit from the global economic balance moving towards the Asian region:

> With China establishing itself as a leading powerhouse for commodities to secure their path of industrialisation, Australian miners, energy producers and farmers can be happy knowing Australia's proximity to the Asian region, Australia's world class, long-life and low-cost resource base provide a one-stop shop for raw inputs needed for the region's industrialisation. (Guy, 2009)

In the field of bulk iron ore resource commodities logistics, Australia has significant competitive advantage in supplying the Asian market purely because of its geographical location compared to its major competitor, Brazil, whose distance from Asia has proved a hindrance to its ability to convince Chinese and other Asian buyers that it is a value proposition equal to Australia. It is an advantage Australia is likely to enjoy for some time as the GFC has forced the Chinese government to restructure the domestic economy away from too high a reliance on exports towards more internal investment. J. P. Morgan China equities Chairman Jing Ulrich states: "Having achieved the primary objective of stabilising the domestic economy, authorities are increasingly turning their attention to improving the quality of growth" (Sainsbury, 2009b, p. 35). China's investment in infrastructure is predicted to continue the nation's increased development and growth, again furthering demand for Australia-type resources (Wyatt, 2009a, 2009b). The fact that approximately 9 million new jobs need to be created annually just to keep unemployment from escalating means that resource-reliant demand for infrastructure, housing and automobiles can only expand. The CCP is no less concerned than its democratic counterparts in other parts of the world as to the political and social instability that can manifest itself when an increasing percentage of the population find that their economic and social aspirations are not being met. Therefore, the question of securing China's long-term resource and energy needs can only be seen as an essentially political one, because the legitimacy of the ruling CCP rests almost entirely on its ability to maintain domestic economic growth. The use of state-owned enterprises to secure these resources can only be seen within the political context of securing the future power base of the CCP. This fact is well-known and understood among senior Australian policy makers and brings a political dynamic to the commercial relationship that is most unwanted (Uren & Sainsbury, 2009).

In 2007, the United States of America became gripped in a financial crisis of its own making – a crisis that quickly began to unravel the financial systems also found in Europe and parts of Asia. Major banks and financial service enterprises in the US, Britain, Ireland, Iceland and further afield all succumbed, and throughout 2008–09 the financial impact crossed over to the broader economy so that in 2010 the United States and Europe remained mired in low growth and high unemployment. The following section explores how Australia avoided such a plight because of China's own successful measures in avoiding an economic downturn by turning to massive infrastructure projects dependant on sourcing Australian iron ore.

## The GFC and impact on Australia–China political economy

At a senate hearing in October 2009 Ken Henry, Australian treasury secretary, stated that "Chinese growth was likely to support relatively high prices for Australian export commodities... for a considerable period of time, quite possibly for decades." This was followed by Glenn Stevens, Australia's Reserve Bank governor, who at a senate hearing in the same month expressed that the export performance of Australia was robust and that China was the basis for this:

> The ongoing structural strength of demand for resources, in China and the emerging world, that's not really a cyclical phenomenon, that is a structural thing which I think is likely to persist for some time. (Anonymous, 2009b)

The following month (November) Stevens went on to further state that "China's importance (to the Australian economy) may be greater for future outcomes than recent past ones" (Korporaal, 2009). In effect he was making it unequivocally clear that the future of the Australian economy, and thereby the prosperity of all Australians, was irrevocably bound to the economic performance of China.

Then Australian Trade Minister Simon Crean, in March 2009, while attending a closed meeting at the Australia–China Business Council, mentioned that investment between the two regions required a mutual flow in both directions:

> Investment is a two-way street. It's not just a question of us considering on a case-by-case basis proposals that come to us from time-to-time. (Berkovic, 2009)

As discussed in an earlier chapter (Chapter 3), the concept of free trade reciprocity is a foundation stone of modern Australian political economy. What Crean, above, is making clear within an Australian political context is that the continuing failure by China to provide open investment access to key domestic markets in resources, agriculture and across service sectors means that any moves by any Australian government to allow Chinese firms unfettered access to Australian acquisitions would flounder on the reciprocity test. Currently, neither the current government nor the major opposition show any inclination whatsoever of dispensing with the absolute requirement that only private-controlled enterprises have largely unfettered investment access to the Australian market. Any Australian government so inclined to break from this bipartisan approach would be met with political outcry: howls of protest by their political opponents, the rallying of commercial interests opposed to such moves and the condemnation of numerous society stakeholders. As this chapter will explore further, for both ideological reasons and on a practical political basis, no major party within Australia has any interest in taking up a fight that would see foreign state enterprises supplant private capital in any key economic sector (notably minerals, gas and agriculture).

At the same time, the then trade minister made it clear that Chinese investment that abided by the political and policy requirements of Australia were not only acceptable but also desirable. Crean also suggested that China explores investing more in new Greenfield projects within Australia compared to existing assets:

> We (Australia) do need foreign capital, that's a constant fact of life for Australia, but in China's case we need even more: its reorientation towards a modern, domestic-demand driven economy will sustain an appetite for our resources for decades to come. (Callick, 2009e)

Overhanging all concerns centred on Australia–China relations is the simple fact that the China economy now underpins the wealth of Australia:

> Strong demand from China in the first quarter of this year was one of the reasons Australia was able to avoid recession, alone amongst developed nations. (Uren, 2009a)

For the first time in modern history the health of the Australian economy, the prosperity of all Australians, relies on the performance of a nation, China, who is not a traditional strategic ally, and has a very different political, economic and legal system to Australia's own. The onset of the GFC (2007) and the difficulties this has created for the nation's traditional investment and trading partners, the US, Britain and Japan, have, combined with the rapid economic development of China in recent years, collectively strengthened the economic relationship between China and Australia within a condensed time frame. At the same time the experience has left both sides unsteady as they have grappled to understand their respective differences in areas of national policy and corporate governance. Australian politicians have been challenged to find a sound regulatory approach capable of harnessing the Chinese minerals investment approaches for the national interests. In turn China's officials and corporate elite have themselves found Australian politicians and enterprises more than willing to question China's own FDI policy as being too restrictive of foreign investors across mining, agriculture, banking and finance. It is truly a relationship in flux with both sides feeling their way, mostly successfully but sometimes awkwardly, within a new post-GFC global political, economic and strategic environment.

## Political reverberations of the failed Rio Tinto–CHINALCO deal

### Political nature of CHINALCO

The following section focuses on the political nature of the Rio Tinto–CHINALCO deal, its eventual demise and the diplomatic repercussions that resulted (the commercial nature of the deal is explored in Chapter 6 of this book). There can be no doubting the highly political nature of any major mining decision within the Australian political and economic landscape. In an open acknowledgement of this fact, CHINALCO hired Hawker Britton, a well-connected government-business consultancy to manage its communications with the incumbent federal Labor government. Paul Skinner, then chair of Rio Tinto, utilised the GFC to justify the deal and upped the political stakes by proclaiming that almost 3000 jobs were at stake if the deal did not go through. What did not have to be stated by Skinner was that the overwhelming majority of these jobs were located in the state of Queensland, the home state of the then prime minister, Kevin Rudd.

On the Chinese political front, CHINALCO is not only a state-owned Chinese enterprise, but one high on the pyramid:

> Just days after the head of state-owned Aluminium Corporation of China signed a $US19.5 billion ($A26.9 billion) deal for part of Anglo-Australian miner Rio Tinto, he left his post to join the China cabinet.
>
> The move by aluminium tsar Xiao Yaqing into politics in February raised a critical question about China's state-owned corporate giants as they step on to the global stage: are they driven by profits, or are they pursuing a nationalist agenda for the Chinese Government? (Oster & Carew, 2009)

CHINALCO, by itself, forms only one part of an extensive network of government-owned enterprises seeking foreign investment:

> China's National Development and Reform Commission has wide-ranging power over China's overseas investments...it selected the Chinese investor before any bid is made for an offshore asset. (Oster & Carew, 2009)

The China Development Bank and China International Capital Corporation are supplying much-needed capital for overseas acquisitions, including those in Australia. Hardly surprisingly, both Rio's and CHINALCO's leadership saw access to China's capital resources as an absolute advantage. Doug Richie, Rio Tinto director of strategy, stated:

> In a capital-constrained world, this will allow us to undertake projects pretty much of any magnitude we wish to. (Sainsbury, 2009d)

CHINALCO's Overseas Holdings president, Wang Wenfu, also made clear the favourable capital access CHINALCO would enjoy:

> Chinese banks are in a better position than those elsewhere in the world. Chinalco is seen by Chinese banks as a blue-chip company. (Sainsbury, 2009d)

CHINALCO's ability to tap into Chinese government-run banks' vast capital was seen by both men as an essential strength of the deal. But in making such statements they showed amazing political deafness within the Australian context, as this very possible corporate strength (access to a deep well of Chinese government capital) was seen as political poison by Australia's political class, and as purely an unfair commercial advantage by the commercial class. The key point was that the deal was driven politically by CHINALCO's access to Chinese banks through the backing of the Chinese government. It was not a purely commercial capital operation, and consequently raised the ire of influential sections of the Australian political and corporate elite.

## Australian political opposition to the deal

The negative political response to the deal from non-government sources was almost immediate. Peter Costello, treasurer for 12 years under the Howard government (1996–2007), proclaimed in March 2009 his opposition to the deal in a column in the *Sydney Morning Herald*, making it clear that he viewed CHINALCO as an arm of the Chinese government and that even if stringent criteria were placed on the deal they would be incredibly difficult to regulate. Costello stated:

> any assurances Rio Tinto or the state-owned Chinese company give about maintaining an Australian presence will be hard to police or enforce because the company is based in London. (Coorey, 2009)

The then (2009) opposition leader, Malcolm Turnbull, suggested "blocking the deal" as a result of CHINALCO being wholly owned by the Chinese government:

> China wants to buy as much of our resources as they can at the lowest price, and China's ambitions are not always in Australia's best national interests... So it is a friendly relationship but it is a competitive relationship... all of these things [Australia–China government and corporate relations] have to be fully disclosed and above board and be transparent, and when they are not they raise legitimate concerns about what is really going on. (Taylor, 2009b)

An influential regional politician, the National Party's Senator Barnaby Joyce from Queensland, backed this position by voicing his complete opposition to state-owned foreign enterprises purchasing national assets (Freed, 2009). Joyce has called for the outright banning of Chinese state-enterprise investment into Australia's natural resource sectors (minerals, gas and agriculture). Joyce stated his support for foreign investment from private enterprises, but on investments from state-owned enterprises he expressed concerns over the interwoven nature of corporate and diplomatic relationships:

> The difference between a corporation and a government is governments have armies, seats at the United Nations and can say the word "no" and you can't do much about it when they do. This is a confusion I don't want my nation to get into. (Uren, 2009a, p. 2)

Joyce speaks here with the confidence of knowing that he has the full backing of his regional Australia constituency, which opposes foreign government investment in natural resources, and from neoliberal-oriented urban constituents who ideologically place the state as having no role in economic activity. He was, of course, attacked for his position by political opponents, with the then Australian trade minister, Simon Crean, asking Joyce to explain if he would leave Australian iron ore capacity underdeveloped if that was the result of rejecting Chinese government-owned enterprise investment (Kitney, 2010). The combustible mixture of political ideology and capital investment decision-making inherent in the question means it remains politically unresolved at the time of writing.

On hearing the views of some Australian political figures, like Joyce's outspoken opposition to Chinese state-owned ownership of Australian resources, Chinese Commerce Minister, researcher Mei Xinyu, stated:

> The opposition parties oppose for opposition only, in spite of the country's strategic interest. (Sainsbury, 2009e)

This statement betrays a lack of knowledge about the nature of Australian political economy over the recent decades. In the Australian political context, state ownership of enterprise is a paradigm that the Liberal Party of Australia is ideologically opposed to, and an ownership position that the Labor Party of Australia has practically moved against via mass sales of public company assets (Qantas, Commonwealth Bank of Australia, Telstra, electricity utilities and suppliers to name a few). Since the 1980s, successive Labor and Liberal federal and state governments have sold off government-owned enterprises with the argument to the public that they are less efficient than POEs. This is also the key current assumption within Australian policy circles for opposing China's SOEs involvement in economic activities. Indeed, the Queensland Labor government is currently in a position of privatising some of the state's largest public-owned assets (most significantly, Queensland Rail). Having taken the ideological and practical position that Australian governments should not own enterprises except under specific circumstances (national and security interests), the political position of allowing foreign government ownership of key national resource assets that are not renewable, or easily subject to competitive forces, is simply unsustainable within the broader context of contemporary Australian political economy. Hence neither the political comfort provided by the FIRB as an independent arbitrator of investment proposals, nor the use of the all encompassing "national interest" test, can be expected to be dispensed with any time soon, irrespective of who holds the federal government benches.

### Collapse of the Rio–CHINALCO deal and political reverberations

With the biggest foreign investment in Australia at the time (2009) becoming a political issue Mathieson (2009) stated that "there were concerns that rejection of the deal, which is China's biggest overseas investment, could damage relations with Beijing".

The extent to which this was a real concern among the political elite within Australia can clearly be seen in the fact that the then prime minister (Kevin Rudd), treasurer (Wayne Swan) and other senior cabinet members (such as the then resource minister, Martin Ferguson) took every possible opportunity to openly express their views that the whole affair was a purely commercial concern. The protestations fooled no one. The very fact that the senior political leadership of the nation was taking such a concerted public and private interest in the Rio–CHINALCO outcome, when normally such a commercial outcome would warrant little or no political interest on the national stage, showed the ingenious nature of the purely "commercial" tag line. This was high-wire commercial diplomacy with an indispensible major trading partner, and everyone knew it.

At the request of the CHINALCO president, the then prime minister, Rudd, held a meeting in June 2009 with the firm's leadership following the failure of the company's proposal to access a larger share in Rio Tinto (Yeates, 2009). Mr Rudd expressed the view that Rio Tinto's verdict to terminate the arrangement was a commercial decision and that Australia was still open to Chinese investment:

> And I think it is very important that our friends in China recognise that fact. (Yeates, 2009; Zappone, 2009)

Treasurer Wayne Swan also denied that the collapse of the Rio Tinto–CHINALCO deal would discourage potential investment opportunities in the future from Australia's largest trading partner due to the government's extensive and long review process of the proposed investment. He stated:

> I completely reject that … There has been a commercial arrangement entered into here by the parties that has occurred completely separate from any examination of this proposal by the foreign investment review board. (Yeates, 2009)

The treasurer also made it clear that Australia's national interest would always be central political criterion for any foreign investment, Chinese or otherwise:

> Australia welcomes foreign investment provided it fits within our national interest criteria. (B. Fitzgerald, 2009a; Yeates, 2009)

Reflecting the political sensitivity of the entire process, the then resource minister, Ferguson, felt the need to state in the wake of the collapsed deal between Rio Tinto and CHINALCO that: "there is some angst in China...to the fact it fell over is obviously disappointing, but in terms of the future, Australia needs China and China needs Australia. I don't expect to see any trade sanctions because in the end I think China and companies such as BHPB and Rio will get through what is really on the agenda at the moment and that's the round of commodity price negotiations" (Tingle, 2009). Just to ensure that this was the case, the Australian government's senior ministers covering natural resources led several delegations of senior officials and commercial players on regular visits to Beijing and Shanghai over the next six months. In fact such is the importance of China's relations with Australia today, and so constant has the diplomatic and commercial interchange become, that the myriad of political and corporate exchanges below the leadership level now barely rates a mention in Australian national newspapers.

Little did Ferguson know, when making the above statement, that for much of 2009 and into 2010 price negotiations themselves would become a major source of commercial tension between Australian resource companies and Chinese government-owned and privately owned buyers. Tensions that would lead BHPB, Rio Tinto and other Australian suppliers to scrap the annual negotiations in favour of a quarterly global pricing system that at the time of introduction highly favoured the seller. This act, in turn, drew further ire from the Chinese government and drew the Australian government into another round of unwanted commercial diplomacy ("Iron prices tipped to soar as Chinese mills feel the pinch", 2010).

### Chinese investment in Australia: The political sales activity post Rio–CHINALCO

It was the belief of the then Australian trade minister, Simon Crean, that Australia needed to continue encouraging investors from China to put their money into Australia:

> I believe we can make the argument as to why Chinese investment is good for the country.
>
> If that investment is expanding our productive activity, if that investment is enabling us to better capitalise on our comparative advantage, that's been the history of this country.
>
> This whole question of investment I believe we can explain to the Australian public. It is in our interest. It is what is going to secure

our economic future. But if we are prepared to be more open and accepting of investment...it has got to be a two-way street. (Yeates, 2009)

He was promptly backed up by Treasurer Swan who made it clear that Australia could not afford to miss the boat on tapping into China's rapid economic growth: "As a resource rich nation on Asia's doorstep, Australia is uniquely placed to capitalise on this Asian century" (Yeates, 2009). Australia's geographic-transport proximity does mean that it enjoys a \$4.30 per tonne freight advantage over the Brazilian iron ore giant Vale (Sainsbury, 2010e).

The FIRB, situated within the Treasury, has been covered elsewhere in this book and as such will only be referred to here in the political context. While Australia does have a well-earned reputation among international business practitioners for political stability and policy consistency, in investment terms that the latter comes with an unstated caveat. This is that any international investments must operate within the international rules and practices that have been laid down by Australia's strategic allies, the US, Britain and Japan, throughout the post-1945 period. China does not play by these rules. The Chinese government's global utilisation of government-owned enterprises, the extension of non-commercial credit and other activities all confirm that China is operating on another international commercial field to the US–European Union–WTO paradigm (Vivoda, 2009; Wilkins, 2010).

It is from the challenge China poses to the Western-derived global commercial behaviour paradigm that Chinese investment difficulties with Australia's regulatory FIRB must be viewed. Indeed, for the purpose of this chapter the Chinese SOEs' efforts to invest into the Australian resource sector hit a critical political hurdle immediately – the Six Principles as discussed in Chapter 3:

1. Whether the investor is independent from its government
2. Whether it generally obeys the law
3. Whether it may hinder competition or lead to undue concentration
4. Whether it may affect Australian government revenue
5. Whether it affects national security
6. Whether it may affect the operations and directions of an Australian business and its contribution to Australia (Moncrief, 2008).

It has been noted by the researchers of this book and others that the federal government has openly and consistently utilised Principle 5, national security, in several public statements to reject significant Chinese investment offers into Australian resources, and thereby not have to utilise Principle 1. This only highlights the keen sensitivity the Australian government feels it faces in addressing the issue of Chinese government-enterprise investment into Australia to the Australian public. As stated previously, the Australian public has, since the 1980s, witnessed their own political class arguing for a limited or no governmental role in enterprise, with federal and state enterprises being regularly privatised. It is, therefore, hardly a stretch to think that this same public would be hostile to any argument advocating Chinese government-ownership of key national assets as being in the national interest. The muted public statements of the Labor government to date suggest that they prefer the Chinese government enterprises to simply go directly to the FIRB – who will politically neutralise the investment type – while the coalition opposition has already stated its outright hostility to any such investment.

Some, like the *Australian Financial Review* (Editor, 2009), have made clear their objections to the FIRB current operations, including the necessity of having such a review process:

> Australia's historic need for foreign funds to develop resources means we should be open to all investment, preferably subject to the protection of national laws, such as those governing competition and taxation, rather than opaque foreign investment approvals.

This all perhaps true from a purely liberal ideological and commercial perspective. What is also beyond dispute is that the FIRB takes very little time to approve investments into Australia that involve strictly commercial actor/s. The only reason, therefore, that the role of the FIRB is being questioned is the presence of entities that are not purely commercial, but political in nature – namely, Chinese SOEs. It is a simple fact that Australian politicians are held accountable every three to four years in ways that commercial operators and newspaper editors are not, and that the perceptions and interests of the Australian voter cannot simply be ignored. The FIRB ultimately provides Australia's political leadership with a regulatory vehicle with the specific mandate to protect the nation's collective commercial and strategic interests.

Australians overwhelmingly see natural resources as *their* resources, with the company involved in extracting it doing so for a "fair value" price. At all times the company must operate within Australian national interests as defined by political, security, commercial and social interests. Breach these criteria and popular support for "any" foreign investment in mining and resources would quickly evaporate. In this nuanced support of the extraction of natural resources Australians are very much like Americans, Canadians, Chinese, Indians and others: they know what a national asset is and know it goes well beyond purely commercial considerations.

## The Rio–BHPB deal: China opposition, Australian political reply and the deals demise

On the heels of announcing the end of the proposed Rio–CHINALCO tie up, Rio and BHPB announced in June 2009 that they had agreed to a $116 billion merger of their giant Pilbara iron ore mines, ports and railways to form the world's biggest iron ore mining operation. The merged company would have become the second biggest business in Australia behind BHPB itself (Chambers, 2009j). Not surprisingly, from their perspective, many Chinese commentators interpreted the announcement and the proposed merger in economic nationalist terms; as a complete snub and humiliation of CHINALCO's leadership and, in turn, the effective owner, the Chinese government. Rightly or wrongly, the commercial consideration of the deal became blurred with political-diplomacy considerations, giving further ammunition to outright opponents of Chinese government investment into Australia, such as Barnaby Joyce and others, as being unwanted and unnecessary. In late October 2010, BHPB and Rio Tinto announced that the planned merger would not take place due to various international regulatory authorities, including Chinese, European and US authorities, expressing firm opposition to the deal. The deal is nevertheless worth studying as it clearly reveals the wide gap in strategic thinking between international iron ore buyers and the sellers of Australian iron ore. The demise of the deal also clearly reveals that iron ore supply to the global economic powers goes well beyond purely market economics, and instead also involves major geo-policy decision-making on the part of national (China, US and Australia) and regional (European Union) authorities.

The BHPB–Rio Pilbara merger would have seen both companies in the Western Australian region combine their iron ore mines, ports and railways into a sole business. Rio Tinto Chairman Mr du Plessis addressed the proposed merger by stating:

> The boards have concluded that the formation of an iron ore production joint venture in Western Australia with BHP Billiton together with rights issues deliver the best solution.

This course of action will assist us to address Rio Tinto's short- and medium-term debt repayment obligations whilst enabling us to retain strategic flexibility, and to preserve and grow long-term shareholder value. ("Rio dumps Chinalco for BHP tie-up", 2009)

The JV will establish an unrivalled iron ore business with world class assets and infrastructure. (Chambers, 2009k)

Furthermore, and in a prescient call, he stated that:

After the agreement is signed the biggest hurdle will be getting the approval of... the European Commission.

BHPB agreed to pay Rio $5.8 billion to bring its share of the JV up to an even 50 per cent. The deal would create the biggest single iron ore exporter in the world, overtaking Brazil's giant Vale (Chambers, 2009j).
Then BHP Billiton chairman Don Argus stated:

The combination of these two asset portfolios will unlock the scale benefits inherent in this world class resource basin. (Chambers, 2009k; "Rio dumps Chinalco for BHP tie-up", 2009)

He also stated that the new merged entity would be in a prime position to accommodate "unprecedented growth due to demand generated by China and in the future India" (Wilson, 2009). Marius Kloppers, BHPB's chief executive, said that:

combining these world-class assets and associated infrastructure which operate side by side – we can get very, very substantial production, development and financial synergies. (B. Fitzgerald, 2009a)

The merged operation would have saved the companies more than $10 billion (Chambers, 2009j, 2009k). Investors openly expressed their support for the new deal over the previous proposed Rio–CHINALCO deal:

"We were not supporters of the Chinalco transaction. We're happy to see this alternative approach to solving Rio's issues with debt... A deal like this was really essential from Rio's point of view," explained Ross Barker, managing director of Australian Foundation Investment Co, the sixth-largest shareholder in Rio Tinto within

Australia and shareholder of BHP. ("Rio dumps Chinalco for BHP tie-up", 2009)

The market response was positive with BHPB shares increasing by 8 per cent on hearing of the collapsed deal between Rio and CHINALCO, and with the expectation that this would signal a JV move by BHPB and Rio in relation to their Australian iron ore assets (Chambers, 2009j).

The Chinese government's response was far less warm. The Ministry of Commerce said that the JV would be reviewed by the country's competition regulators and that both companies would need to apply for permission for their deal to be approved by Chinese regulators. The China Iron and Steel Association (CISA) released a statement:

> The joint venture agreement has a strong monopolistic colour and Chinese steel mills will resolutely oppose the agreement. (Wyatt, 2009a)

The irony of a proxy-Chinese government agency overlooking a sector in which the Chinese government has complete control through either direct ownership of steel enterprises or indirect control over nominally private steelmakers through political and financial means, and claiming monopoly issues has been lost on no one. China's Ministry of Commerce also engaged the highly respected Allan Fels, former chairman of the Australian Competition and Consumer Commission, to provide advice on the merger from an Australian regulatory perspective. Fels stated:

> They are very unhappy about the venture. Officials from the Ministry of Commerce have asked me about the technicalities of the policy and whether it gives them jurisdiction to examine the transaction and I said that it did ...
>
> The question is what BHP and Rio would do if China deemed the venture to be anti-competitive, they would have to think about the short and long-term consequences. (Sainsbury, 2010b)

A counter warning was made by the Australian federal government to China not to inflict any trade sanctions on any future BHPB and Rio Tinto iron ore joint ventures. Treasurer Wayne Swan stated in June (2009),

Obviously any such actions would not be in anyone's best interests including China and the many Chinese businesses that depend on Australian materials.

Furthermore, the Australian resource minister, Martin Ferguson, stated:

> The BHP–Rio Tinto joint venture in iron ore has synergies which will improve productivity and effectively mean that China over time will reap some benefits of that outcome and people shouldn't forget that BHP and Rio will market separately. (Tingle, 2009)

That said the Australian Competition and Consumer Commission (ACCC) immediately launched the required examination of the merger upon the Australian domestic market (namely upon domestic steel-maker BlueScope), while the European Commission also launched an investigation into the impact on European buyers (Tasker, 2010a). The Chinese government and state-owned steelmakers for their part made clear their concerns over increasing prices from a merged identity by noticeably increasing commercial diplomacy operations in key supplier nations such as Brazil and across Latin America, Africa, Russia and Eastern Europe. A $10 billion soft loan to Brazil for the construction of domestic transport projects, and a $20 billion soft loan to Venezuela, are just two examples of China's use of commercial diplomacy to secure natural resource security and can be read as a sign that China, like all buyers, likes price competition and to have a number of purchasing options (Molinski & Lyons, 2010).

## The case of Stern Hu: Iron ore commerce meets international diplomacy

The following month after the BHPB–Rio had announced its proposed Pilbara iron ore merger, July 2009, Rio Tinto Australian executive Stern Hu and three of his Chinese citizen colleagues (Ge Minqiang, Wang Yong and Liu Caikui) were arrested on charges of bribery, stealing state secrets and stealing business secrets. In March 2010 Stern Hu and his colleagues pleaded guilty of bribery and stealing trade secrets and were sentenced to varying lengths of imprisonment (ten years for Hu). For many Australians this event had little to do with the law or justice as no access to an independent lawyer, or his family, was provided to Hu upon arrest. Australian consulate access was severely limited, and at times denied outright. This is not a legal system recognised by many

Australians. The political nature of the trial is clear. China legal expert Professor Jerome Cohen stated:

> the party will decide whether it goes to trial and what sentence is handed down... Instruction from a high party official, or from the Party's Central Political–Legal Committee, headed not by a legal specialist but from a former minister of public security Zhou Yongkang, can determine the outcome of important cases. (Sainsbury, 2010d)

A Chinese foreign ministry official said that authorities in China had sufficient evidence to prove Hu had stolen state secrets and "caused huge loss to China's economic interests and security" (Vaughan, Krestser & Crowe, 2009). Later Beijing downgraded these charges, after months of investigations, to focus on the bribery allegations. The Chinese government-owned media also claimed that the Rio employees bribed executives from 16 of the Chinese steel mills involved in the iron ore price talks, which Rio denies (Frith, 2009). Essentially the government's accusations came to focus on the Rio executives paying bribes for confidential information from Chinese steel mills during the tense negotiations over iron ore prices in 2008–09. The complete absence of state-owned Chinese steel companies from any involvement in the bribery allegations drew immediate responses of indignation from those knowledgeable about their operations (Burrell, Vaughan & Krestser, 2009). The notable absence of government-owned enterprises from the scene of Hu's crimes effectively "portrays China as an innocent victim of the predations of foreign businesses and their government, and presents China's place in the world as being ceaselessly undermined by the wiles of the liberal democracies" (Burchell, 2010b). The importance of this case to Chinese policy makers cannot be underestimated: the iron ore industry was worth $70 billion to China in 2008, and the information gathered through bribery allegedly gave Hu's team at Rio Tinto the upper hand in settling the benchmark price. This is why the issue was dealt with at such a senior political level and why the actions of Hu and his co-accused were deemed to have contradicted China's national economic interests (Kretser & Vaughan, 2009).

Within Australia and internationally, however, the whole case and conviction of corruption against Stern Hu and his colleagues, even given their confessions, is tainted by knowledge of the true extent of China's internal corruption, particularly among government-owned and state-owned enterprises. It is a central concern among China's national political leadership, as it undermines their domestic legitimacy (Callick,

2010a). Furthermore, there is growing concern within international political and business circles over Chinese state-owned enterprises' concerted ability to secure long-term natural resources on favourable terms in nations within Africa, Latin America and other parts of the developing world. This is most notable in Nigeria, the Congo region and other nations where corruption is endemic and a complete lack of transparency in processes is the norm (www.transparencyinterntional).

### The Australian government and opposition response to the Stern Hu case

Reflecting the high level of political and commercial stakes at play as a result of Hu's arrest and detention, the then Australian foreign minister, Stephen Smith, immediately raised the point that if China was going to link standard business practices to national security it was in for a world of questioning:

> As I understand it from the Shanghai State Security Bureau, during China's iron ore negotiations with foreign miners in 2009, Stern Hu gathered and stole state secrets from China via illegal means including bribing internal staff of Chinese steel companies.

This has caused huge loss to China's national economic security and interests.

> Frankly it is difficult for a nation like Australia to see a relationship between espionage and national security and what appeared to be suggestions about commercial or economic negotiations. Having said that, Mr Hu now ... runs the risk of being subject to Chinese criminal, legal and judicial processes. (AAP, 2009a; Vaughan et al., 2009)

During the court trial Smith made explicit the link between the court case and China's commercial relationship with foreign enterprise:

> China has missed a substantial opportunity. This was an opportunity for China to bring some clarity to the notion of commercial secrets...That required transparency, which is one reason why Australian officials and I argue strongly that this part of the trial should be open...
> As China emerges into the global economy, the international business community needs to understand with certainty what the rules are in China. What is unknown as a consequence of the lack of

transparency is whether here we are simply dealing with information that is normally commercially available or whether we are dealing with something more broader than that. (Needham, 2010)

The then Australian prime minister, Kevin Rudd, backed this position and warned China that other foreign governments and companies would be watching closely to see how the Hu affair played out:

> I think it's time for good judgement to be applied – balanced judgment and the best possible actions in support of this Australian citizen... The Foreign Minister is following these developments carefully and we are engaging with Chinese officials closely. (Frith, 2009). And
>
> The world will be watching how this particular court case is conducted. (Kerin, 2010)

The implication was clear, Australia might be a small nation unable to bring much weight to bear on China, but others such as the US and European Union (EU), would be observing proceedings, and altering their commercial relations with China accordingly.

The domestic political repercussion from Stern Hu's arrest, and the subsequent nature of his incarceration, were immediate as the then opposition leader, Malcolm Turnbull, made it clear that he felt the Australian government was less than forceful in its response:

> Mr Hu deserves to be protected, he deserves that protection and the intervention of the Australian Prime Minister... Dismissing this as a consular matter is not good enough. (Burrell et al., 2009)

Turnbull also attempted to link the Rudd government response to its overall connections with China, implicitly claiming a lack of transparency inflicted the government (Taylor, 2009b).

Sheridan (2009c) even went so far as to imply that if the Rudd government did not secure the safe release of Mr Hu within days of his detainment, it would be seen as having no influence at all within Beijing. It is an irrefutable fact that the Australian government requests for information and consular access to Mr Hu were ignored by Chinese authorities until 10 July (Sheridan, 2009c). Opposition shadow minister for foreign affairs, Julie Bishop, asked the question:

> If China is able to ignore the [consular] agreement in these circumstances, are there other circumstances where the consular agreement will not be adhered to?

This would be an issue of great concern to many companies from Australia and also around the world. (AAP, 2010a)

Australian–Chinese government relations at this time would have been defined as *strained* at best, with the then foreign minister Smith stating that it was "in everyone's interests" that a quick resolution be found (AAP, 2009b).

Independent observer Peter Drysdale, professor of economics at the Australian National Universities Crawford School, rejected the notion that the arrest was in any way politically or commercially motivated:

I don't think this relates to any tit-for-tat issue arising directly from Australia's commercial ties with China. There is no evidence of that. But the risk is that Australians overreact and we get locked into a downward spiral. The situation needs a careful and modulated response from the Rudd government. (Kelly, 2009)

A spokesman from CHINALCO also rejected any political interpretation of events, stating, "we have also reasserted that the situation is in no way related to any commercial dealings between Rio and Chinalco" (AAP, 2009a). What cannot be disputed is that the very structure of the Chinese commercial and legal system means that any trial centred on international business practices is political in nature.

When Hu was convicted (March 2010) and sentenced the then prime minister, Rudd, reacted immediately, declaring the sentence "harsh". When Hu, through his legal representation, decided not to appeal, many Australians viewed this not as an admittance of his crime but as an acceptance that the whole process was predetermined. Chinese lawyers, such as the Beijing-based Zhou Ze also expressed this view, stating:

In many cases people decide not to appeal because they see the process as simply a formality where they have almost no chance of success. (Sainsbury, 2009c)

Since the conviction, the near silence from the Australian government on Hu's status has widely been interpreted as an effort to "appease" China in some form of diplomatic "self-censorship" exercise (Burchell, 2010a; Sheridan, 2010). Whatever the case, the lack of transparency of the trial process, the refusal of the Chinese government to grant consular access at vital times throughout and the degree of punishment have all left Australian citizens with a keen awareness that China's legal system differs greatly from their own (Callick, 2010d).[1]

## The Stern Hu trial and the Australian resource sectors commercial diplomacy response

Rio Tinto's initial response to the arrest of their key China-based negotiators came through spokeswoman Amanda Buckley, who said the company was "surprised and concerned" by the allegations and was not aware of any evidence to support them. She further stated: "We remain ready to assist the authorities in their investigation" (Burrell et al., 2009). Rio's iron ore chief, Sam Walsh, went further and insisted that the allegations against Hu and his colleagues were "wholly without foundation" (Sainsbury, 2009g). This position was directly contradicted by *The Australian* newspaper whose unnamed sourced stated: "bribery is almost an open secret in the industry. Everybody knows of it because the (payment) system of state-owned companies (means) the executives do have incentives to sell their information for extra money" (Sainsbury, 2009g). Rio's immediate corporate response was to send in an extensive audit team to ensure that it was not accountable for the accused employees' actions should they be found to be unethical (Stevens, 2010b). It later became clear through the defendants' own declarations in court that Rio Tinto was completely unaware of the employees' actions. The reaction from Rio's executive was swift with Walsh, stating:

> Receiving bribes is a clear violation of Chinese law and Rio Tinto's code of conduct, The Way We Work. We have been informed of the clear evidence presented in court that showed beyond doubt that the four convicted employees had accepted bribes. By doing this they engaged in deplorable behaviour that is totally at odds with our strong ethical culture. In accordance with our policies we will terminate their employment. (Tasker, 2010b, p. 19)

The whole affair led to sweeping changes in Rio's internal governance structures, including contract negotiation processes, according to informed sources (Stevens, 2010b). Hugo Restall (2010) of *The Wall Street Journal* stated what everyone was thinking:

---

[1] David Kelly, professor of China studies at the University of Technology, Sydney, stated: "The real damage is to China's image. The image of the Chinese legal system is in tatters. They don't realise this. The image is now they are the tough guys who do not have to be nice to anyone" (Needham, 2010).

The bosses in Australia made the mistake of leaving their Chinese executives in place for too long with little supervision. The bigger mistake was destroying the trust handshake deals made with Chinese partners in the quest for a little extra margin. That is bad practice anywhere, but especially in China ... Everyone doing business in China should be clear by now on the rules – there is no rule of law. Deals can be done on the basis of mutual trust, which creates some level of certainty.

With Hu pleading guilty of corruption and sentenced, Rio's executive came out of the whole affair looking like less than shining lights in their corporate governance capabilities relating to their most important marketplace. Following Stern's arrest and conviction significant changes were made to Rio's China corporate team and to the regional and contract governance approach, including moving key negotiators out of China and into Singapore with its well-established corporate legal system (Hewitt, 2010, p. 35).[2]

The events surrounding Stern Hu's trial and conviction have had significant ramifications for the Australia–China relationship, with Australians now being more fully aware that China's economic ascendancy will not necessarily translate into it moving towards a politico-legal environment that resembles their own.

## An end to the annual iron ore benchmark pricing system: Political consequences

Clinton Dines, for 20 years BHPB's China chief iron ore negotiator until 2008, made clear the thoughts of most within the iron ore industry on the whole Hu Stern crisis – that the iron ore annual price negotiation system itself was fraught with unsustainable risk:

No other major commodity trade is subject to as much arguing, emotion and hostility between buyers and sellers. No one really trusts the benchmark pricing system. It is seen only as a means to gain negotiating advantage. Every year, buyers and sellers waste months of time and energy on price negotiations. Everyone gets angry and emotional. Every year, relationships are further damaged. (Callick, 2010c)

---

[2] "Rio has moved staff to Singapore, which it said helped with the oversight and supervision by committee" (Hewitt, 2010).

In another interview Dines elaborated even further:

> The Chinese obsession with trying to argue the iron ore price on a short-term basis from year to year rather than taking a strategic perspective to encourage the expansion of low-cost iron ore capacity has been a major contributing factor to the situation they find themselves in year after year.
>
> This mostly reflects a lack of experience in global commodities markets and a slightly suspicious xenophobia, which has prevented the relationship between suppliers and end-users being more civil and productive. (Sainsbury, 2010e, p. 21)

Within a few months of Hu's conviction, both BHPB and Rio Tinto dumped the annual benchmark pricing system in favour of a more market-oriented quarterly pricing structure. They seemed to be laying down a clear commercial verdict that Hu and his fellow Rio negotiators were part of a larger systemic flaw within the annual iron ore pricing system (Hewett & Tasker, 2010).

For the Chinese steelmakers, and particularly SOEs, the outcome of the new pricing mechanism has been to see iron ore prices rise dramatically, from a low range of US$60 per tonne in the middle of 2006 to a high range of US$140 per tonne towards the end of 2009, and they continue to openly and consistently express their dissatisfaction with these significant price increases (Shaw Research, 2009). The fact that BHPB's press release stated that the new pricing system had been negotiated through discussions with "a significant number of customers throughout Asia", but not all, left no one in any doubt that it was China who stood alone while Japan, South Korea and others had struck the deal. Hewett and Tasker (2010, p. 21) stated:

> Beneath the careful language is a revolution that is likely to have an enormous and long-term impact on the national economy, the future profits or iron ore producers, and quite possibly the diplomatic relationship between China and Australia.

The diplomatic nature of the new price methodology was emphasised by the then Australian trade minister, Simon Crean, who made it clear that any political or commercial interference with the resource market pricing would be unacceptable:

> All we ask in return is it acts in accordance with market principles, not seek to get government involved.... For the steelmakers, in

terms of being dissatisfied with the way negotiations have been run in the past, their solution doesn't lie in getting the government to intervene. (Uren & Sainsbury, 2009, p. 19)

The spot price of iron ore in January 2010 remained high; incredibly 84 per cent higher than the price negotiated with Japan in May of 2009 ($131.20 a tonne). There is no fear of these hikes dampening demand, as Malcolm Southwood of Goldman Sachs JBWere, sees seaborne trade expanding by 100 million tonnes in 2010, double the previous 5-year average (Sainsbury, 2010e).

While international iron ore investors are of course delighted by the increased prices, China's Ministry of Commerce spokesman, Yao Jian, made it clear Beijing was very unhappy about the situation and stated that the formal position of the government was that as the world's largest buyer of iron ore China should receive the resource at a lower price. At the same time, an unnamed official from the peak body, China Iron and Steel Association, stated:

> There are not many radical measures the Commerce Ministry can take, without possible violating WTO regulations. (Sainsbury, 2010c, p. 35)

Having joined the WTO in 2001, China has appealed to the body over restrictive US measures on a range of Chinese-made steel products, so it is hardly now in a position to break the same body's rules on the raw material (iron ore) that make up the said product (steel) without raising the considerable political–economic ire of major global trading partners (the US, Japan, the EU, India and Brazil).

At the time of writing, the Australian government's domestic concerns, including a recently held and bitterly contested election, has meant that the long-term impact of this pricing change to Australia's crucial relations with China has yet to be fully appreciated among all but a very small number of trade and resource-oriented political figures. Mining insiders are in no doubt, as one unnamed executive makes clear:

> The significance of what has occurred here has not yet really been understood. We will all look back on this in years to come and realise it was when the floodgates really opened. (Hewett & Tasker, 2010, p. 21)

Now that the new Julia Gillard-led federal Labor government has taken to the parliamentary benches after the 2010 election, it is finding that the economic centrality of China's resource question to Australia's future prosperity is raising questions that can no longer be avoided. Indeed, the Reserve Bank of Australia's decision to raise interest rates once again on 2 November 2010, based on concerns over inflation, highlighted to all that the mining boom created by China's need for resources has cemented successfully, meeting the policy challenges of a "two-speed" economy as *the* defining legitimacy criteria for holding the government benches (Stutchbury, 2010c; Uren, 2010).

The bulk of Australia's iron ore reserves are to be found within the state of Western Australia, along with several other significant metals and huge volumes of natural gas. This makes it, along with Queensland, which possesses equally significant coal deposits and natural gas resources, the premier mining state in Australia. What makes Western Australia unique, and unlike even Queensland, however, is the extent to which it is utterly dependent upon resource extraction to drive its economy, and therefore the degree to which politics, both within and through state-federal relations, is driven by it. This is the topic of the next section.

## WA politics: The premier mining state within Australian political economy

WA is undergoing a series of multi-billion-dollar resource projects aimed primarily at feeding the hunger of China, Japan, India, South Korea and Taiwan for resources in iron ore, gas, gold and other commodities. For those who do not live in Western Australia it is often difficult to appreciate how much political, policy and business thinking centres around the role resources play in the state's prosperity. From our observations, the best way to frame such an understanding is to ask: Is it actually possible to overestimate how much influence mining and other resources have on the thinking of WA's political and commercial elite? The answer, for the researchers of this book, is a definitive NO. It is a mining state in every sense of the word, with all other economic sectors, from agriculture to tourism, keenly aware of the positive and negative impacts this entails. A brief downturn in mining investment in 2008–09, including the closing of some operations and significant retrenchments, provided an unwanted reminder to all of the reality that WA's prosperity hinges on the fortunes of mining and resources.

The current premier of WA, Colin Barnett, has acknowledged that Australian governments and policy makers were slow to appreciate the speed with which China would seek to increase its direct investments into Australian resources:

> While the commonwealth government is engaged in diplomacy they've perhaps been a little slow to recognise that this is all about natural resources and natural resources are Western Australia. I think China wants to know what they can invest in and where they are welcome. (O'Brien, 2009, p. 20)

Mr Barnett then went on to express the view that Australia's relationship with China requires the same considerable work efforts that were invested in developing constructive investment ties with Japan back in the 1960s and 1970s (Japan is now one of Australia's most long-term, trusted and robust investors):

> We need to develop a long-term mature relationship with China.... It comes as a rush, but I don't think this is as hard as Japan would have been in the 60s.... They are a communist state, a one-party state, all the major industries are government-owned. We have to accept the reality of that, recognise that China is not Japan, it's a different type of country, and have a modern, sophisticated approach to it. That has been lacking.... We want to keep them as a customer. We don't have the only iron ore in the world. There are fabulous iron ore resources in Africa that have never been developed, very high grade.... China wants to buy quality assets. It wants to have access to good resources, good projects and be a foundation investor, a foundation customer, and have the status that it sees Japan enjoy. (O'Brien, 2009, p. 20)

Barnett, post-CHINALCO spurning by Rio Tinto, visited China to explicitly reassure both Chinese government officials and investors that they were still very much welcome in WA, and reiterated that Australia needed to do much more to formulate a plan for Chinese investment and communicate this position more effectively to the Australian public (Tingle, 2009). A clear example of the joint WA–China shared interests can be seen in the proposed development of a new iron ore deep-sea port in the Pilbara region of the state, the first such major port in the region since the 1970s. Located at Anketell Point, near the township of Karratha, the port is a joint venture between the WA government, FMG, API Management and the China Metallurgical Group Corporation. It is expected that this proposed port can substantially facilitate WA's iron ore export expansion from 380 million tonnes in 2009 to 700 million tonnes in 2015. The political importance of the project was underscored by Premier Barnett regularly hailing the development on both state and national media forum, and to significant domestic and international business groups (Barrett, 2010).

In 2010 the political divisions between the Australian federal government, led by a Labor prime minister (Kevin Rudd was succeeded by Julia Gillard in June 2010), and the Western Australian government, led by a Liberal premier (Colin Barnett), have widened considerably over questions of resource tax allocations (this will be explored more fully in the following section about super mining tax). Premier Barnett is on record as saying he feels "almost under siege from Canberra" over the revenue push. He said the state's future lay "over the horizon and not over the Nullabor", with its focus increasingly being outside Australia (Barnett, 2010a). He has made it plain that the current, and any future, Western Australian government would be seeking to grow its relationship with not only China, but also Singapore, the Gulf States and India, and reinforce long-standing relations with the US oil and gas sectors due to the high presence of Exxon Mobil and Chevron in the WA economy. High-profile visits to Japan and China in 2009, and a 2010 visit to the US, were all politically and commercially centred around major resource development projects. Barnett justified the trips by stating:

> I'm quite deliberately taking an internationalist approach for Western Australia, and we will continue to forge our future in our region with our major trading partners... I even heard it remarked by someone the other day who had just come back, that WA is seen in China as the most favourable government anywhere in the world. I hope that's true. We're going to continue... [to engage actively]...
>
> The commonwealth and the Prime Minister, I assure you are relying on Western Australia to lead Australia economically, and we'll do that, we'll step up to the plate... but it does not need to be made harder... We are going to take a very international stand as a state government and as a state economy. (Barnett, 2010a)

He has also made no attempt to hide his displeasure at the federal government's attempt to take over mining royalties and to reduce the WA share of the Goods and Services Tax (GST) revenue, being proposed at 68 cents in the dollar compared to 95 cents for NSW, 93 cents for Victoria and 91 cents for QL. In the WA political landscape, one whose history is dominated with talk of succession and significant disputes with the federal government, the political interpretation of this GST imbalance is that WA is carrying incompetent state governments (most notably the current NSW Labor government) on the other side of the country via the federal government's transferral of WA revenue into their budgetary coffers. This may, or may not, be so. But what is not up for dispute, but currently never mentioned by Barnett or other WA-based state politicians, is the fact that in previous decades WA very much enjoyed substantial federal government subsidies derived from the eastern states' revenue base.

The idea that the iron ore and resources of the Pilbara and northern WA are the resources of all Australians, not just Western Australians, is accepted in the contemporary WA parliament (as a majority, not universally). But the idea totally hinges on the continuation of the traditional balance between federal and state rights being upheld, including WA maintaining resource revenue through the state royalties system. Former WA premier, Richard Court, made this states-rights view clear:

> Strengthening the federation by strengthening the states is the answer... Remember, the states created our federation, not the other way around. (Court, 2010)

There can be no doubt that Western Australian politics remains dominated by two interrelated issues: the balance between federal–state relations, and what percentage of revenue WA retains from its China and Asia-bound natural resource assets. These two issues came to a head with the federal government's effort to introduce a super mining tax, and this will be the topic of the next section.

## The politics of the super profits mineral tax

For much of the time of writing this chapter the Australian political landscape was being dominated by a federal government resource tax that is entirely dependent on the continuation of China purchasing Australian resources (Dobson, 2010; Kehoe, Wyatt & Ear, 2010; Kelly, 2010). Through the 2010 Australian budget, the then Rudd-led Labor Party government, on the recommendation of the Henry Tax Review, introduced a mining super profit tax (based on any profits above the 6 per cent Australian government bond rate). The government's economic leadership, then Prime Minister Kevin Rudd and Treasurer

Wayne Swan, immediately spread themselves across the country to sell the tax to the broader population and mining stakeholders. The mining executives, in turn, made a beeline to Canberra to challenge the imposition of this new tax. The Australian mining industry is already the single largest contributor to the Australian tax base: "in 2008–09 Australian miners paid A$10.6 billion in corporate tax and another A$8 billion in royalties" (Stevens, 2010a, p. 25). The response from the Liberal opposition has been a universal public rejection of the new tax. The current leader of the Liberal opposition, Tony Abbott, proclaimed throughout the August 2010 federal election that he would dump the super mining tax altogether. State governments who hold secure constitutional rights over the minerals found within their borders and secure funding in the form of mining royalties (which will continue to be recognised under the new tax) have been more or less vocal depending on their reliance on the mining industry for wealth creation. The premiers of Australia's two key mining states, Colin Barnett of WA and Anne Bligh of Queensland, have, not surprisingly, expressed deep concerns over the nature and form of the tax. Both made it clear they were, and remain, concerned that investors will simply pull out of proposed multi-billion-dollar projects (Stevens, 2010a).

In June 2010 the federal caucus of the Australian Labor Party moved against Kevin Rudd as leader of the party, and thereby, prime minister of Australia, as his popularity throughout Australia, but particularly in the mining states of WA and Queensland, plummeted. The weight that his fellow government members placed on what they viewed as his complete mishandling of the resource super profit tax can be seen through the fact that his replacement, Julia Gillard, immediately placed a brokered deal with the nation's major miners (particularly BHPB, Xstrata and Rio Tinto) on the super tax as her leadership's number one priority. A new deal with the big three was sealed within two weeks, but significant other stakeholders remain opposed (most notably the WA-based FMG led by Andrew Forrest). At the time some commentators suggested forcefully that the mining tax should result in a loss of office for the incumbent Labor government because it represented, in their view, a complete mismanagement of the mining boom (R. Fitzgerald, 2010). They were very nearly right as in the August 2010 federal election the Gillard-led Labor government was nearly swept from office as the mining states of WA and Queensland turned on it and moved to the Abbott-led coalition opposition, with Labor only retaining power through a loose coalition with independent House of Representative members.

While the debate over the tax continues and remains highly contentious, the fact that it would not be taking place *at all* without the
insatiable and continuing demand of China for the foreseeable future is
beyond dispute (Stutchbury, 2010a, 2010b). The current Australian budgetary position is unquestionably entirely underpinned by the international resource market, of which China is the largest buyer. Throughout
the August 2010 federal election neither party leader (Gillard or Abbott)
addressed how Australia's own prosperity is increasingly dependent on
China's own economic performance. Possibly they both knew they did
not have to. The removal of Kevin Rudd, Australia's first prime minister to speak fluent Mandarin, and someone who personally launched a
new $53 million Australian National University China Centre just weeks
before his June downfall, as a result of failing to read the fierce political reaction of a China-driven mining sector and the political weight it
carries, particularly in WA and Queensland, leaves no one in any doubt
as to the centrality of the Australia–China relationship within modern
Australian political economy (Richardson, 2010). Currently, with significant opposition to the resource tax alive and well within WA political
and commercial circles, the opposition of federal opposition and key
federal independents, and BHPB having expressed continued concerns
over the agreement it signed up to pre-August 2010 election, the future
of the resource tax in both form and scale remains an open political
question.

## The global politics of China's economy ascendancy: Australia–China relations within the broader international sphere

China's use of government-owned enterprises to extend its overseas
investment and secure natural resources, its refusal to revalue what
many see as an undervalued currency (yuan) and its widespread use
of non-tariff barriers have led a leading Australian analyst to conclude
that:

> China gets away with behaviour that would never be tolerated from
> other nations because of its economic potential and future assumed
> great power status. (Kelly, 2009, p. 12)[3]

---

[3] "Key elements of the [export-oriented] strategy – including a cheap currency,
regulated interest rates and low energy prices – are stoking discontent in fellow

In this position, he is reflecting a view and concern held by the Australian political and analytical professionals, who have come to view the FIRB as vital to ensuring that national economic sovereignty questions are addressed thoroughly. Analysts in Australia, the US and Europe have viewed China's use of state financing and currency pegging as a form of trade protectionism, which cannot continue indefinitely (Sainsbury, 2009i).[4] In the political realm the validity of the argument either way is currently less important than the view that Chinese investment does currently raise serious concerns among the Australian electorate, or more specifically crucial regional electorates, required for holding government at both the state and federal levels (Onselen, 2010). As this section reveals, Australians are hardly alone in having these concerns over China's growing economic weight.

The rise of China as an economic power has become a continuing theme within the Australian media and commentary, and there can be no doubt of the growing influence it wields (Mitchell, 2010). Having overtaken Germany in 2007 as the world's third-largest economy, in 2009 China became the world's top merchandise exporter, superseding Germany with $957 billion of goods in the first nine months of 2009, compared to Germany's $917 billion (Miller & Walker, 2010). The International Monetary Fund (IMF) projects that China's share of world exports could reach 12 per cent of the global total export in 2014 (Baton, 2010). The financial debacle that has taken place in the major American and European markets since 2007, leaving most major economies with severe public and private debt levels and politically focused on domestic affairs, has left China feeling far more confident to stride the foreign investment world (Stutchbury, 2010a).[5] This does not mean that China

---

developing countries, not just Western capitalism"..."And many economists argue China's export-friendly policies are fuelling inflation pressures at home, placing a burden on the rest of the economy" (Baton, 2010).

[4] "China's policy for the past 18 months, of pegging its currency to the fading US dollar is a form of protectionism" (Sainsbury, 2009i).

"The Americans hate this Chinese exchange rate 'manipulation' because it makes US-produced goods less price-competitive ... China will eventually require a flexible exchange rate regime with open capital markets ... After three decades of liberalisation, product markets have become increasingly competitive and market forces are now generally the main determinant of price formation and economic behaviour" (Strutchbury, 2010b).

[5] "The tarnished credibility of Western-style financial capitalism has raised China's self-confidence in its own economic model over the Anglo-Saxon examples mired in public debt and desperately printing money to stimulate growth" (Strutchbury, 2010b).

is ready to take on a role of global leadership, particularly given that the Chinese leadership themselves face considerable economic and social hurdles at home. International concerns are increasingly being raised over China's export dependency, the level of debt being held by domestic banks, and associated fears in relation to the emergence of property and asset bubbles (Callick, 2009d; Poon, 2010; Sainsbury, 2010h).[6] These challenges collectively mean that:

> The Communist Party believes its legitimacy is dependent on maintaining high levels of economic growth and rapidly rising living standards. (Mitchell, 2010, p. 46)

This often means that the national political elite "make decisions that foster domestic economic growth at the expense of almost everything else, including, some say, the viability of the international currency regime, nuclear non-proliferation and basic rights in resource-rich countries [including widespread use of corruption]" (Metzl, 2010).

The global economic rise of China continues to raise tensions, with the US having taken a number of trade restrictions against Chinese steel producers. The US International Trade Commission found in December 2009 that US steelmakers have been damaged by Chinese suppliers through unfair practices and imposed 10–16 per cent duties on future imports of all Chinese steel pipes used to drill natural gas and oil wells. It was argued by the US steel industry that half of the previous 6000 US workers in steel piping had been laid off due to the unfair pricing of Chinese suppliers. In 2009 the Obama administration placed a 35 per cent import tariff on Chinese consumer car tyres after finding unfair practices existed (Maher & Pulizzi, 2010).

Concerns over China's growing economic reach is hardly confined to the US and the EU, with developing economies such as Indonesia, Brazil, Thailand and Russia all having expressed trade concerns. Ben Simpfendorfer, senior economist with the Royal Bank of Scotland, makes the case for the developing world's rising level of concern:

> There's a potential spoiler for China in relations with the developing world. They've only been exporting and not importing ... It's one thing to produce job losses in the U.S., but it's another to produce job losses in Pakistan – a close military ally of China. (Baton, 2010, p. 25)

---

[6] "China's export data is being closely watched for clues of the state of the world's third-largest economy and for signs of recovery in crisis-hit markets such as the US and Europe" (Poon, 2010).

This point is highlighted most notably by the fact that, in 2009, Asia's other giant, India, laid more WTO complaints against China than any other nation. The two Asian giants do not have complimentary economies, with their agricultural sectors and strategic economic activities (steel, shipbuilding, automobiles, and so on) being direct competitors within the international marketplace. This is most notably the case in the key developing markets of Latin America, Africa and the Middle East. Indian Trade Minister Anand Sharma, like his US and EU counterparts, also pinpoints currency manipulation as an area of dispute:

> A balance of exports and imports is important... China's trade surplus with India grew 46 percent last year to $16 billion, probably aggravated by the weakening of the yuan against the Indian rupee. (Baton, 2010, p. 25)

Most of China's exports now go to other developing countries, with exports to India, Brazil, Indonesia and Mexico growing by 30 per cent to 50 per cent in recent months, according to China International Capital Corporation (Baton, 2010). This process is not without strain, and politicians within those countries will face increasing pressure from domestic enterprises to challenge China's use of artificial currency rates and other measures to gain market share.

The concerns over China's economic ascendancy expressed in Australia and across the developed and developing world, however, do not translate into any meaningful influence. Currently China holds all the trump cards that come with rapid economic growth both domestically and internationally. Australia very much falls within World Bank's framework for Asian growth, which centres on "Beijing's plans to bolster demand by massive infrastructure spending" (Ryan, 2009). Given that Australia's federal and state budgets are all currently underwritten by China's insatiable requirement for mineral and energy supplies, the concerns over China's global economic rise are more than matched by concerns over any signs of significant reduction in that nation's economic growth path. Australia's political, policy and business elite are keenly aware that the greatest threat to China's continued prosperity is a global collapse of consensus as to what form the international economy should take. Influential US Asian analyst, Jamie Metzle (2010), reflected widespread thinking among the American elite that it is time China started carrying international responsibilities reflective of its new power status, and that failure to do so will have negative global consequences:

But if China's leadership will neither do more to support the current international system, nor articulate an alternative, and instead continue to hark back to 19th century models of inviolable sovereignty, they will destroy a global order that, warts and all, has served the world exceedingly well. Those countries that value the current system will increasingly feel the urge to close ranks to defend it.

A scenario in which Australian political elite in the future must choose between explicitly expressing full support for a traditional ally, such as the US taking trade (or strategic) action against a China behaving beyond the established international boundaries, is the stuff of policy nightmares. Australia has gained much from China's rise since the late 1970s, and particularly over the past decade, but it is also becoming apparent that the dividend for the prosperity is a far more complex international environment surrounding the great powers of our region (US, China and India) (Vivoda, 2009; Wilkins, 2010).

## Conclusion

Stephen Smith, the then Australian foreign affairs minister, in a speech to the Australia–China Business Council, stated:

> Such are our shared economic and other interests, it is vital to chart a steady course in the long term with the broader relationship. There will be tensions and difficulties from time to time, owing to our different political systems, histories and societies. (Sainsbury, 2010c, p. 35)

For Australia's political class the balancing of political economy centres on the "sensitive point of contact between ownership by a socialist market economy corporate state, and by a private corporation in a liberal democracy" (Callick, 2009e). An awareness among Australian political representatives of the real economic challenges faced by the Chinese political leadership is currently insufficient across the political spectrum. No one in Australia should underestimate the importance China places in securing long-term resource security, as a failure to secure these (particularly iron ore, coal, gas, oil) would undermine economic growth and, thereby, the central legitimacy of the CCP (Vivoda, 2009). Pricing of iron ore and other essential resources, for Australia, underpins the health of the national budget and, therefore, its ability to fund prosperity and security. As the seller, its incentive is to reach for the highest price for the longest possible time. For China, the question is a political–strategic one at the heart of its future stability, prosperity and security, with the buyer's incentive of securing the asset long-term at a minimal price. These similarities in objectives, but alternative incentive realities, need to be openly recognised and negotiated by each side. Any efforts by Australia to treat China's efforts to achieve resource security as an entirely commercial goal deny the reality of their domestic, political and economic circumstances. Correspondingly, effort by China or others to proclaim that nationally owned enterprises entering the resource market in Australia should be viewed by the Australian public as purely commercial entities is equally ingenious. An open public recognition of Australia and China's differing and concurrent short-term and long-term motivations and objectives has yet to develop, but is an absolute requirement for long-term success in securing Australia's future prosperity and China's future resource needs.

The success, or otherwise, of managing Australia's political, economic and strategic relationships with China over the coming decade and beyond will go a long way to determining Australia's prosperity in the twenty-first century. The absence of addressing the shape and nature of the relationship among the contending prospective future political leadership of Australia leading up to the 2010 federal election did not serve the long-term interest of the nation, which requires a concerted public examination of how a prosperous and increasingly powerful China influences Australia's strategic and economic future. Only a national discussion will provide the public with reference points upon which to determine what levels and forms of Chinese investment into Australia's mining sector (and potentially agricultural in the future) is in their best political–economic interests. Xiong Jin, senior associate at one of the top five Australian law firms, Mallesons Stephen Jaques, states:

> Both sides need to understand each other better, since they have a lot of common interests and the two economies are highly supplementary. (Sainsbury, 2009h)

A formalised and sustained dialogue, rather than the current event-by-event approach that is practised, should be adopted, as this is essential to resolving any public concerns over Chinese investments into Australia's mining sector (and other sectors such as agriculture, telecommunications and information technology).

# 5

# The Investment Process and After-Transaction Integration and Management

## Introduction

While the previous chapters discussed the overall pattern of Chinese investment in the Australian minerals industry, the Australian regulatory framework and Australia–China trade relations, this chapter examines strategic and operational issues at the organisational level. Specifically, it analyses factors considered by Chinese firms when deciding to invest in the Australian minerals industry, the entry process and the managerial issues faced by Chinese firms after they have successfully become part of this industry.

Investing in a foreign country is a complex process; the stakes are usually very high as are the risks and rewards involved. As such, potential investing firms have to comprehensively understand the major steps in the investment process and what key activities and issues are involved in each step. They also need to know the issues and challenges in managing their foreign investments if they choose to establish a WOS or JV with a local firm, or take a controlling stake in the Australian miner invested. In the following sections, the major steps in the investment process will be outlined and the key activities associated with them discussed. Then, the financial returns of several Chinese major investments in the listed Australian companies are investigated. Finally, managerial issues encountered by Chinese-controlled entities after they have successfully entered into the Australian minerals industry are examined, including WOSs, Chinese-controlled enterprises as a majority shareholder and JVs in the post-investment phase and management of these entities. Clearly, Chinese investors could play a substantial role in governing and/or managing their investments in these three types of organisations.

# The entry process: Major steps and factors considered

Broadly, there are three major stages in the entry or investment process. They are pre-investment preparation, negotiation and transaction. Each stage has different objectives and involves various tasks, activities and decision-making processes.

## Pre-investment preparation

Pre-investment preparation represents the first stage in the investment process. Investing in a foreign country is a very challenging managerial decision as it usually involves assessment of both the host and home country's economic, political, legal and cultural environments as well as the target project and the company. Moreover, the financial, HR, technology and management resources of the investing organisation should be reviewed to ensure that its foreign investment goal is achievable.

### *Macro environment analysis*

The pre-investment stage involves a detailed analysis of important issues at both macro and micro levels. At the macro level, environmental analyses in host (Australia) and home (China) countries are crucial. The political environment in Australia is quite a stable democracy that uses preferential voting at state and national levels. Although there are several major political parties in Australia, the Australia Labor Party (ALP) and the coalition (Liberal Party and National Party) have been dominant in governing Australia, with the Australian Green Party growing rapidly since the past decade and exercising more influence on Australia's political agenda. Australia has democratically elected federal and state governments. While there is vigorous political debate aided by a large unregulated press, there is considerable bipartisan agreement on major issues (e.g. defence). Moreover, in modern times, governments usually serve for more than one term (each term lasts between three and four years). This has resulted in a very stable political environment so far in Australian history, despite changes in the Australian government from time to time.

Many publications, books and reports include lengthy discussions of Australia's economic environment. Overall, Australia is a developed country, as a recent global competitiveness report ranked Australia ninth in terms of its economic competitiveness. The report covered 12 areas, including infrastructure, macroeconomic stability, market efficiency of goods and labour, innovation and technological readiness (Schwab, 2009). However, because of its low population of 22.5 million in 2010 (13th largest economy in 2009) and a heavy reliance on commodity exports, its currency can fluctuate strongly (moving in a range between $0.6 and parity to the American dollar in recent years).

The macro environmental issues of the legal and taxation systems warrant particular attention. Australia is legally a federation of six states and two territories, implying that laws are issued at the federal and state levels. Thus, any legal environmental analysis needs to examine the federal laws and regulations and those at the state level. In Chapter 3, the Australian regulatory framework on FDI was described and discussed. However, many other laws and acts, such as corporate law and taxation law, are operational. There are also several laws and acts specially applied to the operations of a foreign entity (more than 15 per cent owned by a foreign interest) or JV in Australia.

*Micro environment analysis*

At the micro level, several important factors need to be considered. These factors can be grouped into three areas: the nature of the target project, the target organisation and the acquiring organisation.

**Project analysis**: Many Chinese investments have been made in mineral projects. Even when investing in a mining company, the key minerals' projects usually represent the major source of the company's value. Factors at the project level cover:

- the value of the project in terms of the quality and amount of resources;
- the costs of mining and processing;
- transportation costs;
- sensitivity of the physical environment; and
- infrastructure, such as rail, port, power, electricity and water supply.

Although these issues are usually dealt with in the preliminary feasibility study (PFS), and in more detail in a feasibility study, it is absolutely necessary to have a broad understanding of these issues at the beginning to identify the likelihood of the target project having economic viability, the likelihood of bringing the project into operation and the likelihood of it passing the threshold of financial performance.

The nature of the target project usually represents the first factor to be considered, such as its quality (mineral grades), quantity (reserve or resources), mining costs (that is, geology conditions) and location, particularly in relation to transportation (main roads, railways and ports). Regarding the mineral resources of the target project, the Australasian Joint Ore Reserves Committee (JORC) (www.jorc.org) has developed minimum standards for public reporting of exploration results, minerals resources and ore reserves. JORC is an independent committee, established by the Minerals Council of Australia (MCA), The Australasian Institute of Mining and Metallurgy (The AusIMM) and the Australian Institute of Geoscientists (AIG). The Australian Stock Exchange (ASX) and the Securities Institute of Australia (SIA) also have representatives on the committee. JORC has classified exploration results into three categories: exploration results, minerals resources and ore reserves. It has then broken mineral resources into three groups: inferred, indicated and measured, which are increasingly operative as the level of geological knowledge and confidence increase; this is usually reflected by the density and depth of exploration drillings in the project field. Ore reserves, which could be more interesting and valuable to potential investors, are converted from mineral resources by considering such moderating factors as mining, metallurgical, economic, marketing, legal, environmental and governmental issues. JORC groups ore reserves into two categories: probable and proved. The relationship between exploration results, minerals resources and ore reserves is shown in Figure 5.1.

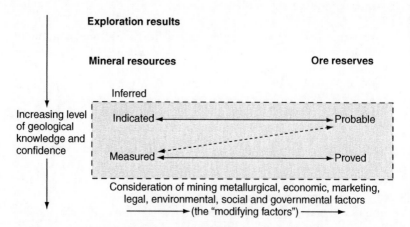

*Figure 5.1*   The relationship between exploration results, minerals resources and ore reserves

*Source*: Joint Ore Reserves Committee (JORC), 2004, reprinted with the permission of The Australasian Institute of Mining and Metallurgy.

The minerals are legally owned by the states in which they are located in Australia. Therefore, the state governments in Australia are responsible for approving a mining project located within their state or territory. Many laws, regulations and acts have to be abided by when exploring and developing a project to the production stage. For example, in WA, these include the Environmental Protection Act, the Aboriginal Heritage Act, the Mining Act and the Harbours Act. These approval procedures may take time to get through, possibly having a significant impact on the project's progress and financing. For information about the target project and government approval procedure in WA, the Department of State Development of WA is a very useful source.

Conducting a detailed project analysis is crucial to any investment in the mining industry. The risk is very high for those projects at the exploration stage because it involves a high level of uncertainty. One Chinese firm recently terminated a JV project because of its low economic viability after three years of exploration, causing the loss of tens of millions of dollars.

**Target organisation analysis:** Analysing the vendor miner or the partner organisation for a JV should include the shareholder structure, the quality of its management and its board, the financial position, the motivation for securing investment and its financial performance. As most of the investment needs approval from the shareholders of the targeted company, the shareholder structure is important. Securing support from major shareholders in a concentrated shareholding is critical. For less concentrated firms, the support of the board is crucial as it can help secure support from the broad range of shareholders.

The quality of the board and management of the targeted company is also important, particularly for potential JVs and minority participation investors. For potential JVs, it is necessary to know the resources and skills of the potential partner organisation, and to assess if they can be used to achieve the potential JV's objectives. A quality board can ensure that major decisions are made in the interest of shareholders, particularly in relation to strategic directions and risk alleviation. More specifically, the quality of a board can be assessed by its composition (number of executive vs non-executive directors, and independent directors), quality (experience, skills and qualifications) and the separation of the chairman from the CEO position.

Additionally, the potential partner's motivation for selling the asset and its financial position should be probed and understood. Those investing as a minority equity participant are not directly involved in managing the target organisation, although they may be offered a seat or seats on the board. If the company's financial position is not strong, further financing may be needed and this may impact on its share price and shareholding structure.

Therefore, having a quality management team and trustworthy board to manage its investment and the company invested in is extremely important. The Chinese Embassy in Canberra and Chinese Consulate-General in Perth, Sydney, Melbourne and Brisbane are good starting sources for Chinese investors to collect information about target organisations.

**Internal analysis**: Conducting an internal analysis helps with making an informed and thorough investment decision. This should cover the strategic motivation, financial strengths and organisational competence. Investment is essentially, if not entirely, an economic decision and non-economic influence should be minimised. Financing the investment could be the most important issue to consider, particularly for those considering setting up a WOS, a controlling entity or JV. Investing in a mining operation at the exploration or development stages not only requires the initial financial layout, but also funds for developing the company or project to the production stage, prior to any cash flow being generated. The initial investment could be relatively small compared with the further investment required for project development. For example, the initial transaction for CITIC Pacific's acquisition of 2 billion tonnes of mining rights from Mineralogy was $470 million. The project is expected to start production in July 2011. So far, the funds CITIC Pacific has provided to develop the project from exploration to production have reached $5 billion. Therefore, a long-term and systematic view of project financing is needed. Otherwise, the project acquired can become dormant, as observed in several Chinese investments that lacked further financing. This circumstance may further undermine the financial position of the Chinese investors. Investing in a large project without properly considering the company's financial position can also restrict its growth because of insufficient funds being available for realising the development opportunities presented for the entire organisation.

Despite the importance of prior-investment preparation to investment success, this has been a common weakness for Chinese investments in the Australian minerals industry and could be one of the major factors contributing to unsatisfactory project performance for many Chinese investors.

**The negotiation stage**

This stage can be very time-consuming, depending on the nature of the project and the amount of the investment. In most cases, contact between a Chinese investor and the target company is made through informal channels or personal contacts. In some cases, the target companies use selling agencies, such as investment banks, to promote a project globally.

Once the connection between Chinese investors and the targeted company is made, information exchange is crucial to the negotiation stage, including the developmental stage of the target project, JORC's report on the project resources and/or reserves, pre-feasibility study report and bankable feasibility report. Field visits are usually made to inform investors of key characteristics of the target project, such as its geographical location, transportation facilities and possibly mining conditions. Minerals samples from the exploration drillings may also be taken for further analyses to cross-verify the technical specifications provided by the target company.

The potential financial performance and return of the target project are also investigated at this stage. This involves detailed examination of the rationale and sensibility of the production processes, capital expenditure, cost structure and detailed breakdown cost items, including transportation costs. Such information is usually provided in more detail in the pre-feasibility or feasibility study reports.

Other information sought and key terms for the negotiation at this stage can vary substantially depending on the entry mode selected: either takeover, controlling shareholder, JV or minority equity participation. Minority equity participation usually requires less time and effort at this stage compared with the other three entry modes. For the latter, the scope of the project investment and the ownership structure are often negotiable at this stage.

Depending on the complexity of the target project or company and the amount of investment, this negotiation stage may take from several months to several years. Because of the differences in language and legal environment between China and Australia, agencies are often hired by both sides for facilitating the negotiations. Once both sides have agreed in principle on the conditions of sale, a heads of agreement is then signed, which states the key terms of sale, including the scope of the target or company for sales, the amount of the investment, timing of the payment, exclusivity, break fees and the approval process. It also specifies share of the ownership and company structure if a JV is agreed.

Due diligence is often conducted after both parties sign the heads of agreement documentation. The target company usually requires the potential buyer to deposit an agreed amount of non-refundable money in exchange for its access to the target project or company's crucial information.

## The transaction stage and several key terms and conditions in the transactions

A formal agreement is signed by two sides if the due diligence confirms the accuracy of the information provided by the target company during the negotiation stage or if no major discrepancy has been found between the information provided by the target company during the negotiation stage and what has been confirmed through due diligence.

Two key components of the agreement are the approval process and the payment terms and conditions. The approval process involves the target company's shareholder approval, FIRB approval (if an investment is made by a SOE "for 10 per cent or above of the target company, or with influence or control over the target investment" (FIRB, 2010b) for less than 10 per cent, or if it exceeds the FIRB's monetary or shareholding thresholds by a private foreign firm) and approval by relevant Chinese authorities (see Chapter 2). The key terms of the transaction for taking a controlling stake and minority equity participation are usually relatively simple, as the former would take control of the target company after the transaction, while the latter often acts as a financial investor. However, the terms for takeover and JVs are quite complex and warrant discussion.

**Key terms of transaction for takeovers**: The payment terms and conditions differ depending on mode of entry. For the four takeovers of established Australian mining companies (see Table 2.1), these were all cash payments. There was no script involved as none of the Chinese investors had a subsidiary listed on the Australian Stock Exchange. Except for Sinosteel's hostile takeover of Midwest, all were friendly takeovers achieved through placing a full takeover bid to the existing shareholders at a "price premium". The key terms for such takeover bids, as specified in their Takeover Bid Implementation Deed, included minimum acceptance (usually 90% in both cases), and approvals from the target company's shareholders, the FIRB and Chinese authorities (such as the National Development and Reform Commission, Ministry of Commerce and the State Administration of Foreign Exchange).

For the three acquisitions of mining tenements or rights made by Shenhua, CITIC Pacific and CHINALCO, no payment conditions were attached. The cash-payment approach could be risky because it does not consider potential variation in the stock market.

Nevertheless, MCC attached conditions for its payment to Cape Lambert in acquiring an iron ore project from Cape Lambert. That is, the last payment of A$80 million out of A$400 million would only be paid when the mining lease was granted and related construction was approved. The terms, conditions and approval process for MCC to acquire the Cape Lambert Project are presented in Table 5.1

**Key terms of transactions for controlling stakeholders:** For those four Chinese investors that entered the Australian mineral industry, taking a controlling stake in target companies (see Table 2.1), two approaches were used: acquiring shares from existing shareholders, and subscribing to a new share placement by the target companies. Hunan Non-ferrous Metals Corporation (now part of Minmetals) and China Guangdong Nuclear Power Corporation (CGNPC) took a majority stake in the target companies through acquiring shares from existing

*Table 5.1* The terms, conditions and approval process for MCC to acquire Cape Lambert Project

| Date | Key steps | Notes |
| --- | --- | --- |
| 26/2/08 | MCC signed an MOU with Cape Lambert Resources | MCC paid A$10 million with A$5 million non-refundable deposit |
| 26/02/08 | MCC started conducting due diligence | Two months for due diligence |
| 28/04/08 | MCC re-lodged the acquisition application to FIRB | |
| 29/4/08 | MCC completed due diligence | |
| 29/4/08 | FIRB approved the sale | |
| 11/06/08 | Both parties signed the sale agreement | |
| 28/7/08 | AGM of Cape Lambert | Approval of the sales to MCC |
| 06/08/08 | Deal settlement | MCC paid A$23 million |
| 15/09/08 | MCC made the second payment of A$80 million | Due on 45 days after the settlement |
| To be announced | MCC to pay final payment of A$80 million | On the granting of a mining lease and related construction approval |

shareholders. The key terms of the transaction were similar to the full takeover, except that they were proportional (70% in both cases) with the minimum acceptance being 50.1 per cent. No further financing conditions were attached to the Chinese investor as it would become the controlling shareholder. Note that these two investments were made in May 2008 before the GFC, and in September 2009, respectively.

Zhongjin and Hanlong acquired a majority share in their target company through subscribing to new share placement. Zhongjin's investment was made in December 2008 during the GFC. Thus, the key terms of its transaction were merely the subscription to the new shares and the approval from Perilya's shareholders, the FIRB and Chinese regulatory authorities, without any further financing conditions attached. However, for Hanlong's acquisition of Moly Mines Limited, further conditions were attached, such as providing a $60 million loan and a $500 million loan facility to the target company for project development. Hanlong also received 35.5 million unlisted three-year options exercisable at CA$1.00 (Canadian dollar) per share, as Moly Mines is a dual-listed company in Australia and Canada.

**Key terms of transaction for JVs:** All these JVs were established at the exploration stage of the project. Besides obtaining relevant approvals similar to those in the takeover acquisition, staged payment is a common key term for Chinese JVs in the Australian mineral industry.

The key commercial terms for the JV between Ansteel and Gindalbie, signed on 6 April 2006, include two-stage development. The first stage involved joint development of the project to the completion of the feasibility study, and the second stage was the decision to mine, at which Ansteel could have 50 per cent of the project on several conditions, including providing 70 per cent of equity funding requirements for the project by Ansteel, and assisting Gindalbie to its 30 per cent of equity funding, if requested. This approach was used by Baotou Steel's JV with Centrex Metals, announced on 27 August 2009, where payments have been structured based on the development of the project – A$8 million for exploration, a further A$8 million to the pre-feasibility study and A$24 million to the feasibility study.

The staged payment approach was also used by WISCo in its JV with Centrex Metals. However, as the payment was structured based on the exploration results, and as the agreement was the most comprehensive JV one between Chinese and Australian firms at the exploration stage, it warrants a close examination. The key commercial terms are outlined in Table 5.2.

*Table 5.2* Key commercial terms in the JV between WISCo and Centrex Metals

| Detail | Terms | Comment |
|---|---|---|
| Participating interest | 60:40 (WISCo:Centrex) | In iron ore rights |
| First resource instalment | A$52 million | Payable 15 days after satisfaction of the conditions |
| Second resource instalment | A$26 million | Payable on the first anniversary of the completion date |
| JORC Inferred Resource milestone | 4 payments of A$27 million each | If and when JORC Inferred Resource reaches 1.25, 1.5, 1.75 and 2 billion tonnes respectively |
| **Subtotal** | **A$186 million** | **When Inferred Resource reaches 2 billion tonnes** |
| Share placement (15% issued capital) | A$10.09 million | Centrex to issue approx 40 million shares |
| **TOTAL** | | **A$196 million** |
| Work commitment | A$75 million. Once the A$75 million has been dispensed, Centrex and WISCo will pay promised sums into Eyre Iron Pty Ltd in proportion to interest held in the joint venture | WISCo to sole fund first A$75 million in work commitments with:<br><br>• A$50 million payable into the joint venture on the completion date, and<br>• A$25 million payable to the joint venture on the first anniversary of the completion date |
| Sheep Hill Port participating interest | 50:50 (Centrex:WISCo) | Centrex and WISCo to jointly develop a capable port at Sheep Hill. |
| Project financing beyond bankable feasibility study | | WISCo to arrange project financing |

*Source*: www.centrexmetals.com.au.

Such a staged payment has linked the resources to the payment, which will not only reduce the risk level of the Chinese partners, but will also increase the commitment of their Australian partners in speeding up their exploration process.

## Entry considerations and their impact on financial performance

Understanding the major stages in the entry process and key activities involved in each of these stages is very important as this can better prepare business executives for their investments and help them develop a list of alternatives when making investment decisions. Fast but comprehensive decisions are crucial to M&A in today's competitive and volatile international market.

Several external and internal factors can influence the share prices of the Australian companies in which investments are made. The external factors include commodity prices, and thereby type of minerals invested, timing of the investment made and the overall performance of global share markets. The internal factors cover the developmental stage of the company/project investment, shareholding structure, financial resources, management and governance and the outcome of negotiation (for example, price, rights and obligations). Timing is important because of the cyclical nature of commodity price and the dynamics of the international competitive environment. This can impact on the financial return of ODI in general. Minmetals' Minerals and Metals Group (MMG), a newly established Australian subsidiary of Minmetals consequent upon its $1.35 billion acquisition of most of OZ Minerals' assets, reported a net profit of $180.7 million (A$198 million) in March 2010 for 2009, covering the first seven months since it was established after the acquisition (Behrmann, 2010). This represented a 13.4 per cent of return on its investment in the first seven months, or 22.9 per cent annually, which may have been partly due to the quick recovery of the global commodity price. For the three remaining takeovers, the Australian companies were delisted after being taken over by Chinese companies. Thus, their financial performances are difficult to evaluate because of the scarcity of available financial information.

Four Chinese companies have taken a controlling stake in Australia's listed companies, and remained listed after their investment. As mentioned previously, many factors influence their financial performance. Moreover, an ODI is usually a long-term commitment; thus its financial return should be calculated on a long-run basis. These four Chinese firms invested in Australian miners for less than three years; therefore, it would be premature to assess their financial performance up to the present. Nevertheless the changes in their share prices between the date prior to their investment announcement and 2 July 2010 were used and compared with those of the All Ordinaries Index and Small Ordinaries Index of the Australian stock market. For a broad comparison, the financial performance of two Chinese investments as minority participants are also examined, albeit at the production stage; they are Valin's investment in the FMG and the Shougang (Capital Steel) investment in Mt Gibson. The financial return of these Chinese investments in the listed Australian mining companies is presented in Table 5.3.

As the financial return for investments is often a long-term consideration, it may be too early to draw conclusions at this stage. Nevertheless three factors seem very important to the financial performance of the investment: the developmental stage of the company or project, types of minerals and timing of the investment. Investments in the hematite (or direct shipping ore) at the production stage to FMG and Mt Gibson made Valin and Shougang a hefty return on their investments besides securing off-take agreements for a specified amount of iron ore. Both have invested as minority equity participants. Similarly, the financial performance of Zhongjin's investment in Perilya is very good as one of Perilya's major mines (Broken Hill in New South Wales) has already been in production since 2002. All three Chinese firms made their investment in the Australian companies at the production stage and during the GFC.

The ownership control is another relevant factor. Except for Zhongjin, the three other major Chinese investments in the listed Australian junior miners, through taking a controlling stake, have underperformed their peers based on the All Small Ordinaries Index. Although this may be partly explained by the developmental stage of the target company (all of them were in the exploration or development stages), it could be a reflection of the financial market's perception of the Chinese-controlled entities, or "governance discount" (Lattemann, 2009). This has raised the importance of corporate governance in the international financial markets in general, and in Australia in particular. Another plausible explanation is the strategic motivation of the Chinese investors, whereby market-rate profitability may not be their primary goal. Instead, they may be more interested in securing the supply of minerals for their production in China.

The above analysis (see Table 5.3) has also raised a very important question about control of the entity, Chinese firms having been criticised for their obsession with control. The cases analysed above show no clear pattern between ownership control and financial performance. Rather the Chinese-controlled entities are more likely (three out of four) to underperform compared with the benchmark indices.

*Table 5.3* The financial performance of six Chinese investments in listed Australian mining companies

| Chinese subsidiary or Australian firm invested | DoA[a] | Share price on DoA (A$) | Share price bought by Chinese investor | Share price at 2/7/10 | Change in the share price (%)[b] | Change of All Ord. Index between DoA and 2/7/2010 (%) | Change of ASX small ordinary between DoA and 2/07/10 | Chinese share (%) |
|---|---|---|---|---|---|---|---|---|
| Perilya | 9/12/08 | 0.15 | 0.23 | 0.38 | 160 (69.57) | 20.71 | 39.18 | 50.1 |
| Moly Mines | 19/10/09 | 1.22 | 0.747 | 0.55 | −54.9 (−26.7) | −11.17 | −13.14 | 55 |
| Energy Metals | 8/9/09 | 0.96 | 1.02 | 0.46 | −53.1 (−55.9) | −5.79 | −8.83 | 66 |
| Abra Mining Limited | 13/5/08 | 0.75 | 0.83 | 0.095 | −88.5 (−89.64) | −27.5 | −34.59 | 74 |
| Mt Gibson (Shougang) | 3/11/08 | 0.40 | 0.60 | 1.54 | 285 (156.7) | 2.2 | 14.34 | 20[c] |
| FMG (Valin) | 9/3/09 | 2.54 | 2.48 | 4.08 | 65.9 (N/A) | 36.62 | N/A | 17.4 |

[a] Date of announcement.
[b] changes of the share price between DoA and that on 2/07/10 (between that bought and that on 2/07/10) (%).
[c] it was reduced to 14 per cent in early 2010.

## After-transaction integration and management

Investing or entering into the Australian minerals industry is only the first step for many Chinese investors. There are challenges in the after-transaction integration and management for Chinese-controlled entities and JVs, which will be examined in this section. The four entry modes mentioned in the previous section involve different managerial tasks and governance roles from a Chinese investor's perspective. They also demand different business strategies and impose various operational challenges for Chinese WOSs, controlling entities and JVs. Here the WOSs and controlling entities are grouped as one, and called "Chinese-controlled entities". In this section, we focus on the strategic and operational issues in the Chinese-controlled entities and JVs.

Table 5.4 lists these Chinese organisations along with several key characteristics of their investments. As can be seen from the table, seven Chinese companies have their WOSs in Australia, four with a controlling stake and five JVs with 50 per cent or 60 per cent of the entity.

The seven WOSs were established after 2005, reflecting the growth of Chinese ODI after 2003; their parent companies are all SOEs. The two major acquisitions of large established Australian companies were made during the GFC in 2009. In addition, Sinosteel made a hostile acquisition of a partly established junior Australian miner in 2008 just before the GFC and paid a top market price for this acquisition. Yanzhou Coal also acquired a small coal miner in 2005 after it was closed due to fire disaster. The remaining four investments were made between 2006 and 2008, before the GFC, with two in magnetite mining and one in coal or bauxite exploration.

For the four companies in which the Chinese have a controlling stake, three were invested in after the GFC, and Hunan Non-ferrous Metals (now Minmetals) acquired its controlling stake in Abra Mining in May 2008, before the GFC. All of these four Australian companies were junior miners at the exploration stage.

All five JVs were project-based and were established at the exploration stage of the project. Four of them are in magnetite mining and one is in tin mining.

*Corporate governance and senior management appointments*

Effective corporate governance is crucial to the survival and prosperity of an organisation. Corporate governance is the system by which

*Table 5.4* A list of Chinese-controlled entities and JVs in the Australian minerals industry with some characteristics of their investments

| Chinese firm | Targeted Australian firm | Share (%) | Year | Entry mode and developmental stage | Transaction | Major type of minerals |
|---|---|---|---|---|---|---|
| **100% ownership** | | | | | | |
| Yanzhou Coal | Southern Land Coal | 100 | 2005 | Production | A$32m | Coal |
| Yanzhou Coal | Felix Resources Ltd | 100 | 2009 | Acquisition (Production) | A$3.54bn | Coal |
| CITIC Pacific Mining (2007) | Mining right of 2bn tonnes | 100 | 2006 | Greenfield | A$470m | Iron ore |
| Minmetals | OZ Minerals | 100 | 2009 | Acquisition (Production) | A$1.7bn | Precious and base metals |
| Sinosteel | Midwest | 100 | 2008 | Brownfield | A$1.4bn | Iron ore |
| MCC | Cape Lambert mine | 100 | 2008 | Greenfield | A$400m | Iron ore |
| CHINALCO | Aurukun Project | 100 | 2007 | Greenfield | N/A | Bauxite |
| Shenhua Energy | Watermark Project | 100 | 2008 | Greenfield | A$300m | Coal |
| **Majority ownership (>49.9–90%)** | | | | | | |
| Hunan Non-ferrous Metal Corp (now Minmetals) | Abra Mining Limited | 74.27 | May 2008 | Greenfield | A$70m | Base metals, copper and gold |

| China Guangdong Nuclear Power Holding | Energy Metals | 66 | 2009 | Greenfield | A$81.4m | Uranium |
|---|---|---|---|---|---|---|
| Hanlong | Moly Mines | 55 | 2010 | Greenfield | US$140m | MO and iron ore |
| Zhongjin | Perilya | 50.1 | Dec 2008 | Greenfield | A$45.5m | Zinc, lead and silver |
| EJVs | | | | | | |
| WISCo | Centrex | 60 | 2009 | Greenfield | A$186m | Iron ore (M) |
| Baotou Steel | Centrex | 50 | 2009 | Greenfield | A$40m | Iron ore (M) |
| Ansteel | Gindalbie | 50 | 2006 | Greenfield | A$372.06m | Iron ore (M) |
| Chonggang Dev. Inv. Ltd | Asia Iron | 60 | 2010 | Greenfield | A$280m | Iron ore (M) |
| Yunnan Tin Group | Metals X | 50 | 2010 | Greenfield | A$50m | Tin |

business corporations are directed and controlled (Cadbury, 1992, p.14). According to the OECD (2004),

> Corporate governance involves a set of relationships between a company's management, its board, its shareholders and other stakeholders. Corporate governance also provides the structure through which the objectives of the company are set, and the means of attaining those objectives and monitoring performance are determined. Good corporate governance should provide proper incentives for the board and management to pursue objectives that are in the interests of the company and its shareholders and should facilitate effective monitoring.

Corporate governance can impact on the firm's strategic decisions, managers' accountability and the firm's productivity and profitability. Good corporate governance ensures the firm's strategic and operational activities are aligned with the interests of its key stakeholders, and thus the firm can be developed sustainably. This is very important to those firms operating in the Australian resources sector because this impacts on the firm's performance and alleviates the general risks to which the firm is exposed. Moreover, its key external stakeholders, such as the Australian and state governments, institutional investors and regional communities have a high demand for sustainable development in the resource sector.

There are 11 Chinese-controlled entities in the Australian minerals industry, including seven Chinese WOSs and four with controlling stakes. This subsection examines several characteristics of corporate governance in these entities or subsidiaries, including the nationality of the chairperson, the composition of the board, CEO duality, the proportion of independent directors on the board and the appointment of the senior management team to these entities. The boards' composition and their senior management appointments in the three Greenfield acquisitions by Chinese firms are not available. For the remaining eight Chinese-controlled entities, their board composition and senior management appointments are presented in Table 5.5.

For these eight Chinese-controlled entities, Chinese investors have appointed a chairman from their own parent company to the board, except in the case of Moly Mines (controlled by Hanlong, a private company) where its chairman is an Australian. Moreover, all the Chinese investors also have 50 per cent or above of board members in their controlled entity. This is in line with the principle that board

*Table 5.5* The appointment of board and senior management positions at Chinese-controlled entities

| Chinese subsidiary | Chinese director(s)/No. of directors | Chairman | CEO | Other senior managers | Chinese share (%) |
|---|---|---|---|---|---|
| Minerals and Metals Group | 5 (4 NED)/7 | C (NEC) | A | 5 (A) 1(C) | 100 |
| Yancoal Australia | 4 (2 NED)/7 | C (NEC) | A | N/A | 100 |
| CITIC Pacific Mining | 4/8 (all ED) | C (executive) | C (duality) | 5/10 | 100 |
| Sinosteel Midwest Corp | 7(6 NED)/8 | C (NEC) | C | 11 (A) | 100 |
| Abra Mining Limited | 6 (all NED)/8 | C (NEC) | A | 4 (A) | 74 |
| Energy Metals | 3 (2 ED)/5 | C (NEC) | A | 3 (C) | 66 |
| Moly Mines | 3(2 NED)/8 | A (NEC) | A | 7 (A) 1 (C) | 55 |
| Perilya | 3 (NED)/6 | C (NEC) | A | 2 (A) | 50.1 |

*Notes*: NED = non-executive director; NEC = non-executive chairman; A = Australian; C = Chinese.

members represent the interests of shareholders. Additionally, most of the Chinese directors are non-executive, reflecting commonly adopted Australian corporate governance practice that encourages the separation of the board from the management. Except in the case of CITIC Pacific Mining, all CEOs or managing directors are separated from the chairmanship. Therefore, the establishment of corporate governance in terms of the separation of chairperson and CEO in the Chinese-controlled entities has largely followed the best practice recommendations proposed by the ASX Corporate Governance Council (2003).

Most senior management positions in the Chinese-controlled entities are held by Australians. In the case of top management (CEO or managing director positions), only two companies (CITIC Pacific Mining and Sinosteel Midwest Corporation) have internal appointments from their parent company. An Australian CEO or managing director has been appointed at the other Chinese-controlled entities.

Two factors may contribute to the appointment of senior managerial positions in the Chinese subsidiaries, including the parent company's competence in international business and the characteristics of the target company or project. The level of the parent company's international experience influences the appointment of the CEO or managing director position in their subsidiary. The more experienced the parent company in international business, the more likely that they have made internal appointments of senior managers to their subsidiaries. Sending expatriate managers to a subsidiary has several benefits, including their high level of loyalty to the parent company, the trust placed by the parent company due to its understanding of the competence and track record of the expatriate managers appointed, easy communication and smooth coordination between the parent company and the subsidiary. For example, Sinosteel has appointed its managing director to its subsidiary, Sinosteel Midwest Corporation, partly because it has a long history of international business operations. CITIC Pacific appointed its executive chairman to CITIC Pacific Mining (CPM) after its parent company, CITIC Group, held a majority of its shares, because CITIC Group could leverage its experience in international project construction and management. The executive chairman of CPM was the former deputy executive chairman of CITIC Construction, another subsidiary of the CITIC Group. CITIC Group also appointed three other senior managers to CPM from its other subsidiaries to manage the construction of its Australian project. Moreover, the remunerations for expatriates may be lower than the locally recruited executives, as we have found during our interviews with executives in several Chinese-controlled entities; although this is not a major factor in appointing senior managers to their subsidiaries.

The characteristics of the company or project invested in are other important factors affecting the management appointment in the Chinese subsidiaries. The managerial expertise of the target company has often been retained by the Chinese investors after the acquisition. For example, Minmetals and Yanzhou Coal kept most of the senior managers, even the managing director, of the target companies, OZ Minerals and Felix Resources, after their acquisition. However, this does not suggest that the parent company would not leverage its international business experience or skills. In fact, both parent companies have also appointed expatriates to their subsidiary as senior managers, possibly to assist the managing director to coordinate and communicate with the parent company. Learning from the Australian managers is another consideration that the Chinese investors take into account when retaining Australian senior managers after their acquisitions.

For those Chinese parent companies with little international experience, their only option is to appoint Australians to their senior management positions. This can have a number of benefits if done properly because Australian managers are familiar with Australia's legal and social environment. They also have fewer language problems in communicating with local governments and business communities than expatriates. Lack of human resources in a Chinese investor's firm may be the major reason contributing to such a low level of participation in management and operations. This includes experience in managing international business, language difficulties and cultural differences. Nevertheless this can be expected to change over time as more Chinese executives gain international experience and education.

Senior management appointment has been regarded by many Chinese investors as the most crucial decision in their after-transaction integration and management because this could have a substantial impact on operations. Because of a relatively short history of Chinese investments in the Australian minerals industry, the effectiveness of these two modes of senior management appointment is so far inconclusive, as is their impact on the organisation's financial performance.

*Strategy and structure*

A low-cost strategy has been dominant in the resources sector as most of minerals can be regarded as commodities, and the Chinese subsidiaries in Australia are not an exception. It is difficult for an individual firm to influence commodity prices. Depending on the developmental stage (exploration, development or production) of the project or company acquired, a low-cost strategy is reflected in two areas:

- operational excellence or efficiency for reducing costs; and
- sustainable development for satisfying stakeholders.

Operational efficiency has been the major strategic issue, for example, within the Metals and Mining Group (Behrmann, 2010). This could cover process design, construction and contract management for outsourcing and risk management. Sustainability is quite high as a strategic initiative in all Chinese subsidiaries, as indicated by the strategic statements in their companies' websites, including obligations to the environment and heritage, partnership with the local communities and aboriginal groups (Sinosteel Midwest Corporation), acting as a responsible corporate citizen (Yancoal and CPM), and "sustainably operating resources projects" (Minerals and Metals Group – MMG, a subsidiary of Minmetals in Australia).

Some Chinese-controlled entities have also incorporated sound corporate value in their strategy statement, particularly respect and integrity. For example, for MMG, an established company in the production stage, the strategies are:

- **Growth:** Create value by nimbly discovering, acquiring and developing quality opportunities.
- **Operations:** Manage a portfolio of quality assets to deliver consistency and growth in returns.
- **People:** Develop capable people in a safe working environment, who have a commitment to teamwork to deliver our business plans.
- **Business Excellence:** Continually improve standardised, systematic approach and apply innovation to achieve superior outcomes.
- **Reputation:** Build and sustain credibility and trust.

For the Sinosteel Midwest Corporation, which is still at its development stage, its vision is to: 1) enable people, 2) seek excellence, 3) act with integrity and respect and 4) proactively manage social responsibility.

All Chinese subsidiaries in Australia have a functional structure. This could reflect their growth stage as most of them do not have a diversified portfolio and have a relatively simple operation. However, the functional structure becomes more complex as these organisations move from exploration to development and production. At the exploration stage, the major functions are relatively simple, mainly covering exploration, government approvals and community liaison. Nevertheless, as the project progresses to the developmental stage, construction may become a major function. The liaison between the Chinese subsidiary and their parent company can become more complex. Some construction work or equipment can be sourced from China. Thus, coordination between the Chinese subsidiary and Chinese firms could be very important. This could lead to the establishment of an additional office in China, which can help ensure smooth communication between the two groups and foster knowledge-sharing and opportunities to identify synergies (Tasker, 2010c).

The organisational structure of a Chinese subsidiary at the development stage is presented in Figure 5.2.

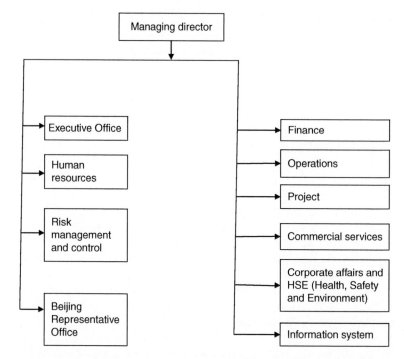

*Figure 5.2* The organisational structure of a Chinese subsidiary at the development stage

A subsidiary's office in China could also play a marketing role in the Chinese market. Thus, such an organisational structure has been adopted by those Chinese entities at the production stage, such as MMG, Yancoal Australia and Sinosteel Midwest Corporation.

*Operational characteristics*

Chinese-controlled entities in the Australian minerals industry have displayed several interesting characteristics in their operations, including financing, project management, coordination with parent company, cross-cultural management and communications and HR management.

**Financing**: Financing is probably the most critical issue for those Chinese-controlled entities at the exploration or development stage as a substantial amount of funds is required to move the project forward. There are two broad funding approaches: bank loan and share placement. For those listed in the Australian Stock Exchange, such as Moly

Mines and Energy Metals, funds can be sought from a share place-ment or rights issue. Share placement is often offered to institutional investors while a rights issue is made to existing shareholders. This is an approach used by Energy Metals. Getting a bank loan is another financ-ing approach that is adopted. For example, Hanlong was responsible for seeking loans from Chinese banks. The financing approaches by the four Chinese-controlled listed entities are listed in Table 5.6.

**Project management**: For those investing in the exploration stage or a Greenfield project, project management has been one of the greatest challenges. Three WOSs (CPM, Sinosteel Midwest Corpora-tion and MCC), and three JVs (Karara Project, Eyre Peninsula Project and Bungalow Project) fall into this category. There are three major objectives in project management: exploring and identifying minerals resources of the project, completing its feasibility study and obtaining environmental approval from the state government.

While CPM and Karara JV Project (between Ansteel and Gindalbie) have progressed well into the development stage, progress on sev-eral other Chinese-controlled or JV projects has been slow, partly due to financing difficulties. Examples of this include MCC Mining and Sinosteel Midwest Corporation.

**Coordination with parent companies**: This is more of an issue for those Chinese WOSs as, for example, accounting reports need to be prepared based on the Australian and Chinese accounting systems. Thus, the Australian subsidiaries are requested to prepare monthly accounting reports at two points of time: one as an Australian entity,

*Table 5.6*  Financial approaches adopted by some Chinese-controlled entities or JV partners

| Company | Share placement | Rights issue | Bank loan | Date of transaction completion |
|---|---|---|---|---|
| Energy Metals | Yes | Yes | No | 09/12/09 |
| Moly Mine | No | No | Yes. The Chinese investor (Hanlong) is responsible for this | 16/3/10 |
| Perilya | No | No | No | 9/2/09 |
| Abra Mining | No | No | No | 22/09/08 |

and one as a subsidiary of their Chinese parent companies. Major strategic decisions, such as investment and appointment of senior managers in the subsidiary, must be approved by their parent company. Monthly meetings may be held between top managers of the parent company and the subsidiaries for discussing key issues relating to their operations.

**Cross-cultural management and communications**: Cross-cultural management has been long regarded as a challenge in international business and JVs. There are big cultural differences between China and Australia. According to Hofstede (1980), differences in power distance and uncertainty avoidance between China and Australia are very large. Specifically, China is a large power distance country where decisions are usually made centrally while Australia has a small power distance, the Australians often preferring a decentralised decision-making process. Regarding the uncertainty avoidance, Chinese again has a much larger index than Australians. This suggests that Chinese managers have a high level of need for security and rely more on experts while their Australian counterparts are more willing to accept risks and are less structured in conducting their business activities (Wang, Zhang & Goodfellow, 2003). Such differences often become problematic as the number of Chinese employees has increased in the Chinese subsidiaries in Australia, particularly at the managerial level. Moreover, Australia is ranked high in individualism, indicating that they would look after themselves and their immediate family members, although there is a strong workplace mateship ethos in Australia. Conversely, the Chinese tend to look after each other in exchange for loyalty. Therefore, these cultural differences are often sources for conflict in the decision-making processes, leadership style, project management and communications between Chinese and Australian employees. Melding very different Chinese and Australian business cultures has been reported as one of the biggest problems that Minmetals faces within its Australian subsidiary (Sainsbury, 2010f).

**HR management**: The importance of good human resources management practice in international business cannot be overemphasised, particularly in the Chinese international subsidiaries, for two reasons. Firstly, managing an international operation not only requires experience and knowledge of the host country, but also the ability to deal with cultural diversity, communications and adaptation. Many Chinese MNCs are not very experienced in conducting international business. Thus, it can be difficult for Chinese expatriates to hold key positions in their international subsidiaries. Secondly, trust is another issue for

Chinese international subsidiaries. It is widely known that the Chinese emphasise a high degree of trust and personal relationships in doing business. They prefer to use managers who can be trusted, particularly at the individual level. This may further limit the scope for filling senior management positions in their international subsidiaries. Broadly, HR issues in Chinese subsidiaries in Australia can be broken down into two categories: management and skilled workers.

At the management level, HR issues include management selection, remuneration and performance appraisal. As shown in Table 5.5 above, Chinese subsidiaries in Australia recruit most of their senior managers from Australia, and have a relatively small number of expatriates in managerial positions. In fact, most of the Chinese expatriates in the Chinese-controlled entities and JVs have been recruited internally. Management experience could be the most important selection criterion, followed by the technical expertise and language ability. Thus, HR strategies in these subsidiaries are not ethnocentric, but reflect a polycentric strategy (Perlmutter, 1969). This could indicate a greater need for local responsiveness and some degree of global integration between the parent and subsidiary. It is not certain if the internal recruitment policy has resulted in the smaller number of expatriates in Chinese international subsidiaries. In this respect, China is following the well-trodden path of Japan and South Korean investment in the Australian resource sector.

Remuneration for expatriate Chinese managers is another problem in some Chinese subsidiaries. Locally recruited managers in Chinese-controlled entities are paid the market salary rate. However, a salary package for expatriate managers in some Chinese-controlled entities could be much lower than their local counterparts, but higher than their peers in China. In addition, some Chinese expatriate managers are not allowed to bring their family members with them. This could be a problem for the expatriate living in Australia, and may also have negative impacts on their work. Some Chinese parent companies also displayed a tendency to "rotate" their expatriate managers every three years. All these aspects point to a lack of strategic HR management.

Performance appraisal for managers in the Chinese subsidiaries seems very soft for two reasons. Firstly, many strategic decisions, such as investment and the appointment of senior managers, are made by the parent companies. Secondly, it may be difficult to replace managerial positions, particularly while Chinese subsidiaries are competing for skilful, experienced managers in local markets.

At the front-line level, Chinese subsidiaries only recruit a number of skilled workers (most of them from China) due to the strict requirements imposed by the Department of Immigration and Citizenship (DIAC) on employing overseas skilled workers. These requirements include their professional skills qualifications, English language proficiency (at least IELTS 5.0 in each of four test components of speaking, reading, writing and listening) character requirements (e.g., police certificate) and health and insurance requirements (DIAC, 2010). Moreover, DIAC also requires employers to pay market salary rates for the skilled workers recruited from overseas. The shortage of skilled workers has been a major problem for Australia. Yet the procedures for bringing in overseas skilled workers are quite lengthy.

Integration of workforces could be a challenge in some Chinese subsidiaries, particularly during the development stage when a large number of Chinese construction workers are employed. Given the differences in work ethics, leadership styles, culture and values between Chinese and Australian employees, it may be difficult to resolve these differences and integrate such diversity in line with organisational goals. To alleviate these issues, cultural awareness training has been provided in several Chinese subsidiaries for new staff members. They have also invited external consultants to hold seminars for their managers, to promote awareness of business practice differences between China and Australia.

A related issue is industrial relations. Australia has traditionally a strong union in its workplace, although its role has been weakened over the past two decades. Moreover, Australia has many laws and regulations on industry relations that are very different from those in China. Both could become a substantial challenge for Chinese managers in managing their workforce and contracted firms, as has been reported recently by Australian and Chinese media (Chen, 2010; Fuhrmann, 2010; Klinger, 2010).

As most of the Chinese investments in the Australian minerals industry occurred after 2006, it is too early at this stage to determine their success. It may take another decade for Chinese firms to achieve their investment objectives, making it more appropriate then to identify factors that influence the success of the Chinese-controlled entities in the Australian minerals industry.

# 6
# Why the Proposed CHINALCO Investment in Rio Tinto Failed

On 12 February 2009, the board of Rio Tinto ("Rio" hereafter) announced that it had struck a deal of $19.5 billion with CHINALCO. This was by far the largest deal in Chinese and Australian corporate history. If this transaction was successful, the deal could deliver great strategic and financial benefits to CHINALCO and Rio, such as helping Rio to meet its $18.9 billion debt maturities before October 2010. This would enhance Rio's ability to obtain further funds for major project development, increasing CHINALCO's share in the Rio Tinto Group from 9 per cent to 18 per cent for a relatively low price. Strategically, the partnership between Rio and CHINALCO could leverage the complementary strength of both parties, particularly CHINALCO's ability in delivering infrastructure projects and Rio's operational efficiency. Nevertheless, Rio informed CHINALCO on 5 June 2009 that it had terminated the agreed deal and would pay CHINALCO the agreed break fee of $195 million. This was only ten days before the due date for Australia's FIRB to make its decision on CHINALCO's investment application and 114 days after the deal announcement.

Why such a deal failed is the question asked by the business community, governments and the worldwide public, and particularly by Australia and China. This question is both pertinent and complex as many interacting players were involved, and many factors influenced the deal's outcome. Ostensibly, Rio and CHINALCO were the key players. However, others were also actively involved, such as BHPB, the Australian and Chinese governments, the media and the public. The actions and interactions have brought many factors into consideration, including economic, competitive, political and cultural issues at the national, industry, organisational and individual levels.

This chapter will examine these players and their influence on the fate of CHINALCO–Rio deal. Before this, background information about CHINALCO's proposed investment (the deal hereafter) must be first provided.

## The background of the CHINALCO–Rio deal

Rio is the third-largest resource company in the world. The group's headquarters is in the UK; it has two listed companies: Rio Tinto plc (77%) in London and New York Stock Exchange (NYSE); and Rio Tinto Limited with the Australian Stock Exchange (23%). Despite its large size, Rio has been a target for merger and acquisition (M&A), particularly by BHP Billiton, since July 2002, when the former BHPB's CEO, Brian Gilbertson, initiated discussions with Rio's chairman, Bob Wilson (Thompson & Macklin, 2009). The major reasons for such a merger were both synergy between the two companies and the resultant dominant market power in the global iron ore industry. The initiative failed mainly because the then BHPB's chairman, Don Argus, feared the loss of BHPB as an Australian national icon. Consequently, the proposed merger was aborted and Brian Gilbertson "resigned" as BHPB's CEO in January 2003.

Partly driven by the worry of being swallowed by BHPB, Rio successfully acquired Alcan, the largest Canadian aluminium company, at a top market price of $38.1 billion in 2007. This was a major debt restructure of Rio, resulting in the significant increase of Rio's debt. Thus, it was considered by many industry analysts as a barrier to further potential M&A because it could make Rio less attractive owing to its size, financial performance and asset quality. However, this did not prevent BHPB's proposal for merging with Rio in November 2007, which was based on 3 BHPB shares for 1 Rio share, thereby valuing Rio at $150 billion. The deal was immediately rejected by Rio's board who maintained that "it is not in the best interest of shareholders" as its then chairman, Paul Skinner, told the media (Rio Tinto, 2007). Rio adhered to this decision even when BHPB increased its offer to 3.4 BHPB shares for one Rio share on 6 February 2008. BHPB finally dropped its formal proposed merger with Rio on 25 November 2008 due to the global financial crisis and price slumps in the commodity market.

The GFC greatly stressed Rio's senior management and the board because most of the acquisition funds for Alcan were bank loans. The two debt maturities were October 2009 and October 2010, with debts being $8.9 billion and $10 billion, respectively. With the free fall of

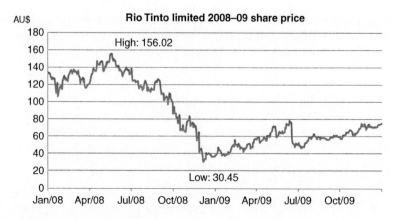

*Figure 6.1*   Share price of Rio Tinto Ltd from 2008 to mid-2009
Source: Yahoo Finance, 2010.

commodity prices, Rio's share price had slumped from A$156.02 on 19 May 2008 to A$30.45 on 5 December 2008 (see Figure 6.1).

CHINALCO, in partnership with Alcoa, spent $14.05 billion on 1 February 2008, acquiring 12 per cent of Rio Tinto plc on market (about 9% in Rio Group). The market price CHINALCO paid was very high (60 UK pounds per share). Many believed CHINALCO's acquisition of Rio shares was strategic, not financial, and was partly aimed at blocking BHPB's potential acquisition of Rio.

## The proposed strategic alliance between CHINALCO and Rio

Rio's management and board recommended a transaction with CHINALCO to their shareholders on 12 February 2009. The following terms are the highlights of this transaction.

The key term of this deal was the delivery of $19.5 billion in cash to Rio. The cash proceeds were divided into two parts:

1. CHINALCO to invest $12.3 billion to acquire part of Rio's assets in iron ore, copper and aluminium through establishing joint ventures and exploring project development opportunities. As depicted in Table 6.1, the joint ventures included bauxite mining and aluminium smelting in Queensland (Weipa, Yarwun, Boyne and Gladstone), copper mining in Chile (Escondida, La Granja), copper-gold mining in Indonesia (Grasberg), copper mining in the USA (Kennecott) and iron ore mining with Hamersley in WA (Rio Tinto, 2009a);

2. CHINALCO would pay $7.2 billion in cash to the Rio Tinto Group in exchange for the issuance of convertible bonds by Rio Tinto plc and Rio Tinto Ltd. The conversion had a 60-year maturity time frame and the bonds would be redeemable by Rio after seven years. These bonds had 9 per cent and 9.5 per cent of interest for seven years for Rio plc and Rio Limited, respectively, before they were to be converted into normal shares. Each of the Rio Tinto plc and Rio Tinto Ltd Bonds would be split into two tranches. Tranche A of the bonds would be converted at the initial price of $45 per share with a total issue size of $3.1 billion, while tranche B would convert at the initial price of $60 per share with the total issue amount of $4.1 billion. If fully converted, CHINALCO's interest would be raised to 14.9 per cent in Rio Tinto Ltd and 19 per cent in Rio Tinto plc: a total of 18 per cent in Rio Tinto Group (Rio Tinto, 2009a).

Other key clauses in the proposed strategic alliance included:

1) establishing a jointly owned sales company between Rio and CHINALCO to supply the rapidly growing Chinese market. The company would be managed by Rio Tinto and would market 30 per cent (about 30 million tonnes at 2008 production rate) of Hamersley's output on commercial and arms-length terms; and
2) being bound by a "break" fee and having exclusivity. Rio would pay $195 million to CHINALCO in the event that the boards of Rio Tinto withdrew their recommendation. Rio Tinto agreed not to solicit any third party competing proposal prior to completion, and its fiduciary obligations to consider superior offers remained.

## Analytical framework and data collection

To gain a depth of understanding for the reasons why the CHINALCO–Rio deal failed, an analytical framework has been developed based on methods used by researchers in industrial buyer–seller relationships and networks (Dwyer, Schurr & Oh, 1987). This analytical framework involves the following key elements: actors (players), elements and process of interaction (e.g., activities and events), atmosphere and environment (Håkansson, 1982). It has also taken into consideration the time order as an analytical tool for qualitative data analysis (Miles & Huberman, 1994).

In the following sections, the key players from the approval perspective are firstly identified, as well as important stakeholders from

Table 6.1  Details of CHINALCO's investment in Rio's assets

| Asset | Country | Strategic alliance | Rio Tinto's existing economic interest (%) | CHINALCO's proposed share of Rio Tinto's economic interest (%) | Rio Tinto's resulting economic interest (%) | Attributable values of CHINALCO's proposed share ($ million) |
|---|---|---|---|---|---|---|
| Hamersley Iron | WA, Australia | Iron ore | 100 | 15 | 85 | 5,150 |
| Weipa | QL, Australia | Aluminium | 100 | 30 | 70 | 1,200 |
| Yarwun | QL, Australia | Aluminium | 100 | 50 | 50 | 500 |
| Boyne[a] | QLD, Australia | Aluminium | 59.4 | 49 | 30 | Bundled with Gladstone |
| Gladstone Power Station | QLD, Australia | Aluminium | 42.1 | 49 | 21.5 | 450 |
| Escondida | Chile | Copper | 30 | 49.75 | 15 | 3,388 |
| La Granja | Chile | Copper | 100 | 30 | 70 | 50 |
| Grasberg | Indonesia | Copper | 40 | 30 | 28 | 400 |
| Kennecott | USA | Copper | 100 | 25 | 75 | 700 |
| Development fund[b] | | | | | 50 | 500 |
| Total | | | | | | 12,388 |

Note: [a]Bundled with Gladstone; [b]The development fund is proposed to be jointly owned by Rio Tinto and CHINALCO. The $500 million included in the transaction is for the acquisition of project developments, including from Rio Tinto.

the economic and competitive perspectives. Then the key activities conducted by each of them are processed and discussed, and their interactions between the deal announcement and its termination (12 February–5 June 2009), taking into consideration the changes in the global financial market and Rio's share price. This is followed by a discussion of their overall impact on the deal outcome. Finally, the causes for the failure of this deal are suggested.

## Identifying key stakeholders

Several approvals were required for the proposed CHINALCO–Rio deal, from governments in Australia, China and the USA, regulatory organisations in stakeholder countries, shareholders of the Rio Group and CHINALCO and other approvals, for example, relevant CHINALCO financing approvals (Albanese, 2009). These were regulatory and legal hurdles that the deal had to pass. The deal also required approval from the ACCC from a competition perspective. While all these approvals are important and act like a series of chains, the most critical ones were those from the Australian government – as nearly 70 per cent of the assets acquired by CHINALCO were in Australia – and from shareholders of Rio Group, both in Australia and UK. Therefore, besides CHINALCO and Rio, other key stakeholders included the Australian government, Rio's shareholders and BHPB as a competitor. Australian politicians, the media and the public were also involved to various degrees in this deal through their direct and indirect influence on the Australian government's decision. The key stakeholders in this deal are outlined in Figure 6.2.

## Data collection

The potential impact of the proposed deal on the Australian economy and society attracted much attention from the Australian media, particularly in newspapers, which gave a very comprehensive coverage of its major events and developments. *The Australian* and *The Age* are two of three newspapers that have a national coverage. The Australian Broadcasting Corporation (ABC) is Australia's most trusted and independent source of news. Thus, three different searches were conducted on the Factiva database, each attempt dedicated to one of the three sources mentioned. In each search, the keyword was "CHINALCO" with a time frame limitation of 1 January 2008 to 29 October 2009, and the newspaper title restriction. After eliminating replicated entries, all articles were downloaded and saved for later review. The results found for each

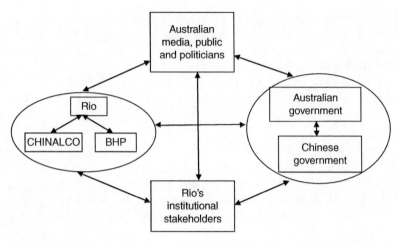

*Figure 6.2*    Key stakeholders in the proposed CHINALCO's investment in Rio

title are shown in Table 6.2. In a preliminary examination, most results seemed to relate to the CHINALCO–Rio Tinto partnership. Many of the downloaded articles were published in 2009 (76%), with most reports being published during the deal consideration period. *The Australian* had the most entries with 681 stories (60.4%) on the CHINALCO–Rio Tinto tie-up. This is no surprise because the newspaper has maintained its own comprehensive mining section that has in-depth coverage of mining and related issues. Next, further searches using Factiva were run to check the number of entries on the CHINALCO–Rio Tinto affiliation that other major Australian newspapers had published. *The Sydney Morning Herald* came second with 352 entries. As *The Age* and *The Sydney Morning Herald* are owned by Fairfax Media Limited, we decided to retain our initial choices of three sources – *The Australian, The Age* and ABC News.

*Table 6.2*    The number of articles retrieved from three key resources

| Period | *The Australian* | *The Age* | ABC news | Total (%) |
|---|---|---|---|---|
| 2009 | 501 | 242 | 113 | 856 (75.95%) |
| 2008 | 180 | 69 | 22 | 269 (24.05%) |
| Negotiation period (Feb–Jun 09) | 376 | 176 | 93 | 645 (57.23%) |
| Total | 681 (60.4%) | 311 (27.6%) | 135 (12%) | 1,127 |

In addition to the articles retrieved from these three sources, materials were gathered from international sources, such as the BBC and Reuters, *The Times UK*, Bloomberg and *China Daily*, which also, when necessary, provided supplementary information as several sections in the report referred to foreign players involved in the CHINALCO investment in Australia. The websites of the involved organisations (Rio Tinto, BHPB and CHINALCO) were also searched, along with the FIRB for detailed information about the key events and activities relevant to this deal.

## Actions and interactions among key players on the deal

This section describes the key actions and interactions among the key players, including Rio, CHINALCO, BHPB and the Australian and Chinese relevant authorities. It provides a detailed account of the behaviours of each key player under the dynamic changes of international economic environment, Australian politics and institutional shareholders. We began this with the examination of activities conducted by Rio's board and management and their dynamic interactions with key stakeholders as the international, national and organisation contexts changed.

### Key activities conducted by Rio and its interactions with other key stakeholders

There is no doubt that Rio was the central player that had the most at stake in the deal as it needed to secure funds to pay its massive debt of $18.9 billion that was to mature in October 2009 and October 2010. To pay this debt, Rio would have had at least three options (Frith, 2009a):

1) selling part of its assets and issuing convertible securities to CHINALCO;
2) issuing shares to existing shareholders; and
3) selling a substantially larger part of its assets than that in option 1.

In comparison with the convertible bonds issued to CHINALCO, the rights issued to Rio's existing shareholders (option 2) would be deeply discounted and was estimated to raise about $6–8 billion. Even if fully converted, this option alone would not generate enough cash proceeds to meet the maturing $8.9 billion debt for the 2009 term. As a result, Rio was also considering selling off assets across its diversified portfolio (option 3) to make up the debt repayments. This option was not in the best interest of its shareholders due to low commodity prices in late 2008 and early 2009, as the commodity price was at the bottom of the market cycle. Rio was also considering a JV with Japan's Mitsui in the Robe River iron ore operation in WA. This partnership could give Rio up to $5 billion in assets sales, but still not enough to pay its debt. Thus, option 1 seemed relatively attractive.

To get option 1 (CHINALCO–Rio alliance) through, Rio's board and senior management had to deal with two major stakeholders, particularly institutional investors and the Australian government, because most of the assets to be sold were in Australia. In the following subsections, the activities conducted by Rio and its interactions with key stakeholders in the deal will be analysed. Rio's activities and interactions with its key stakeholders are broken down into two periods: those before and after its annual general meeting (AGM) in Sydney on 20 April when du Plessis took over Rio's chairmanship from Paul Skinner, and the incipient recovery of the international share market.

## Activities conducted by Rio from 12 February to 20 April

*Initial responses and concerns from Rio's shareholders*

As the proposed deal with CHINALCO required approval from Rio's shareholders, the imminent task for Rio's board and senior management was to communicate with its shareholders the benefits of this proposed deal, and convince them to agree to it. Because over three quarters of Rio's shareholders were based in the UK, Rio's then chairman, Paul Skinner, and CEO, Tom Albanese, held meetings with the major institutional shareholders in the UK, a day after the announcement. The group's chief financial officer, Guy Elliot, went to Australia to talk to Rio's shareholders there.

The initial reaction from the UK shareholders was very negative as they had three major concerns about various aspects of the proposed deal: (1) the value of the stakes being acquired by CHINALCO; (2) the price of the bond issue; and (3) the timing of the commodity market (Chambers & Tasker, 2009).

Firstly, regarding assets sales, Rio succeeded in securing a 124 per cent premium to the then current enterprise value for all assets sold to CHINALCO – a very positive development. The $12.3 billion tag came close to an independent estimate of $14 billion by Goldman Sachs (Chambers & Tasker, 2009). However, some shareholders complained that these figures did not take into consideration the long-term strategic values of those assets, and that the 15 per cent stake in Hamersley iron ore in WA was quite a bargain because the $5 billion tag was deemed to be on par with its net present value (Stevens, 2009f).

Secondly, Rio's shareholders believed that the terms of convertible bonds issued to CHINALCO seemed to advantage CHINALCO. Industry analysts had assumed the average annual growth rate of both Rio Ltd and plc to be 4 per cent, while the usual appreciation of shares for most major resource companies throughout the cycle is 10 per cent annually. Based on such calculations, CHINALCO could make money after seven years when the bonds matured (Stevens, 2009f).

Thirdly, the fact that commodities prices were at the bottom of the cycle made the CHINALCO–Rio alliance seem less attractive for Rio shareholders because it undermined the financial value of Rio's assets in monetary terms, let alone the strategic implications for these assets.

In addition, several of Rio's institutional shareholders questioned the board on the principle of pre-emption, meaning that all share-holders should have the option to participate in capital-raising. The London-based Legal & General, Rio's second biggest shareholder after CHINALCO, said that it would be active in designing a rights issue deal acceptable to all shareholders (Chambers, 2009c). It also claimed that this could raise up to $12 billion from an offer to existing shareholders in London (Costello & Robertson, 2009). This option was backed by ten of Rio's 12-largest UK institutional shareholders.

On the Australian side, Tom Albanese had delayed his visit to Australia in early March 2009 by three weeks, presumably because of the unex-pectedly strong reactions of British shareholders. During his visit, Albanese also talked to the Australian government and the FIRB, met with the new CHINALCO boss, Xiong Weiping, who arrived in Australia a few days earlier to discuss CHINALCO's application to the FIRB with Treasurer Wayne Swan.

Despite the efforts of Rio's senior management to communicate with key Australian shareholders, the latter were not convinced of the deal's merits. On 16 March, the Australian Foundation Investment Company (AFIC), Rio Tinto Ltd fourth-biggest shareholder, joined a long list of UK shareholders to raise their concerns (Chambers, 2009d). The AFIC chairman voiced the same issues as those of UK investors, saying that the move delivered too much control to China and was loaded with potential conflicts of interests. He also advocated the rights issue option to Rio's existing shareholders. Tensions also came from Rio's Australian shareholders who pressed for more voting power against their British counterparts (Chambers & Tasker, 2009) as about 70 per cent of the asset sale under the CHINALCO deal came from Rio Tinto Ltd in Australia.

Despite the initial grave concerns raised by Rio's key shareholders, Albanese and Rio's board insisted that there was no viable alternative because the rights issue would not generate enough cash and asset sales seemed too difficult given the market conditions (Chambers, 2009f). They were determined to guard their "Chinese solution" and still believed that the situation Rio faced gave them no choice other than convincing the reluctant Rio shareholders to approve the deal. Nevertheless, Rio did have its "Plan B" as revealed by is chief financial officer, Guy Elliott, at a mining conference in Singapore on 26 March, just "in the eventuality that either the various governments or the shareholders prevent the deal going through" (Tasker, 2009d). Plan B included rights issues, assets sales, debt rescheduling or the combination of these strategies. This strongly suggests that Rio had explored different options, or "Plan B", at the beginning of the proposed deal.

Another important event was former British American Tobacco chairman, Jan du Plessis, a South African, being nominated as the Rio's new chairman on 18 March after the former designated chairman, Jim Leng, suddenly resigned his directorship on 9 February, three days before the deal was announced. Media reports suggested that Leng was opposed to the deal and favoured a rights issue to all existing shareholders. Du Plessis was an accountant by profession and joined the Rio board in September 2008.

On 4 April 2009, Albanese was back in Australia before Rio's annual general meeting in a final bid to win support from local shareholders and government for his Chinese solution (Tasker, 2009a). He continued to stress that the CHINALCO deal remained the best option for reducing debt. However, he also began emphasising that it was prudent for Rio to consider other debt-refinancing options (Chong, 2009).

The above description of Rio's activities before its AGMs in London and Sydney showed that the primary outcomes of the interactions were the strong opposition of Rio's shareholders to the proposed deal and their demand for right issues. These outcomes were mainly based on economic and strategic perspectives. However, Rio's management and board were adamant about the proposed deal, something that partly reflected the good relationship of senior management between Rio and CHINALCO. Nevertheless Rio did have its Plan B and remained open to other financing options.

### Dealing with the Australian governments and regulatory authorities

Like other stakeholders, Rio also attempted to influence the Australian government's decision regarding its deal with the Chinese. Specifically,

Rio pressed that failure to approve the CHINALCO agreement could cost Australia 2150 existing and 750 planned jobs. As stated previously, all but 100 of these jobs would be in Queensland, the home state of the then prime minister, Kevin Rudd, and treasurer, Wayne Swan (Chambers, 2009h). Rio's voice was echoed by Queensland premier, Anna Bligh, who urged the federal government not to stand in the way of CHINALCO's rescue of Rio Tinto because mining and tourism were most vulnerable to an economic downturn in her state (Parnell, 2009).

The CHINALCO deal also needed approval by the Australian regulatory bodies, including the FIRB and the ACCC, which considered whether the proposed deal could have a substantial impact on competition. This has a narrow focus and is often more straightforward.

CHINALCO submitted its investment application to FIRB on 1 March. On 16 March the FIRB informed CHINALCO that it would extend its approval process for 90 days until mid-June 2009, the maximum time for approving an FDI application. This was understandable given the application's size and potential impact on Australia's national interest. This also gave Rio's stakeholders an additional 90 days to express their opinions and gave CHINALCO and Rio more time to address those significant concerns. More importantly, it could provide critical time, whether deliberately or unintentionally, for the recovery of the global financial market. The ACCC was quick to make its decision, and announced on 25 March 2009 that it did not oppose the proposed CHINALCO deal because it would be unlikely to result in a substantial lessening of competition. This cleared the first regulatory hurdle for the deal.

## Activities conducted by Rio after its 2009 AGMs

*Activities and interactions with shareholders*

Rio's board and management began repositioning their stance on the deal after Rio's 2009 AGMs because of its shareholders' strong opposition to the deal and the rapid recovery of the international share market. Rio held its AGMs for Rio Tinto plc in London on 15 April, and for Rio Tinto Limited in Sydney on 20 April. During both AGMs, Rio's shareholders in the UK and Australia upheld their preferences for rights issues. The responses from Rio's AGMs changed the position of Rio's board and senior management on the CHINALCO deal, perceiving that the proposed deal would not gain the approval of its shareholders if not substantially amended.

The recovery of global financial markets in April and May 2009 further agitated Rio's shareholders, senior management and board about the terms of the proposed deal. April 2009 witnessed a positive sharp turn in the global bond and equity market. By the time of AGM in Sydney, Rio Ltd's shares had appreciated by 16 per cent since February. Rio took this opportunity to raise $3.5 billion bond money at a 9 per cent coupon with no conversion rights on 15 April through the open market (Tasker, 2009e). In particular, Rio would pay 8.95 per cent on $2 billion of five-year bonds, and 9 per cent on $1.5 billion of ten-year bonds. The interest of these two tranches of bonds was slightly lower than those of bonds to be issued by CHINALCO on convertible rights. These suddenly made Rio bonds start to look like a huge bargain for CHINALCO. It should be pointed out that Rio's bonds were issued three weeks after BHPB had successfully secured $4.14 billion on bond issues with coupons at only 4–6 per cent interest on 26 March. It is widely believed that BHPB was testing the financial market and set an example for Rio to benchmark its CHINALCO deal and to make progress in raising money to pay its debt.

The change of chairmanship at Rio may have also helped it move its position on the deal. Du Plessis took the chairman post on 20 April at the AGM in Sydney saying that Rio would scrap the CHINALCO deal if shareholders were opposed. Unlike his predecessor, Paul Skinner, who had a hostile relationship with then BHPB's chairman, Don Angus, du Plessis met with Argus on 20 April, the day he formally became chairman (Freed & Garnaut, 2009). The meeting was more than just an informal introductory greeting because, directly after the meeting, both parties made clear their intention to create a strategic alliance between BHPB and Rio in case the CHINALCO transaction could not obtain government and shareholder approval (Wilson, 2009).

The further quick recovery of the global financial market in May 2009, coupled with the consistent and strong opposition by its shareholders and offers from BHBP for JV through its meetings with BHPB's board and CEO, had driven Rio's towards a negative position on the deal. Rio's board and management became openly less enthusiastic about the deal, thereby becoming more serious about its "Plan B". May 2009 witnessed more increases in Rio's share prices. On 4 May, Rio Tinto Ltd closed at $49.50, which meant it was trading at 10 per cent of premium of CHINALCO's first tranche of $45 per share. Rio's boards had reversed their defence of CHINALCO's value around that time, and commenced using hesitant statements in early May. This was reflected by the talk of Rio's director of global strategy, Doug Ritchie, during a meeting with the Committee for the Economic Development of Australia. He maintained that it remained uncertain if the CHINALCO deal was still a good trans-action. Richie was believed to have visited CHINALCO officials during the same week to discuss investors' opposition to the deal and suggest revisions to the bond portion of the transactions (leaving the asset part untouched).

Du Plessis met UK shareholders on 13 May for the first time, 23 days after he took over the new post as Rio's chairman. These 23 days had provided him and Rio time to consider alternative options under the recovering global financial market and strong pressure from the shareholders. The board and its new chairman seemed more receptive to other alternatives than previously. Du Plessis was reported to have told London shareholders that all options were on the table, not just the CHINALCO alliance. When he attended a Merrill Lynch Global Metals Mining and Steel Conference in Barcelona on the same day, Albanese's discussions aimed to convince the whole industry that the CHINALCO deal was still worthwhile (Litterick, 2009). However, watch-ers of Albanese giving his speech at the conference could spot that the CEO's tone had become less enthusiastic about the CHINALCO deal (Chambers, 2009g).

Albanese also met BHPB's CEO Marius Kloppers who was also attend-ing the conference. Although the conditions in Rio's agreement with CHINALCO specified that Rio would not seek any competing proposal at the same time, they did not preclude any third party approaching Rio. Thus, it made sense for BHPB to be the first to revive contact with Rio. Many believed that Kloppers may have initiated some discussion with Albanese on what BHPB's attitude was towards the proposed Rio–CHINALCO transaction. That week also saw a steep fall in the price of Rio shares in both Britain and Australia (Chambers, 2009g). This steep fall happened because of strong speculation that Rio was preparing for its massive rights issue to replace the CHINALCO rescue package.

### The final stage of deal negotiation (late May–4 June 2009)

By late May, it seemed that Rio's board and management had sub-stantially changed their view on the proposed deal with CHINALCO, and were considering cooperating with BHPB in the Pilbara region as the preferred option for two reasons. Firstly, they had considered it to be an insurmountable task to convince its increasingly dissatisfied shareholders of the benefits of the proposed deal due to the quick recovery of international financial market. Secondly, the improved rela-tionship between Rio and BHPB at the top level, thanks to their long and established working relationship at middle management level, seemed to rekindle one alternative to Rio's Plan B, a JV with BHPB.

On 22 May, du Plessis was reported to have informed CHINALCO of Rio's intention to cancel the proposed deal and explore other options to the CHINALCO–Rio alliance, such as inviting CHINALCO to participate in its newly proposed JV with BHPB. Albanese flew to Beijing on 23 May to hold a face-to-face meeting with CHINALCO's president, discussing details for further changes and other options. Albanese's unambiguous comments had taken Xiong by surprise. Albanese said, "...on the balance of probabilities, we are going to have to withdraw our recommendation for this transaction and look at other options" (Mathieson, 2009b). It was reported that Rio had offered CHINALCO a 5 per cent ($5.8 billion) stake in its proposed $116 billion deal with BHPB, but without board representation. However, CHINALCO did not want to participate in the proposed Rio–BHPB JV, but was prepared to further modify the deal. Their proposed changes, outside of reducing its convertible bonds and dropping its marketing JV with Rio, included opening the bond issue to other shareholders, taking a reduced stake in some mining projects, paying more for some assets and accepting one board seat rather than two. However, Rio's management and board had foreseen the difficulties in getting the deal through its shareholders no matter how much change CHINALCO was prepared to make.

Du Plessis started his Australian visit on 26 May, two weeks after he met Rio's UK shareholders. His one-week tour was to meet Australian institutional shareholders. One agenda item on his schedule was to meet with CHINALCO's president. It was widely supposed that du Plessis had more options to discuss with Australian shareholders than he had when appointed as chairman. In contrast to everyone's expectations, his objective seemed to be to inform Australia's shareholders of the decision that Rio's board had already made, rather than discussing alternatives with them. This was demonstrated in the speech by Rio's iron ore chief executive officer, Sam Walsh, at the Mineral Week Conference in Canberra on that night. He commented that, after consulting its shareholders, Rio would make many changes to the agreement with CHINALCO, "Once we have heard shareholders' views, we will determine action" (Behrmann, 2009). Furthermore, Walsh did not decline the possibility of joining BHPB in an iron ore joint venture in the Pilbara, "If anyone makes a proposal, it's the Board's duty to consider it while looking at the overall merits of the strategic alliance with CHINALCO. So if such a situation (with BHPB) arose, we could consider it", he said (Behrmann, 2009; Williams, 2009b).

Next day, on his Australian tour, du Plessis met with key stakeholders in Melbourne, and then headed to Canberra on the same day to attend the Mineral Week Conference. Later in the evening, du Plessis was joined by BHPB's CEO Marius Kloppers at the Minerals Council of Australia's Annual Dinner. On 29 May, the Rio chairman continued his tour by meeting with the Australian Shareholders Association. Meanwhile, Albanese returned to Australia, along with iron ore boss Sam Walsh, to host a media tour of the company's Pilbara assets and planned automated mining facilities (Chambers, 2009e).

CHINALCO's president, Xiong Weiping, arrived in Australia the same week, and held final negotiations with du Plessis on 31 May and 1 June. Shortly after this, du Plessis cancelled his meeting with Sydney shareholders to return to London due to a "family emergency" (Murdoch, 2009). Du Plessis did not give any interviews to the media nor speak publicly while he was in Australia. Furthermore, the audiences in all meetings with the chairman were limited to the top 12 local shareholders (Chambers & Callick, 2009). Suspicions increased when the most outspoken shareholders declined to comment on what was discussed in these talks. Perhaps Rio was contemplating some changes to its Chinese solution that might be too controversial to reveal to wider audiences.

On 5 June, Rio Tinto Group announced to its shareholders and the public the abandonment of the deal. Rio "notified Chinalco that it cannot proceed with the deal" (Mathieson, 2009a). Under the agreement, Rio Tinto was to pay a $195 million breaking fee to CHINALCO plus other financial advisory and underwritten costs. This was surprising as the decisions from the FIRB and Rio's shareholders were yet to come. The FIRB was supposed to announce its stance on the Rio–CHINALCO tie-up within ten days. On the same evening, it was believed that the Rio Group's shareholders had become aware of the alternatives to the CHINALCO transaction. These included the massive $15.2 billion rights issue and the JV in which Rio would receive $5.8 billion from BHPB as Rio had more iron ore resources in the JV than BHPB.

## Activities conducted by CHINALCO's senior management

The announcement of the alliance with Rio Tinto was positive news for CHINALCO. From a purely commercial viewpoint, the agreement would see CHINALCO acquire shareholding to strategic levels in Rio's most valuable assets, such as the Hamersley iron ore in WA and the Escondida copper mine in Chile. From a long-term strategic perspective, integrating backward with one of the world's largest suppliers could give CHINALCO critical understanding of the corporate governance and strategic management of one of the largest mining companies, including the price negotiation process between miners and steelmakers. Importantly, the proposed partnership would double to 18 per cent CHINALCO's share in the Rio Tinto Group, the level at which it could act to prevent the giant miner BHPB from any anti-competitive move towards Rio Tinto. Thus, CHINALCO's alliance with Rio not only offered a direct benefit but would also have helped maintain a competitive market for mining resources. Consequently, CHINALCO became very keen to complete the transaction. Understanding the difficult task of obtaining Australian government approval, and the negative sentiment existing in the Australian public, CHINALCO's effort had been concentrated on these two areas rather than on influencing Rio's institutional shareholders.

### Dealing with Australia's public perception of SOEs

CHINALCO's new president, Xiong Weiping, visited Australia on 1 March, two weeks after the deal announcement (Chambers, 2009a). He was appointed to this new post on 26 February after former CHINALCO president, Xiao Yaqing, was appointed to be the deputy secretary-general of China's State Council. The new president did not take long before moving to his first international mission – completing the Rio Tinto acquisition. A key objective on his visit was to convince Australians of the benefits of the deal, to improve the public perception of SOEs, to lodge the investment application to the FIRB and to meet with Rio's shareholders.

Xiong held a media conference in Sydney on 2 March, stating that CHINALCO would not achieve any "control in any sense" of Rio and natural resources in Australia (Keenan, 2009). He also emphasised that CHINALCO's investment would be "beneficial to Australia in terms of helping it withstand the impact of the global financial crisis and its economic recovery" (B. Fitzgerald, 2009b). At the same time, he also tried to downplay the state-owned status of CHINALCO, which could indirectly influence commodity prices and resource development decision-making through its alliance with Rio. During answers to questions from the media, he intimated, "although we are a state-owned enterprise, ever since our establishment [in 2001], we have been run as a separate and independent commercial enterprise" (B. Fitzgerald, 2009b).

As part of CHINALCO's public relations strategy, a corporate communications consultancy firm FD Third Person was hired to deal with public perceptions about the deal to ensure that "Chinalco's bid was not played out in the court of public opinion" (Canning, 2009). The role FD Third Person played was to demonstrate to the public and the authorities that while CHINALCO might be a state-owned enterprise, it was not "an agent" of the Chinese government (Canning, 2009). Through FD Third Person, CHINALCO funded A$250,000 for surveying Australian attitudes towards Chinese investments, plus A$30,000 sponsorship for Australia's National Council and a membership fee for the Queensland brand, because CHINALCO was developing a A$3 billion bauxite project in north Queensland (Callick, 2009b). UMR Research was commissioned to conduct a survey of 1000 Australian respondents on their attitudes regarding Chinese investments in general. The survey results indicated that the Beijing Olympics had contributed to a significant positive opinion shift in attitudes towards China. Furthermore, attitudes towards foreign investment remained positive and stable, and opposition to Chinese investment had dropped significantly compared with a similar survey in April 2008 (Milne, 2009).

In addition to the effort of its senior management to convince the Australian public positively, CHINALCO also hired a lobby firm to win over the Australian government and other stakeholders for its proposed partnership with Rio Tinto. As stated in Chapter 4, the strongly Labor-connected public relations firm Hawker Britton was commissioned to lobby the Australian government and test the government's view towards an appropriate investment threshold for a foreign entity. Former Labor staffer Simon Banks headed the Hawker Britton team advising CHINALCO; he had served as chief of staff to former party leaders Simon Crean, Kim Beazley and Kevin Rudd. This lobbying firm, which has a history of making financial contributions to the Labor Party, also backed CHINALCO in 2008 when the Chinese first acquired 12 per cent of Rio's London shares (Sainsbury & Tasker, 2009).

*Dealing with Chinese banks to secure financing for the deal*

CHINALCO secured a loan from a Chinese bank syndicate for its $19.5 billion investment in Rio on 1 April 2009. This syndicate was led by the China Development Bank and three other banks (Export-Import Bank of China (Eximbank), the Agricultural Bank of China and the Bank of China). It agreed to provide CHINALCO with $21 billion, most of which would be dispersed by paying Rio. The remainder would be channelled to CHINALCO's other development projects.

The conditions for this bank loan were exceptionally attractive, although the bank syndicate would secure the loan against some of Rio's assets, in which CHINALCO would have a stake if the deal went through successfully. Under the financing contract, CHINALCO would only pay 90 basis points (less than 1%) over the benchmark six-month of LIBOR. The interest rate and the 15-year length of the contract were described as "unheard of" and would not be possible from a commercial bank (Tasker & Mathieson, 2009). When compared with the loan obtained by BHPB at the same time, the terms in CHINALCO's loan seemed unrealistically superior. BHPB, which was much bigger in assets and financially stronger than CHINALCO, agreed to pay 345 basis points above the LIBOR on a five-year bond, and to pay 390 basis points over a ten-year bond, in a capital raising in the US and EU in March 2009 (Stevens, 2009c). With a market value of $125 billion and a strong balance sheet, investors were confident that BHPB would have no problem repaying $6.25 billion in debts and annual interests when due (Stevens, 2009c). However, financial experts found it difficult to understand how a company with only $7 billion in net assets like CHINALCO could afford to invest $19.5 billion (Durie, 2009). Annual interest from this debt alone would cost the company $1.6 billion. Moreover, CHINALCO had already pumped in $14 billion of borrowed money to acquire 9 per cent of Rio Tinto shares in 2008. Many contended that it would not be possible for CHINALCO's small balance sheet to obtain a total of $35 billion debts if it was not funded by those generous Chinese state-owned banks (Stevens, 2009e).

*Negotiating with Rio for the deal amendments*

CHINALCO's stance towards the deal changed after the deal announcement, in part as a response to Rio's shareholders' strong opposition to the deal, and the quick recovery of international financial markets. Before Rio's AGMs in April 2009, CHINALCO approached the deal rigidly and wanted to keep the original terms of its Rio alliance, despite the message that Rio's shareholders were unfriendly during its meetings with Rio's executives and its shareholders in March 2009. On 26 March, Rio CFO Guy Elliot suggested that Rio was still open to Plan B in case the CHINALCO deal failed (Tasker, 2009d). This upset CHINALCO who blamed Rio for not trying hard enough to sell the deal to its shareholders (Tasker, 2009c).

CHINALCO's attitude started to change after Rio's AGMs in 2009. It had become more vocal in defending itself and was prepared to renegotiate the original agreement while remaining inflexible on certain aspects of the deal. At this stage, CHINALCO was prepared to modify terms for its convertible bonds, but wanted its asset package untouched. However, CHINALCO became increasingly prepared to amend the structure of its deal with Rio Tinto in May 2009, mainly because the global financial market had improved substantially, and Rio's shareholders were working hard against the deal. It was prepared to change both the asset and bonds sections of the deal to win over all major stakeholders. The new scenario of a partnership between Rio and BHPB further worried CHINALCO. Rio came to CHINALCO in late May 2009 with an important update for these two companies' partnership. Under the new scenario, Rio offered CHINALCO a shareholding of up to 5 per cent (worth $5.8 billion) in the iron ore joint venture between Rio and BHPB in the Pilbara region of WA (Stevens, 2009d). This offer was to replace the original controversial $19.5 billion acquisition that would be derailed by institutional shareholders in London even if the FIRB approved it. From that moment on, the prospect of a Rio–CHINALCO alliance began to vanish. CHINALCO ultimately turned down the invitation because it involved significant change to the original deal and the controversy of the Rio–BHPB JV, and because they were not offered a director's seat.

CHINALCO was trying harder to save the deal in the final days despite Rio's loss of interest and was prepared to rescue the deal by offering more changes. Xiong flew to Sydney to discuss the potential changes to the deal with Rio's chairman and CEO at the end of May. He held a meeting with du Plessis on 31 May and 1 June in Sydney (Mathieson, 2009b). After the meeting, Xiong told the media that, "... certainly there have already been changes in the market and according to these changes we and Rio are together looking into the present situation" (Rabinovitch, 2009). Rumours abounded that CHINALCO was prepared to lower its proposed stake from 18 per cent to 15 per cent, and to abandon iron ore's marketing terms and reduce the seats of director from two to one (Chambers, 2009b). However, Xiong asserted that all details about CHINALCO's attempted changes were "market rumours" (Rabinovitch, 2009).

Rio announced on 5 of June that the negotiation of its alliance with CHINALCO had failed and that the company would pursue other options to finance its debt repayments. Xiong remained diplomatic, saying that the failure was due to a purely commercial issue, despite other speculations. He also refused to comment on whether Rio's behaviour had dishonourably made use of CHINALCO. Xiong confirmed prior speculations that CHINALCO would have reduced its stake to less than 18 per cent and cut its ownership of Hamersley iron assets from 15 per cent to 7.5 per cent: "We said we would simplify marketing and corporate governance structures around iron ore assets", said Xiong (Sainsbury, 2009f). In July 2009, CHINALCO took up its full entitlement, spending $1.5 billion in Rio's $15.2 billion capital raising (Murphy, 2009). Regarding this acquisition, CHINALCO issued a statement saying that it had put emotions aside and made "an economically rational decision" (Murphy, 2009).

## Political and competitive activities conducted by BHPB

When Rio Tinto and CHINALCO first announced their alliance, the tie-up seemed to be a real threat to BHPB's market position for two reasons. Firstly, the agreement would allow the Chinese to have stakes in several Rio strategic mining projects, especially 15 per cent in Hamersley iron ore – Australia's biggest iron ore deposit – and 15 per cent in the Escondida copper mine, the world's largest. The transaction, if approved, would also have allowed CHINALCO to increase its stake in Rio up to 18 per cent and thus would enable the Chinese to effectively prevent any future bid from BHPB in Rio Tinto (Frith, 2009a). These outcomes would crush BHPB's dream of acquiring Rio Tinto to create one of the world's largest companies. Secondly, the CHINALCO deal would provide the Chinese with a presence on Rio's board, which potentially could allow them to manipulate marketing and iron ore pricing. Thus it could have an immediate impact on the negotiation process of iron ore price between miners and Chinese steelmakers, not to mention any potential restructuring of the industry. Therefore, BHPB, as the world's biggest mining company, was very eager to monitor the unfolding of the Rio–CHINALCO deal. It also foresaw the two potential deal-breakers. Without the approval of the Australian government and Rio's shareholders, CHINALCO's deal could not be finalised. Hence, BHPB and its Public Affairs and Government Relationship team had been very active even before the official announcement of CHINALCO–Rio Tinto alliance (Hewett, 2009b).

As soon as Rio announced the Chinese solution on 12 February, there was strong speculation that BHPB would launch its counter offer bid on Rio's assets, including iron ore (Hewett, 2009c). However, it was still too soon for BHPB to do anything about the Rio–CHINALCO alliance. Firstly, BHPB had been held back by the legislation after its failure to acquire Rio a year earlier, with its ruling that BHPB could not make any similar hostile bid for Rio until November 2009, one year after it abandoned its initiative to merge with Rio. Second and more importantly, BHPB understood that many things could go wrong with this deal (e.g., the agreement terms, the Australian government, Rio shareholders and the global market), and that it would take time for Rio to address issues with each of these "deal-breakers".

Thus, the "big Australian" actively waited to see how the CHINALCO deal would unfold in the face of the market situation and to slowly weaken the already shaky confidence of Rio's shareholders in London (Hewett, 2009c). It did little to confirm the counterbid speculation but indicated its interest in acquiring shares in many of Rio's strategic assets, being joined by Japan's Mitsui in the chase for a share of the rich pool of Australian assets. Nevertheless BHPB had been quietly working on several areas to win Rio back from CHINALCO, including politics, executives, shareholders and finance.

## Political activities conducted by BHP Billiton

It was in the political area that BHPB had advantages over both Rio Tinto and CHINALCO. Its Government Relations team was headed by former Labor national secretary Geoff Walsh (president) and Bernie Delaney (vice-president). Walsh, who joined BHPB as director of public affairs in November 2007, was previously chief of staff to Victorian Premier Steve Bracks. He had also been an adviser to both Prime Ministers Bob Hawke and Paul Keating. The effectiveness of BHPB's Government Relations team was summed up by one former government official who said, "E-mails from BHP were circulating at the highest levels, copies in to Minister's offices, about all the 'China Inc' stuff" (Garnaut, 2009).

The BHPB's Government Relations team was not only working hard to promote the company in Canberra, but its board and management, especially in relation to the CHINALCO deal. BHPB's then chairman, Don Argus, seemed to take a personal interest in this matter, wanting to ensure that BHPB's view about the Rio–CHINALCO alliance was heard in Canberra. BHPB's tireless chairman was often seen with his own annotated version of the 600-page CHINALCO deal agreement. He and BHPB CEO Marius Kloppers put their views about CHINALCO's tie-up to the government at the highest levels. While Rio and CHINALCO were busy convincing the world about their deal's values, Argus and Kloppers met with the then Australian prime minister, Kevin Rudd, and then finance minister, Lindsay Tanner, to brief them on BHPB's view of the alliance (Maiden, 2009a). Argus had also arranged meetings with the treasurer, Wayne Swan, during the FIRB assessment of CHINALCO's transaction. Clearly BHPB was trying its best to exploit the "policy dysfunction" so as to bend policies in its favour (Garnaut, 2009).

In contrast, Rio had very little political capital and credibility in Australia. First, it is headquartered in London, only having three Australian-based directors out of 15 on its various boards. In addition, while half of its Group income is generated from Australia, three quarters of the shares are British registered. Hence, Australian interests in Rio are in the minority when compared with those of British investors. Secondly, Rio Tinto did not seem to have good credibility in Canberra since its dual-listing transformation in 1995. Rio promised it would maintain two independent headquarters in London and Melbourne in 1995, but broke this promise in 1996, sacking 100 employees and taking three out of six global divisions away from Melbourne (Mayne, 2007). This change made London Rio's only headquarters. Therefore, the Australian government did not see the CHINALCO transaction as one between an Australian company and a Chinese company but one between two foreign entities with significant Australian national interests. In fact, the term, "national interests", had been used predominantly and was deemed more appropriate than "nationalism" when the media reported the Australian government's stance on the CHINALCO transaction.

With little experience in dealing with Australian authorities, CHINALCO had to rely on Rio Tinto and its PR firm, Hawker Britton, to do the lobbying. CHINALCO's efforts in lobbying the Australian government, including visits by CHINALCO's president to Australia, were widely regarded as being purely educational. Thus, its perspective might not have been heard fully in Canberra (Fitzgerald & Sharp, 2009). In general, CHINALCO was not a winner in political lobbying in Australia when compared with BHPB.

*Moving Rio's board and management away from the deal and luring them to form a JV with BHPB*

The constant yet subtle approach that BHPB used in dealing with Rio's management and boards was very effective in moving Rio away from the deal (Freed & Garnaut, 2009). With the help of the international financial market, BHPB ultimately changed Rio management's view on the CHINALCO transaction and made its own offer to form a JV acceptable to Rio. In doing so, BHPB employed two channels. The first was through middle management levels. Ever since the failure of its hostile bid for Rio in November 2008, BHPB had constantly sent the message about the possibility of a strategic alliance in Australia between the two companies through to Rio management in meetings at below-executive level. These discussions, mainly about Rio assets sales, were unknown to the media as they only involved middle managers. The second channel was through contacts between BHPB's board and senior management with their counterparts at Rio. The appointment of du Plessis as Rio's chairman changed the game considerably for BHPB because it did not have good contact at the executive level with Rio under Paul Skinner's reign. The relationship restarted when the congratulatory card conveyed in mid-March 2009 from BHPB's Argus to his Rio counterpart, du Plessis, expressed a wish to meet and "exchange resources and industry experiences" (Maiden, 2009b). Both chairmen met after Rio's Sydney AGM and discussed the potential alliances in the iron ore of Australia. Subsequently, the two companies' most powerful men met on several occasions.

At the CEO level, Albanese met briefly with Kloppers at a Mining Conference in Barcelona in May 2009. Du Plessis was met on 27 May by Kloppers at a Government Conference in Canberra, where Kloppers publicly aired concerns about the CHINALCO deal and urged the Rudd government to be cautious (Williams, 2009a), "Australia needs to be careful that it does not forfeit the economic merit of our resource sectors" (Chambers, 2009i). At that point, BHPB's CEO did little to quell rumours that BHPB and Rio were in talks about an alternative iron ore deal. BHPB's persistent efforts began to pay off in terms of weakening Rio's executives' stance on the deal.

*Seeking support from Rio's shareholders for blocking the deal*

BHPB also worked on the expectations of Rio's shareholders through the media, which were told it believed that "the deal will go ahead [and] don't see any legal reason why Chinalco can't increase its stake" (Tasker, 2009b). The aim was to encourage Rio's shareholders to block the deal from a corporate governance perspective. BHPB also explicitly indicated that it would not be gatecrashing the alliance between Rio and CHINALCO (Wighton, 2009), that it had no appetite to pay more than what the Chinese had indicated and that it would not be rushing into a counter offer. All these intimations were part of BHPB's strategy to communicate with Rio shareholders. There was speculation that BHPB would approach them directly if it failed in making a counter-bid through Rios' boards (Robertson & Power, 2009). Regardless, BHPB did not have to be too active as Rio's institutional shareholders had been consistently opposed to the CHINALCO transaction. Rather, it focused on the preparation of its war chest for the final task of luring Rio to form a JV.

BHPB also raised $4.36 billion in the US bond market in April 2009 (Stevens, 2009c), with terms much better than those convertible bonds offered by CHINALCO to Rio. Despite no confirmation on the matter, putting "corporate general purposes", as BHPB put it, as justification to generate more cash seems more obvious than it needed to be. Speculation had it that BHPB might be preparing its pocket for the "alternative option", or the "Plan B" that Rio had always been looking for in case the CHINALCO deal was scrapped. Indeed, BHPB's US marketing team confidently announced to its investors that BHPB had the balance-sheet muscle and cash resources to conduct a "double-digit billions" acquisition very quickly should the right opportunities arise (Stevens, 2009c). The question one might ask then is: What other options, rather than Rio, the giant miner was considering at that time?

Overall, with gradual, persistent and effective strategies, BHPB quietly changed the negotiating environment and the outcome of CHINALCO's deal in its own favour. Many might consider that it was Rio sharehold-ers' strong opposition that "sank" the deal. They are only partly correct. Without BHPB's bond raising in the open market and its proposed strate-gic alliance, the Rio board might still be unsure if the bond issues to existing shareholders and other asset sales might be sufficient to save the Group's financial situation in the long term. From politics, board and management, to institutional shareholders, BHPB used a well-devised strategy to win Rio over. BHPB's experience and skill in conducting political and competitive activities perhaps accumulated rapidly after the failure of its initial bid for Rio in 2008.

## The Australian government's actions

The decision whether to grant permission for CHINALCO's investment in Rio Tinto was considered as one of the toughest the Australian gov-ernment had ever faced in assessing FDI applications. In 2008, the FIRB already approved CHINALCO's acquisition of a 9 per cent share in the Rio Group. It was also made clear at the time that a further increased share in Rio Tinto Ltd should expect a more intense review as that would incur anti-competitive implications (Frith, 2009a; Stevens, 2009b). Hence, CHINALCO's proposed deal, which could double Chinese inter-ests in Rio, would have posed the Australian government with an even more difficult challenge.

## Factors considered by the Australian Government in assessing the CHINALCO–Rio deal

The broad term used by the Australian government in considering an FDI is "national interest". As discussed in Chapter 3, national interest covers three areas: political, economic and social benefits and con-cerns. Because the CHINALCO–Rio alliance has been the largest FDI in

Australian corporate history, and CHINALCO is a state-owned MNC of China – the largest Australian trading partner, many specific factors must be considered. Thus the Australian government was very cautious in its deliberations on this deal, using the most fundamental guiding principle, national interest, to evaluate the potential benefits and problems the deal may have in the economic, social and political areas.

*Economic considerations*

From the economic perspective, the key issue in considering an FDI in the minerals industry has been "commerciality" or "resource scarcity", the terms used by OECD's deputy director of financial and enterprise affairs, Blundell-Wignall (Uren, 2009b). The central issue is the economic rent of natural resources. Unlike other goods and services, scarce resources like mines deliver economic rents that cannot be competed away (Uren, 2009b). However, such economic rents from a country's natural endowments will decrease as these resources are used. Thus, a country's economic welfare depends on its ability to capture most effectively those economic rents for its citizens. One might say that the easy and most effective way to keep those economic rents inside a country is to prevent foreign ownership in the national resource sectors. This is not easy for the Australian government to adjudicate as FDI has been a driving force for the Australian mining industry in general, and became more important during the economic downturn. Therefore, it is not a question of whether to allow foreign ownership to be part of Australian resource firms, but a question of how the government should regulate those investments in the country's best interests.

Nevertheless FDI may lead to a problem of foreign control, an issue that worries the government in the host country most. Of all methods controlling economic rents, investment control is often regarded as less preferable than tax-based approaches, such as royalties, resource rent tax, production taxes, product sharing and equity participation, as it might be less effective in preventing foreign companies from engaging in aggressive tax accounting or transfer pricing to lower their input costs. These tax-based tactics would take away part of the economic rents that are the supposed entitlements of resource-rich countries. However, this does not mean they are flawless. Even with strict and comprehensive tax policies, it is very difficult to pursue court action against a foreign MNC when tax-transparent issues arise. This was of legitimate concern in the CHINALCO case because of the strong tie the Chinese conglomerate has with its own government (Geoff, 2009).

A specific factor in this deal involved the issue of market power, which is another option for governments from resource-rich countries to use to maximise rent from their resource sector; that is, by relying on the invisible hand of the market to set prices in accordance with the market situation. The current giant size of BHPB and Rio gives them strong bargaining power in setting up mineral prices, thereby maintaining healthy economic rents for the Australian governments at the federal and state levels. However, ownership structure within these miners could undermine this bargaining power. In particular, many worry that CHINALCO could use its significant stake in Rio to drive down Rio's export price to the advantage of the home country (Mathieson, 2009b). In addition, with major voting power, CHINALCO could use its pre-emptive right to stop BHPB buying out Rio in its effort to create the world's largest mining company. This would further enhance BHPB's superior bargaining power to China and other countries as buyers of mining products (Sheridan, 2009b). In general, this concern points to the classic vertical integration issue where a buyer holds critical voting power within a seller's organisation, thus having significant impact on the pricing and competition situations in the market.

Nevertheless China was Australia's largest trading partner, its second-largest export destination and its largest import country in 2009. Such an important trade link was also an important factor for the Australian government. Moreover, Australia and China had been negotiating their bilateral free trade agreement (FTA) since May 2005. A total of 15 rounds of negotiation had been held before June 2010. In the latest rounds of negotiation, Australia had asked China to open its financial, education and agricultural product markets, while China requested Australia to be more transparent in its FDI approval process. Thus, the Australian government may use this as a bargaining stake for the FTA negotiations.

Handling this deal was a predicament for the Australian government from the economic perspective, particularly under pressures caused by the global financial crisis. On the one hand, many feared that opening up to CHINALCO would lead to the rise of Chinese investment in Australia and consequently lead the Australian economy to rely even more on Chinese investment. On the other hand, saying no to CHINALCO immediately could spawn many ramifications in Australia's relationship with its most important trading partner. Australia's hesitance could send Chinese investors to Latin America or Africa where investments such as CHINALCO's would be more than welcome. Africa is the "new" destination having attracted around $40 billion in Chinese investment in 2008 (Anonymous, 2009a). Furthermore, an unwelcoming attitude to CHINALCO might harm the negotiation process of the FTA between the two countries (Sainsbury, 2009a).

*Political and social considerations*

Politically, CHINALCO's state ownership concerned the Australian public and thus the government because CHINALCO's national strategic objectives, rather than commercial goals, could have shaped the way it influenced Rio Tinto's trading. While Australia and China have much common ground in the economic area and benefited from such investment, the political and value systems of these two countries are vastly different. China was considered as a potential threat to Australia's security because it is a socialist country governed by a Communist Party. Thus, since the tie-up between a company bearing Australian interests and a state-controlled Chinese conglomerate was announced, some Australians believed that the government should block CHINALCO's bid despite the economic benefits provided by the deal (Taylor, 2009a). Other voices against the investment of CHINALCO included well-known politicians like the then opposition leader, Malcolm Turnbull, the former head of treasury, John Stone, the former treasurer, Peter Costello, National Party Senator Barnaby Joyce and the Australian Workers' Union (Coorey, 2009; Costello & Robertson, 2009; Franklin & Berkovic, 2009; Hewett, 2009a). Australia is a democratically elected country and its government usually pays attention to public opinion on various issues that concern society.

Traditionally, Australia's most important trading partners have also been its key security partners (Britain and the US), or at least an ally of these partners (Japan), all of whom are politically democratic. However, Australia's largest trading partner in recent years has been China, who is often regarded as being authoritarian, quasi-mercantilist and a strategic competitor of a major [Western] ally (Sheridan, 2009b). Some Australians feared that China, through economic investments, was seeking to translate its economic power to geopolitical influence, backed by rapid growth in its military and a blue-water navy (Anonymous, 2009a). Although this issue might be at the heart of the Australian government's concern, the diplomatic Rudd and Swan declined to comment publicly on the political aspect and did nothing to stop Senators Barnaby Joyce and Nick Xenophon in their anti-CHINALCO TV campaign and outspoken attitudes. "It is great for the Australian people that…we do not have the complications of the Communist People's Republic of China's Government owning the wealth of Australia", said Joyce (Mathieson, 2009b). Overall, significant political considerations made handling this

CHINALCO–Rio alliance proposal extremely difficult for Swan and his FIRB team.

*Actions taken by the Australian government*

The Australian government had been carefully deliberating CHINALCO's application so as to protect Australia's "national interest" and quell public perception about Chinese investment even before the deal's announcement. Just one day before Rio announced its alliance with CHINALCO to its shareholders, federal Treasurer Wayne Swan announced the amendments to the Foreign Acquisition and Takeover Act 1975 (FATA) (Chambers & Berkovic, 2009). These new amendments treated convertible debt as equity, with the change coming into effect immediately (Swan, 2009c). It targeted exactly the type of acquisition CHINALCO was planning with Rio. Under the new legislation, CHINALCO's stake could go up to 18 per cent immediately rather than after the normal waiting period of seven years required for the convertible bonds to be converted into shares. In addition, this meant that the transaction would require regulatory approval such that any foreign company investing in Australia requires if the stake crosses the threshold level of 14.99 per cent, and any investment irrespective of its size if it comes from a state-owned company at that time.

The following months witnessed more decisions from the Australian government bodies regarding investments from other Chinese companies into Australia. These decisions set guidelines for what would be the key considerations of the government in the CHINALCO case. In the face of mounting criticism from the stakeholders, the FIRB, on 16 March, informed CHINALCO that it would delay its decision on the CHINALCO transaction until mid-June 2009. In its correspondence with CHINALCO, the FIRB particularly emphasised the then newly issued Six Principles for assessing foreign investments in Australia. The message to CHINALCO from the Australian government at that point was that it could invest in Australia but not to overdo it (Sheridan, 2009b). However, different parties, including the Australian government, had different interpretations on what constituted the appropriate investment threshold into Australia.

The ACCC approved the CHINALCO deal on 25 March, stating that the deal posed no real threat to industry competition (Stevens, 2009a). However, the ruling of ACCC did not include consideration of Australian national interests, which was expected to be the key consideration on FIRB's agenda (Sheridan, 2009b).

The FIRB conditionally approved Hunan Valin Iron and Steel's investment of $1.2 billion in FMG on 1 April 2009 (Frith, 2009b). The conditions imposed by the FIRB (see Chapter 2) provided CHINALCO with a good understanding of what it might expect from the FIRB in its case. Based on this decision, many were positive about the acceptance of CHINALCO investment while others were sceptical (Taylor & Sainsbury, 2009).

The FIRB kept sending positive signals regarding its stance on Chinese investments in Australia. On 24 April, Treasurer Wayne Swan approved Minmetals' revised investment application after it excluded OZMs' Minerals' Prominent Hill asset in accordance with the FIRB's guidelines (Tasker, 2009f). This approval entailed several provisions that guided Rio Tinto and CHINALCO in drafting their proposed alliance. This time, the treasurer was particularly concerned about the pricing terms in OZMs' alliance. In particular, he maintained that prices must be set on an "arms-length basis" from state-owned Minmetals, in line with international benchmarks (Tasker, 2009f).

The Australian government once again extended the list of issues Rio Tinto and CHINALCO needed to address for their FIRB application. In May, the FIRB had made it clear to them that a significant restructuring of the deal was needed before the approval could be granted (Mathieson, 2009b). The message did not come as a surprise to CHINALCO because they had been following FIRB's decisions on similar transactions very closely. It was reported in the media that FIRB, in its correspondence with CHINALCO, asked that part of the proposed deal be changed, including reducing convertible bonds from $7.2 billion to $4.8 billion. This would effectively lower CHINALCO's share in Rio from 18 per cent to 14.99 per cent – the maximum percentage of Rio's share CHINALCO can hold as approved by the Australian government in CHINALCO's application in February 2008. Another key change the FIRB asked for was that the marketing by the JV of 30 per cent of iron ore produced by Hamersley Iron be abandoned.

On another front at that time, senior Australian government officials, including the then minister of trade, Simon Crean and the then minister of foreign affairs, Stephen Smith, visited China several times while the FIRB was assessing the CHINALCO application. Such a high level of contact between two countries was believed to focus on some of the sticky terms of their FTA, including the opening up of Chinese markets for Australian direct investments in the resources sector as a bargaining chip for the Australian government to approve CHINALCO's deal.

Rio's decision to abandon its deal with CHINALCO on 5 June 2009 was a huge relief to the Australian government as it was saved from making a difficult and controversial decision because, on the one hand, the Rudd government would have been keen to demonstrate its bona fides towards Chinese capital flows to the Australian mineral industry, particularly junior miners (Hewett, 2009b); on the other hand, it needed to secure Australian public support for its decisions on FDI.

## Activities conducted by the Chinese government

While the Australian government was struggling with an array of issues in the economic, political and social areas arising from the CHINALCO's deal and other Chinese investment applications, the Chinese government was also involved in the deal with its diplomatic approaches through a number of channels, such as placing the deal on the agenda of a senior Chinese government delegation to Australia, using its diplomatic agency in Australia and meeting with the Australian government and business delegations in China.

Li Changchun, a member of the China's Politburo Standing Committee in charge of propaganda, media and ideology, visited Australia on 21 March 2009. He is ranked number five in China's nine-member Politburo Standing Committee and dispatched three central messages during his meeting with the then Australian prime minister, Kevin Rudd (Sheridan, 2009a). Two of them focused on the CHINALCO deal: support from the Australian government was sought for the bid, and a definition of CHINALCO's status as an independent commercial entity run at more than arm's length from the Chinese government despite its state-owned status. Another message he released was to the effect that Australia must not support Tibet's Dalai Lama as Tibet was considered as a core and non-compromising issue for the Chinese government in its diplomatic policies.

At the time, the then Chinese ambassador to Australia, Zhang Junsai, had sought to address the concerns of the Australian public and politicians about the deal, particularly on the matter of Chinese control of Australian resources. He acknowledged publicly that there were fears in Australia that Chinese enterprises, being state-owned, could seek to control Australia's energy and mineral resources. He told the Australian media that he believed these concerns were "understandable but unnecessary" (O'Malley, 2009). He also strongly insisted that Beijing no longer had management control of state-owned enterprises after three decades of reform. Zhang further emphasised that "China doesn't intend to control Australian energy and resources industry nor is it possible for China to do so" (O'Malley, 2009).

As the concerns from the Australian public and Rio shareholders were soaring, Zhang had to reiterate the stance of the Chinese government on the CHINALCO investment. He warned against an overly emotive debate about Chinese investments in Australia and suggested that, "... arguments for or against investment by Chinese companies are not surprising", but the subject should be approached "... in a rational and comprehensive manner rather than using emotive language" (Callick, 2009c). Zhang also emphasised that the healthy bilateral trade between the two countries had had an impressive 36.1 per cent annual growth rate in 2008. Regarding public concerns about the control of Australian resources by Chinese state-owned enterprises like CHINALCO, he further insisted that, "... state-owned enterprises are no longer entities under a highly centralised planned economy", and that "like companies from other countries, they seek a long-term, sound and reliable supply of energy and resources" (Callick, 2009c).

Senior Chinese government officials also met Australian government delegations in Beijing several times. It was widely believed these talks involved the CHINALCO deal and the FTA between Australia and China.

## Factors causing the failure of the proposed CHINALCO–Rio alliance

The proposed CHINALCO–Rio alliance was the largest Chinese ODI in Chinese corporate history and the outcome could have had a major strategic impact on the global mining industry. Thus, it is understandable why not only key players of this deal, such as Rio, CHINALCO and BHPB conducted extensive and intensive corporate, political and competitive activities, but that the Australian and Chinese governments, the public and the media were actively involved in the associated issues. These key stakeholders had different interests and levels of power in the deal. Thus the outcome of this deal was influenced by the actions and/or interactions of these key players or stakeholders. Figure 6.3 summarises the discussion of actions and interactions among key stakeholders on this deal.

Although many key players engaged with the issues and each other to influence the outcome of this deal, and there were intricately entangled connections between these players, as shown in Figure 6.3, several factors causing the deal's failure can be derived based on the above analyses

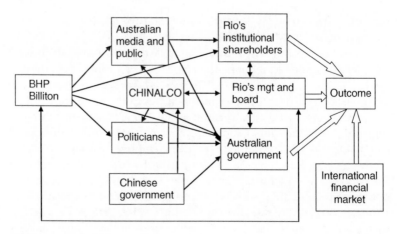

*Figure 6.3*   Key players and their actions and interactions for influencing the outcome of CHINALCO's deal

and discussions. These factors can be broadly categorised at two levels: environmental and organisational.

### Environmental factors

Two environmental factors contributed to the outcome of the deal. First, the rapid recovery of the global financial market improved the financing environment and lifted commodity prices. This substantially increased the value of Rio's assets, its investors' confidence and expectations and galvanised opposition by Rio's shareholders.

Second, the extension of the investment assessment process by the Australian government had unintentionally provided crucial time for further global financial market recovery. It is understandable that the FIRB extended its assessment process given the challenge in assessing the impact of this deal on Australia's national interest, particularly in assessing the economic benefits, the public concerns in Australia and the large diversity of conditions that might be imposed if the FIRB approved the deal, regarding balancing the related economic benefits and public concerns. These conditions could include substantial changes to the convertible bonds, the proposed marketing JV and CHINALCO's seats on Rio's board. These are similar to those conditions imposed on Valin's investment in FMG (see Chapter 2). In hindsight, the most significant impact on the deal from this extension was the crucial time it provided for the global financial and commodity markets to recover. Many governments around the globe had already spent thousands of billions of dollars to lift their national economies out of recession. Consequently, this meant that massive funds were available to corporate borrowers and that the global economy quickly turned around, particularly in Australia.

## Organisational factors

At the organisational level, there were several factors contributing to the failure of the proposed deal. First, the consistent and strong objection of Rio's shareholders was the most critical factor that caused its failure. From the moment of the deal's announcement, Rio's major institutional shareholders were opposed to it, and were unhappy about the terms of asset sales and convertible bonds. These were two key components of the deal.

The second organisational factor concerned the intensive and extensive political and competitive activities conducted by BHPB. This had a major impact on the deal from several perspectives: influencing Rio's shareholders' perception about the deal; lobbying the Australian government; offering competitive terms for setting up a JV between Rio and BHPB; and revealing to Rio the possibility of raising money on the open market with reasonably good terms.

Third, the limited experience and competency of CHINALCO in striking the deal with Rio also contributed to the failure. On the positive side, CHINALCO had defended the deal on several fronts. Its senior management actively lobbied the Australian governments at the federal and state levels, had direct dialogue with the Australian media and displayed its professional skills in dealing with Rio's board and senior management. It also hired an Australian political lobbying firm to influence the Australian government and individual politicians, and commissioned a PR company to conduct a survey of Australian public opinions on Chinese investment in Australia. In this regard, CHINALCO can be viewed as one of the best Chinese investors in Australia in defending its investment and lobbying the Australian governments. CHINALCO had also developed a strong relationship with Rio's senior management and board. However, it seems that CHINALCO did not do enough in exploring alternatives in the deal from a decision-making perspective. Developing alternatives is one of the crucial steps in the strategic decision-making process. A close examination of this deal indicates that CHINALCO may have lacked risk management in structuring this deal. The deal consisted of three major components and could have been better structured to obtain the approval of Rio's shareholders. In this case, "One bird in hand is better than two birds in flight." Whether the packaged deal was the best option is questionable.

Finally, the change of Rio's chairman may also have contributed to the outcome of the deal. The newly appointed chairman (du Plessis) had adopted a more neutral stance towards the deal than his predecessor, Paul Skinner, and improved Rio's relationship with BHPB at the top level. Both could contribute to the softening of Rio's stance on its deal with CHINALCO. This is another factor at the organisational level that tipped the deal in BHPB's favour.

# 7
# Chinese Investment in the Australian Minerals Industry: Concluding Comments, Organisational Challenges and Policy Implications

Chinese ODI is a relatively new phenomenon. Hence, research on the characteristics and influencing factors of Chinese ODI is still at the developmental stage. The main purpose of this book is to explore Chinese investment in the Australian minerals industry, and thus contribute to the literature on FDI in general, and knowledge and understanding of Chinese ODI in Australia specifically.

China has recently emerged as an important source of capital. This has been underpinned by several factors at both the macro environment and organisational levels. At the macro environment level, rapid economic development over the past three decades made China the second-largest world economy by the end of June 2010, driven primarily by its capital investment, domestic consumption and export. On the one hand, this has resulted in its foreign currency reserve amounting to $2.454 trillion at the end of June 2010; on the other hand, China lacks natural resources to sustain such economic growth.

Institutionally, China accessed the WTO in November 2001, and is committed to integration with the world economy and business system. In addition, the Chinese government formally launched its "going out" policy in 2002 and during the past eight years has stipulated several policies to encourage its firms to go international, and develop facilities and services, such as banking, insurance and international settlements that support them when conducting their business abroad (Zhang, 2009).

At the organisational level, Chinese firms, particularly large SOEs, have gained substantial experience and developed competencies in

175

competing in global markets over the past three decades since China implemented its "open door" policy in 1978. These are expected to expand further into international operations in the future, although they still have to go a long way to catch up with their international competitors.

All these reasons underline the importance of Chinese ODI to its future economic development. With its large foreign currency reserve, China will remain an important source for investment in the global market.

This book has focused on several important issues surrounding the Chinese investment in the Australian minerals industry. First, it provided an overview of such investments and an analysis of its entry modes, size and minerals distribution. Second, the Australian regulatory framework on FDI, and the impact of Chinese investment on the Australian political economy were discussed and examined. Third, it dealt with the motives and entry processes into both the Australian minerals industry and explored several strategic and operational issues in Chinese-controlled entities and JVs. Fourth, it analysed the activities and interactions among the key stakeholders of the proposed CHINALCO's investment in Rio Tinto in early 2009, thereby identifying the causes for the failure of this proposed investment.

This concluding chapter is not intended to summarise all the aspects mentioned above; rather it concentrates on some key characteristics of Chinese investment in the Australian minerals industry, the entry process and after-transaction integration and management. More importantly, it proposes organisational challenges for Chinese investors and policy implications for both Australian and Chinese policy makers based on the research findings herein.

## Key characteristics of Chinese investment in the Australian minerals industry

Based on the data gathered and interviews with Chinese managers working in their Australian entities, an examination of the characteristics of Chinese ODI in Australian minerals industries is made and its patterns and trends explored.

Overall, Australia was the fourth-largest destination of Chinese ODI at the end of 2009 (Ministry of Commerce, 2010). Chinese ODI stock reached $5.863 billion (Ministry of Commerce, 2010), but accounted for less than 2 per cent of the total FDI stock in Australia (UNCTAD, 2010), far less than that of US, UK and Japan. As shown in Figure 1.2, China's share of Australia's total trade was about 20 per cent in 2009. Therefore, China is underinvested in Australia if compared with its two-way trade percentage.

### Mineral distribution and the stage of entry

Chinese investment in the Australian minerals industry has been concentrated on iron ore and coal. Australian iron ore industry investments, particularly in the magnetite, have been underpinned by several factors, including the structure of the Australian iron ore industry, which is dominated by the three largest established iron ore (hematite) producers: Rio Tinto, BHPB and FMG; the rapid increase of China's steel production and thus its demand for iron ore; and the lack of domestic iron ore supply in China. Magnetite usually contains less iron (about 30%) when compared with hematite (usually more than 50%), which can be directly shipped to steel mills without further processing. Magnetite requires beneficiation processes before shipping to steel mills, thus substantially increasing the capital investment and production costs. Therefore, magnetite mining incurs much higher overall costs than hematite. Moreover, magnetite projects are usually very big, partly to justify the large capital investment for their development and production. In fact, all the magnetite projects in Australia under development and production at the end of the first half of 2010 were owned, either partly or wholly, by Chinese investors: ranging from 46 per cent (Shasteel) to 100 per cent (CITIC Pacific Mining). China is a large coal producer, but lacks enough coking coal for supplying its huge steel industry. Thus most investments, such as Yancoal's acquisition in Felix, are in coking coal aimed primarily for export to Chinese steelmakers.

Other minerals in which Chinese firms have invested include base metals, uranium and gold. Base metals are crucial to economic development; for example, copper is used mainly in building construction, infrastructure and equipment manufacture, accounting respectively for 25, 15 and 60 per cent in 2008 (international copper study group, 2009). All three areas of investment are crucial to China's economic development at this stage. Copper is also of strategic importance to China because it was the world's largest copper consumer in 2008, using 29 per cent of the world's copper consumption, but only mining 5 per cent of the total world production. Thus it was the largest importer of copper ore and concentrate and refined copper (28% and 20% of the global import, respectively) in 2008. However, its consumption intensity of refined copper use was only about 4 kilograms per capita, much smaller than those in Japan (9 kg), the EU (8 kg) and the USA (7 kg) (international copper study group, 2009).

Much recent Chinese investment in the Australian mineral industry has been made at the stage of exploration and in the junior miners, except for the acquisition of most of the assets of OZM by Minmetals, and the takeover of Felix Resources by Yanzhou Coal. The earlier the stage of the miners/projects invested, the higher the risks involved and possibly the higher the potential profits. Moreover, junior miners are usually lacking in the finances necessary for their development. Thus, they are keen to secure investment from international investors.

## Ownership by Chinese investors

Large Chinese SOEs, or their controlled enterprises, are the dominant investors in the Australian minerals industry. By and large, Chinese ODI in the natural resources sector has been driven by China's shortage of resources, as these are insufficient for supporting its economic growth, particularly in its resource-intensive manufacturing industries, such as steelmaking and non-ferrous refining, which are dominated by Chinese SOEs. Nevertheless large Chinese private firms have been active in investing in such Australian minerals industries as Hanlong and Creat. Investment in the minerals industry usually requires considerable capital – upwards of many millions of dollars. Thus SMEs may well feel that they do not have the necessary financial resources for such investment.

More importantly, Chinese SOEs have the backing of Chinese governments, particularly at the central and provincial levels, for financing. They are thus usually able to secure loans from Chinese banks more easily than their private counterparts. In addition, Chinese SOEs are more experienced in conducting international business than private ones, which have been only allowed to make their ODI since 2003.

In this regard, China seems to follow Japan's investment trajectory wherein large trading houses, such as Mitsui, Itochu, Kobelco and Sumitomo Corporation, and large manufacturing firms, including JFE, Nippon Steel and Mitsubishi, are dominant in Japan's ODI in the Australian minerals industry.

## Entry approaches by Chinese firms

An overwhelming majority of Chinese investment in the Australian minerals industry has been through acquisitions, except in a few cases where Chinese investors bid for exploration permits (Greenfield investment). This largely reflects the fact that most of the minerals exploration tenements have already been acquired by local or international firms in Australia. In addition, Greenfield investment is normally more risky than acquisition as it involves a higher level of uncertainty.

Four entry approaches into the Australian minerals industry have been used by Chinese investors. They are: takeover, majority-owned, JVs and minority equity participation. A takeover usually requires a large amount of investment as well as expertise and experience to set up and operate a foreign subsidiary after the transaction. Thus, it has so far only been adopted by large Chinese SOEs (see Figure 2.1).

Acquiring a majority of shares in a listed company was another method adopted by Chinese investors. As with the takeover, this approach requires approval by the FIRB and the shareholders of the target company. Compared with takeovers, however, this approach requires less capital and could be preferred by the FIRB as the company will still remain publicly listed and thus must comply with the information disclosure and corporate governance requirements of the ASX and the Australian corporate legal framework. Nevertheless the benefits and costs of such approaches need to be carefully considered and balanced and will be elaborated later in this chapter.

EJV has been used by several Chinese firms, including Ansteel, WISCo, Yunnan Tin Group, Chongqing Steel and Baotou Steel. All these EJVs were established after 2006 and are project-based. Except for Yunan Tin Group with Metals X, the remaining four EJV are in magnetite mining, invested at the exploration stage. Given the high level of uncertainty and large amount of capital requirement in such a project, a staged approach was used by three Chinese investors, typified by the case of WISCo with Centrex Metals.

Three marketing JVs were established before 2005, pioneered by the JV (Channar Project) between Rio Tinto and Sinosteel (formerly China's Metallurgical Import and Export Corporation), when the global iron ore market was predominately a buyers' market. These marketing JVs are all with the two super-powered iron ore miners, Rio Tinto and BHPB. The market conditions, the mineral invested and the competence of foreign partners contributed to the success of these three marketing JVs.

Finally, many Chinese firms invested in the Australian minerals industry as minority equity participants. This could reflect the motives of Chinese investors for seeking financial return, and/or securing supply of the minerals invested and their limited financial resources, and the limit of foreign ownership imposed by the FIRB and Australian corporate laws. Australian corporate law requires an acquiring firm to launch a takeover bid if its ownership of the target firm is over 19.9 per cent unless otherwise agreed by the majority of the shareholders of the target company.

## Operational and managerial issues and future challenges

As shown in Figure 2.1, a number of Chinese firms have established their WOS, taken a majority stake in an Australian company or set up a JV in Australia. Thus, they have accepted certain responsibilities in governing and managing their entity or JV.

### Ownership and corporate control

Information on the size and composition of the board of directors was collected from eight Chinese-controlled entities, four being WOS and four majority-owned. The number of directors in each company varied from five to eight. Among the four WOSs, a majority of directors were Chinese, thereby reflecting the ownership control. The managing director from both Australian companies acquired (Felix and OZ Minerals) were kept, and still hold their position after the transactions, indicating a strong learning motive for the Chinese investors and, possibly, their desire for operation stability as both companies acquired were well-established and already at the production stage. The remaining two cases are quite different. Sinosteel's acquisition of Midwest Corporation was hostile as it encountered strong opposition from the former managing director. Thus, it became impossible for Sinosteel to employ the previous managing director of Midwest Corporation. In the case of CITIC Pacific Mining, it appointed a local manager as managing director after it acquired the mining rights from Clive Palmer, an Australian mining magnate. However, the managing director resigned a week after revealing an $835 million cost blowout and a substantial project delay in May 2010. His term of office had lasted for three and a half years before his resignation.

For the other four Chinese majority-owned entities, the Chinese investors have at least half the number of directors and have appointed their chair to the board. The exception is Hanlong's investment in Moly Mines where the Chinese investor entity has less than half the directorships, with a non-Chinese being appointed as the chairman. Unlike the other three Chinese investors, Hanlong is a large Chinese privately owned conglomerate and has a relatively short history of international operations.

Hanlong presents a good case for corporate control of an Australian company. It has a majority stake in Moly Mines, but a minority of directors in the board. Both the chairman and managing director are non-Chinese. However, the performance of Moly Mines was ranked the second among the four Chinese-controlled entities (see Table 5.3). This raises an important issue of corporate control, particularly the relative importance of external and internal corporate governance mechanisms. Chinese investors in the Australian minerals industry have been criticised for being too obsessed with control, but Hanlong's case shows that Chinese investors can rely on Australia's external corporate governance mechanisms, while at the same time actively making use of such internal mechanisms for selecting a competent chairperson and appointing senior management for controlling their investment's performance.

## Senior management appointment and remuneration

Most Chinese-controlled entities appointed senior managers from the local talent pool. This reflects primarily the need for local knowledge in dealing with local operations, business networks and government departments in Australia. It is also part of the learning process for Chinese firms to gain experience in conducting business. In some cases, Chinese investors have appointed senior managers from within the organisation. However, this depends on whether the Chinese investing firm has experience in managing international business activities relevant to its operations in Australia. In this case, large Chinese SOEs, such as Sinosteel and the CITIC Group, are more likely to appoint senior managers within the organization to their Australian subsidiaries.

The remuneration for senior managers in the Chinese-controlled entities varies substantially, hinging on the HR systems within their parent companies. People who are recruited locally are paid according to the market rate. For expatriates, market-based remuneration is paid to them in some Chinese-controlled entities. In other cases, their monthly stipend is mainly based on their salary in their home country, plus international living allowances. In all cases, there is no share option for them.

Such a relatively low salary, with a living allowance package for expatriate mangers in some Chinese-controlled entities, could create problems in motivating such employees to work towards the company's strategic objectives. It may also increase the level of turnover as they may be "headhunted" by competitors. Some expatriate managers are not allowed to bring their families with them. This could add more difficulties or impose stress on their living conditions in Australia.

Some Chinese investors still adopt the approach of rotating their senior managers in Australia, usually every three to four years. Therefore, management performance is being difficult to evaluate, given that most investment projects are of a long-term nature.

## Challenges in corporate governance

Effective corporate governance is crucial to the long-term survival and prospect of business organisations as it can ensure strategic decisions are made in line with the shareholders' goals for the organisation, thereby enhancing shareholder value, reducing the costs of financing and stabilising the national economy. Corporate governance has become increasingly important in Australia as recent changes in corporate laws emphasise governance more, place greater liabilities on companies and hold firms more accountable to society through reputation and risk management (Young & Thyil, 2009).

Governing a Chinese-controlled entity in Australia is challenging for several reasons. First, Chinese firms usually lack experience of implementing corporate governance in China. The concept of corporate governance in China is relatively new as the Code of Corporate Governance for Listed Companies in China was only introduced in 2002. Thus, many Chinese companies are still not familiar with existing corporate governance practice (Deloitte, 2010).

Second, a big difference exists in the corporate governance system between Australia and China. Australia adopts the Anglo governance system, which is referred to as being market-based with a diversity of shareholders (Young & Thyil, 2009), while corporate governance in Chinese firms has been historically weak and relationship-based (Lattermann, 2009). Although China has been gradually developing its market-based corporate governance system, which has primarily applied the European "insider" system of corporate governance with concentrated shareholders (Clarke, 2009; Lattermann, 2009), it is still a challenge to the Chinese to adapt to Australia's corporate governance system. In particular, the listed entities are challenged as they have to comply to Australia's corporate governance codes and develop internal control mechanisms for their local context.

Third, the Australian government has placed much emphasis on the corporate governance of foreign investors. For example, national interest is the fundamental criterion the Australian government uses to assess an FDI proposal. In further explaining the national interest, it has issued a detailed statement regarding the factors considered in assessing whether a proposed investment is in line with its national interest (FIRB,

2010b). One of these factors is investor character, whereby corporate governance is used explicitly as an indicator for good investor character. Moreover, the FIRB dictates the manner in which the target company should be governed after acquisition, such as the number and nature of company directors, information disclosure and ownership structure. These are the conditions for approval of Chinese investment proposals as exemplified in the cases of Minmetals' acquisition of OZM and Yan Coal's takeover of Felix Resources. The FIRB has even demanded the relisting of the Australian company acquired, as in the case of Yan Coal's takeover of Felix Resources. All these conditions stress the importance of corporate governance in the Chinese-controlled entities or JVs.

*Establishing an appropriate corporate governance framework*

To take up the challenge in corporate governance, Chinese-controlled entities in Australia should establish a quality corporate governance system that can appropriately comply with the local context and, at the same time, satisfy the requirements of the parent company. Such a corporate governance framework could be principles-based as adopted by the Australian regulatory institutions, such as ASIC and ASX, in guiding corporate governance in Australian-based entities. Such a framework should aim to achieve accountability, transparency and fairness, and cover the establishment of the corporate governance committees and relevant corporate policies such as the appointment of a board of directors, the decision-making processes deployed and policies for the conduct of business.

A well-functioning corporate governance system involves two sets of mechanisms: external and internal (Grant, Butler, Hung & Orr, 2011). The former is a set of legal, social and institutional systems for the corporation, while the latter covers issues such as the composition of the board of directors, governance committees, the responsibility and remuneration of management and the decision-making mechanisms. Australia is a developed country and provides stable and advanced external mechanisms for corporate governance. In this regard, the Chinese subsidiary in Australia could play a leading role in corporate governance for sustainable development within its corporation.

While the detailed statutory regulatory framework in Australia has been well-established and demands compliance, developing and implementing appropriate internal governance mechanisms could be difficult in the Chinese-controlled entities.

There are three major internal corporate governance mechanisms: ownership, the board of directors and executive remuneration (Hanson,

Dowling, Hitt, Ireland & Hoskisson, 2008). As we focus on the Chinese-controlled entities, ownership is concentrated by Chinese companies. Thus there is a need to investigate the other two internal mechanisms.

### Board of directors

Regarding the boards of directors, their composition (external vs internal) and occupational diversity (expertise, knowledge and experience) are important. Appointing external, experienced directors to the board may present a challenge to many Chinese-controlled entities in Australia. Currently most of the Chinese directors are appointed from among those holding managerial positions within the parent company. Although these appointees can represent the parent company's interest in the entity well, whether they are the best candidates for the board in terms of experience, knowledge and skills is highly questionable.

One of the problems in appointing directors to the board for Chinese firms relates to the difficulty of communication between Chinese and foreign directors. Language can be a big barrier inhibiting Chinese directors from communicating with their Australian peers, and can substantially diminish the role Chinese directors are expected to play in the corporate decision-making process. This can be overcome by appointing directors from other Chinese firms and/or overseas-Chinese.

For the board's occupational diversity, appointing directors from other Chinese SOEs could be a good option. Operating at different stages in a different industry requires a different set of expertise and services from those held by the board members. For example, Chinese firms have invested heavily in magnetite mining. While magnetite mining is relatively new to Australia, several Chinese steel companies, such as Benxi Steel Company and Anshan Steel Company, have a long history of magnetite mining and processing, and are thus very experienced and competent in this area. Therefore, such experienced Chinese managers can be appointed to the board. Project construction in international markets is another area in which several large Chinese SOEs, such as CITIC Construction and MCC, have already accumulated rich experience and developed expertise as they have undertaken many international construction projects as a complement to their expertise in domestic markets.

Providing knowledge and skills in dealing with local political, economic, legal and social issues is another role of the board. This can be done through appointing Australian directors. In this regard, employment of experienced and knowledgeable overseas-Chinese could be advantageous as they usually have little problem with the language and share common cultural values.

Conducting a well-functioning corporate governance practice is probably the biggest challenge for Chinese-controlled entities. While establishing a solid corporate governance framework and appointing experienced and skilled external members to the board are challenging, they are relatively easy when compared with the conduct of required corporate governance practices. Traditionally, this is weak in many Chinese SOEs because: interference by the bureaucracy in the decision-making processes is massive; insider power is strong and heavily influenced by such traditions as *guanxi* (personal relationships); and an effective board is often absent. These issues are made worse by being coupled with a weak and poorly enforced legal system and highly concentrated ownership by the state (Latterman, 2009). Additionally, the heavy presence of the boards' members from within the parent corporations in the Chinese-controlled entities or in their parent companies can hamper the conduct of the corporate governance framework, even if well-established, in its subsidiary in Australia. The independence of the board is necessary for achieving good corporate governance practice.

### Issues and challenges in financing

Financing is crucial as mining businesses are usually capital-intensive and long-term oriented. Currently, most of the Chinese-controlled entities primarily rely on the funding from Chinese banks and their parent companies' capital and, to a lesser degree, the issuing of shares to existing shareholders or institutional investors. Investing in the mining industry is risky mainly due to the uncertainty involved in exploration and global commodity prices. The risk in exploration decreases when the project moves from exploration to production, but changes to global commodity prices is an ongoing concern throughout a project's life.

Given the level of uncertainty involved, different financial options should be considered, including bank loans, own capital, share issuing, bonds and strategic equity alliances (consortia or JVs), to better balance the risks, control and returns. This is particularly critical for those investing in large projects at the exploration stage because the projects involve a high level of uncertainty in resources, take longer and require increased funding levels to move them from exploration to production, where cash flow can be generated. For example, in the case of CITIC Pacific, it spent about $470 million in March 2006 to acquire mining rights to 2 billion tonnes of magnetite, but has invested over $4.8 billion more to move the project into production, something that is expected to happen in July 2011. Using its own capital or bank loans solely could be very risky and incur a huge financial cost.

This circumstance can also hinder organisational growth and/or mean that opportunities for business development in other areas are lost.

Given the capital-intensive nature of the mining industry, financing models need to be reviewed as well. The issue of ownership structure needs to be considered carefully before the investment is made. Moreover, banks are notoriously risk-averse. As the privatisation of Chinese banks continues, it can be expected that they will be more market-oriented in the future. It is highly questionable that Chinese banks would continue financing high-risk projects at relatively low interest rates. Therefore, financing investment projects could become more challenging and other options will need to be thoroughly explored.

## Other operational challenges

Operating an international organisation is a big challenge for many Chinese firms. There are several critical issues involved in the operation, such as management styles, human resources management, cross-cultural management, business contractors and risk management.

There are big differences in management styles between China and Australia. The decision-making process by Chinese managers is often top-down with a centrally controlled hierarchical organisational structure. However, Australian managers are often used to a more horizontal organisational structure and a high level of autonomy. Coupled with a lack of international management expertise and experience, Chinese managers may find that their leadership style is one that Australian employees find difficult to accept. This may become less of a problem as Chinese managers gain more understanding and experience in managing and leading international entities.

Another operational challenge is the area of human resources management. At the senior management level, the demand for executives with international experience has rapidly increased as Chinese firms expand their international business. However, Chinese MNCs in general are still disadvantaged in the pursuit of talent compared to their international competitors in terms of pay and prestige. Thus, the challenge for Chinese-controlled entities in Australia is how to recruit and retain senior managers. At the skilled labour level, the source of recruitment to complete a project on time is challenged by the importance of meeting the requirements established by the Department of Immigration and Citizenship.

A related operational challenge is the management of cross-cultural issues. There are large differences in national culture between Australia and China. More specifically, Chinese firms have quite a different culture at the organisational level and thus cultural clashes happen in the Chinese-controlled entities. These cultural differences are a source of problems in leadership style, human resources management and coordination of operations. Differences in values, work attitudes, motivations and goals between Chinese and Australian employees make coordination within an organisation difficult. Coupled with the problems of language and thus communication, employees' morale could be lowered and manpower turnover increased.

Managing business networks in Australia is another challenge for Chinese entities, particularly those relying on Chinese expatriates. Depending on the size of the investment project, this may involve tens of contractors and thousands of construction workers. Coordinating these contractors to make sure that they can complete the contracted work on time is very challenging.

Finally, risk management is crucial across all stages. Areas of high risk include environmental impact, and occupational safety and health. Mining is a high risk business and such risks could have a devastating impact on an organisation's financial performance. The impact of resources sector operations on the environment could be huge as demonstrated by the recent BP oil spill in the Gulf of Mexico, causing the biggest loss in British corporate history.

## Policy issues for Chinese investment in Australia

China's growing economic and political power is the phenomenon of this century. Trade relations between China and Australia have become increasingly strong, reflected by their increased bilateral trade volume. It is expected that two-way trade between China and Australia would reach A$100 billion in 2010, the first time ever in the history of this bilateral arrangement, indicating the strong interdependence of these two economies.

China relies heavily on Australia for the supply of natural resources to feed its economic growth. It is expected that China will surpass Japan to become Australia's largest export destination in the near future. While the rapidly growing trade between these two countries has been welcomed by the general public, politicians and business communities, China's fast increasing investment in Australia, particularly in the Australian minerals industry, has raised concerns among Australia's public and politicians. It is the first time that an Australian major trade partner derives from a different political regime with vast differences in national culture. Additionally, the rise of China as a geopolitical power has several crucial implications for the Australian government in dealing with its Chinese counterpart as Australia is traditionally a close ally of the US, who may perceive China as a threat to its dominance in Asia (White, 2010). Such political and security issues can make the relationship between Australia and China more complex, subtle and challenging. Consequently, policy issues concerning Chinese investment in Australia must be carefully dealt with within a broad context.

This section focuses on the policy issues that have arisen from, or are continuously important to, Chinese investment in the Australian minerals industry only. We will discuss these issues for Australian and Chinese governments as they relate to attracting, directing and facilitating Chinese investment in the Australian minerals industry.

## Policy issues for Australian governments

There are several important policies that the Australian governments can use to direct and facilitate Chinese investment in Australia, including its FDI policy and screening processes, mineral taxes and infrastructure and project approval procedures at the state government level.

### *Australian FDI policy and its screening processes*

Chapter 3 has discussed the Australian regulatory framework on FDI. Currently, proposed investments by foreign governments and their agencies (for example, state-owned enterprises and sovereign wealth funds) have been assessed using stricter criteria when compared with those applied to the private sector. According to Australia's Foreign Investment Policy updated in June 2010, "...all foreign governments and their related entities should notify the Government and get prior approval before making a direct investment in Australia, regardless of the value of the investment" (FIRB, 2010b). In addition, these conditions also apply to their establishment of a new business and acquisition of urban land. The key concern for the Australian government is whether their investment is "commercial in nature or if the investor may be pursuing broader political or strategic objectives that may be contrary to Australia's national interest" (FIRB, 2010b).

Several issues have arisen from such government approval regulations. Firstly, there is little evidence that an SOE that has acquired an Australian subsidiary or firm has behaved uneconomically or against Australia's national interest. Examples of correct thinking in this regard can be exemplified by the following: the Pohang Iron and Steel Company's (POSCO) (a South Korean steelmaker) investment in Rio Tinto iron ore, and the SingTel (a Singaporean telecommunication company) investment in Optus (an Australian telecommunication company). Both POSCO and Singtel were SOEs when making their investments in Australia. More specifically, Chinese SOEs, after more than three decades of economic reform in China, now operate more independently of the Chinese government than ever before. Thus, it is questionable whether stricter regulations for SOEs are necessary from an economic perspective.

The second issue is whether the Australian FDI regulations should differ based on the size of the company or project invested. While a large company or project may have an economic and social impact, junior miners usually have difficulties in obtaining financing. Thus, such a strict regulation on SOEs, particularly those investments in the mining industries that are typically risky and capital-intensive, can be a problem for many Australian junior miners as they struggle for survival.

Third, a case-by-case approach has created uncertainty for potential Chinese investors, although it offers flexibility for the Australian government in assessing inward FDI and the FIRB has approved an overwhelming majority of investment proposals over the past decade (see Table 3.1).

For Chinese investment proposals more specifically, the FIRB has approved more than 170 such proposals from China, with only five proposals being required by FIRB to be revised, and then being approved with conditions; investment in only two projects by Chinese investors were withdrawn. In this regard, the Australian government has a very low level of intervention in Chinese investment in Australia, although the transparency of this approval process can be improved.

Regarding the conditions imposed on Chinese investment so far, they were largely related to the ownership structure and corporate governance factors and, to a lesser degree, local community welfare and employment. In this matter, the Australian government has played a shareholders' role on boards of directors, rather than a regulator role. Australia has well-developed external corporate governance mechanisms, including relevant corporate laws, such as the Australian Investment and Security Commission (ASIC) and the Australia Stock Exchange (ASX). The FATA has clearly specified the thresholds for both ownership structure (15%) and investment transaction (A\$231 million in 2010); the conditions imposed on corporate governance, such as the number of the Chinese directors, informational disclosure, venue of annual board meetings and so on, could be left to the Australian corporate governance system to handle – it may not be necessary for the Australian government to impose these conditions on Chinese investments in Australia.

With regard to conditions concerning local community welfare and employment, these were designed to help local communities who might be affected by the Chinese investments. Their effectiveness is difficult to gauge so far, but the degree of impact seems small. In fact, these conditions may principally play a political role (as the Australian government is democratically elected) in allaying public concerns about Chinese investment.

*Minerals tax and benefits of inward FDI*

It is widely acknowledged that the Australian economy depends heavily on its minerals industries. Thus, minerals taxes have been an important part of the Australian government's revenue. The Australian government announced its intention to introduce resource super profit tax (RSPT) in late April 2010 for all minerals as a crucial part of the tax reform package. The RSPT was then changed in June to the minerals resources rent tax (MRRT) due to the wide and strong opposition from the minerals industry. The MRRT was proposed to apply only to iron ore and coal mining. This was widely regarded as a key concession to Australian miners as the headline rate of the tax was dropped from 40 per cent to 30 per cent. Besides it is limited to the iron ore and coal industries, which effectively reduced the number of Australian miners affected from 2500 to just 320.

From society's perspective, the principle of minerals tax is welcome as every Australian is entitled to a fair share of its national natural resources. However, questions have been raised by the Australian business communities regarding whether such a tax reform is fair to enterprise and also whether it enhances productivity. In particular, Australian mining executives have argued that mining tax in Australia should be internationally competitive and not retrospective. Otherwise, it may put the Australian minerals industry at a competitive disadvantage, thus driving away future investment in the Australian mineral industries. It could also affect the financial performance of the existing mining companies as their investment decisions would be based on the tax rates in the past, rather than the newly proposed tax rate. The proposed changes in mining tax as outlined by the MRRT so far are quite broad, but have created uncertainties for FDI in Australia, particularly for those Chinese investors who have invested heavily in iron ore and coal.

Iron ore has dominated Australia's exports to China. In the 2008–09 Australian financial year, Australia exported nearly three quarters (262 out of 353 million tonnes) of its iron ore production to China, accounting for 41.7 per cent of China's total iron ore import. This shows that China depends heavily on Australia for its iron ore supply. The proposed MRRT seemed to be designed to bank on the rapidly growing Chinese economy and specifically its increasing demand for iron ore; it has thus been dubbed "China's tax" (Treadgold, 2010a), because the Chinese demand for iron ore has driven up its price, thus generating super profit for the global iron ore industry. China is expected to absorb the future increase in prices and pass them onto its customers.

There are two important issues that the Australian government may take into consideration in refining its MRRT: the global supply of iron ore and the differences in profit between hematite and magnetite. The investment in the global iron ore industry has rapidly increased over the past several years and thus could substantially increase the global iron ore production in the near future. For example, the joint venture signed between Rio Tinto and CHINALCO in July 2010 to develop the Simandou iron ore project in Guinea, an area comparable to the Pilbara iron ore region in WA, aimed to provide an annual production of 70 million tonnes of iron ore (Rio Tinto, 2010a). The largest iron ore producer, Brazilian Vale, has spent heavily in recent years to boost its output from 301 million tonnes in 2008 to 450 million tonnes in 2013 (Onstad, 2008). Moreover, three major Australian iron ore producers, Rio Tinto, BHP and FMG have their own production expansion plans, with Rio planning to expand from 220 to 330 million tonnes by 2015 (Rio Tinto, 2010b), BHPB lifting its production to 240 million by 2013 (Ashby, 2010) and FMG ambitiously planning to develop its production from 40 to 155 million in the future (FMG Group, 2009). Such rapid increases in iron ore supply in the near future could have a negative impact on the iron ore price, thereby potentially reducing the profit margins of the Australian iron ore industry. Moreover, with the development of iron ore in other countries, such as Africa, the proposed MRRT may threaten the competitive position of the Australian iron ore industry in the global market, particularly in China.

Regarding iron ore more specifically, the MRRT may need to vary, based on the type of iron ore mined: hematite or magnetite. The value of magnetite is relatively low compared with hematite as it requires further processing for enriching its iron content. Thus, magnetite mining is more capital-intensive and costly than hematite. The magnetite production in Australia is very small currently, compared with that of hematite. In 2009, the entire Australian iron ore industry produced less than 1 million tonnes of magnetite concentrate.

The rapid expansion of global production of iron ore could pose a severe threat to the survival of the Australian magnetite industry as it has a much higher cost structure than hematite. Its large capital requirements make magnetite more vulnerable to fluctuation in the global iron price. Nevertheless Australia has a vast reserve of magnetite. In WA alone, there are currently 16 magnetite projects with tens of billions of tonnes of magnetite reserve worth upwards of $40 billion (AAP, 2010b). These projects, if developed, could generate more than 10,000 ongoing jobs in Australia and billions of dollars of royalties and tax to the Australian governments. Moreover, a new magnetite mining industry in Australia could bring more benefits to Australia, enhancing its competiveness in the global market (Huang, Austin, Zhang & Grainger, 2009). However, the proposed MRRT could deter the investment and development in these magnetite projects (Treadgold, 2010b), thereby reducing tax revenue for the Australian governments at the federal and state levels. Thus, magnetite miners may need to be considered exempt from the proposed MRRT to attract further investment in this area and encourage existing investors to develop their magnetite projects to the production stage.

*Infrastructure and state government project approval process*

Infrastructure is crucial to the Australian minerals industry. The development of infrastructure depends on the volume of the minerals resources discovered. In some cases, this has become a "chicken and egg" dilemma. While the miners demand that state governments develop infrastructure, the governments must consider whether the needs are sufficient for such infrastructure, particularly power, gas, railways and ports, and whether they can justifying such investments in it.

Transportation infrastructure, such as railways and ports, has been a major problem for the Australian minerals industry, particularly for high volume commodities, such as iron ore and coal. Australia's infrastructure was ranked 25th by the World Economic Forum, ten places behind its national competition index (Schwab, 2009). Its port facilities were ranked 50th – a crucial bottleneck to the growth of the Australian economy as it depends heavily on this export mode of economic growth.

WA exported 97 per cent of the iron ore in Australia in 2009 (Department of Mines and Petroleum WA, 2010c). Currently there are four major ports for exporting iron ore in WA: Port Dampier, which exported 117 million tonnes of iron ore for Rio Tinto in 2009 (Dampier Port Authority, 2009); Port Hedland, which exported 154 million tonnes of iron ore in 2009 and is used by BHPB, FMG and several junior miners, such as Atlas Iron (Port Hedland Port Authority, 2009); Cape Lambert Port (80 million tonne capacity), which is owned by Rio Tinto (Rio Tinto, 2009); and the Port of Geraldton, which was used by Mt Gibson to export 4.17 million tonnes of iron ore in 2009 (Geraldton Port Authority, 2009). These existing port capacities have become bottlenecks for Australia's minerals export trade.

While port capacity is a problem for the whole Australian iron ore industry, railways present a specific problem for junior iron ore miners. Currently, only three major iron ore producers, BHPB, Rio Tinto and FMG, have their own railways. The legal battle for BHPB and Rio to open up their railways to other iron ore miners has been going for many years without an outcome. FMG has offered its railway services to a junior iron ore miner, BC Iron. However, the cost for BC Iron would be enormous because it would have to give half of its iron ore project to FMG in return for using its railway to move BC Iron's ore to a port.

The public–private partnership (PPP) to develop infrastructure in the Midwest region in WA is a good model for the Australian minerals industry. This project primarily consists of the construction of Oakajee Port, 25 kilometres north of Geraldton in WA, and a railway, which has the capacity to carry 80–100 million tonnes per annum (http://www.opandr.com/). The port and railway facilities will cost A\$3.5 billion. The first-stage capacity of the port is expected to be 45 million tonnes per annum with plans for expansion in stages as demand grows. It is planned to be operational by 2014. However, financing for the proposed project is still a problem because of politics involved in its development and management. This can delay the operation of the proposed port and railways.

Early in 2010, the WA government agreed to develop another port, Anketell, with a maximum capacity of 350 million tonnes in the Pilbara region, mainly for iron ore export (Mills, 2010). It is expected the WA government will adopt the PPP model, emphasising the financial commitment of the private partners.

The Chinese investors are also concerned about the project approval process at the state level, regarding it as inefficient, tedious and bureaucratic. For example, environmental approval can be very time-consuming yet is critical to the survival of the investment project as it can either limit the mining scope (Environmental Protection Authority, 2009), or even totally ban the project from that area. However, until a field examination is undertaken, there is not enough information available on what the major environmental issues in the proposed mining area are. Therefore, there can be substantial costs and risks for investors and delays for the project developers. For example, the environment approvals for Gindalbie's Karara Project took more than three years to complete for several reasons, including environmental sensitivity and diversity in the mining areas, the frequent changes of government staff processing the proposal and the speed and quality of the applications and revisions submitted by Gindalbie to the state authorities. This process was urged to be streamlined and more open and transparent. Recently, the WA government has restructured the organisations involved in the process and also streamlined the process, aiming at "making the approvals system for the State's resources sector more efficient and transparent" (Department of Mines and Petroleum WA, 2010b, p. 17). Significant improvements have been made so far by the WA state government in processing mining project applications, as indicated by the Business Council of Australia in its recent report on the overall performance of the regulation-making systems at the state government level in Australia (Business Council of Australia, 2010).

### Skilled labour shortage and Australian immigration policy

Skilled labour shortage was a major problem for the Australian mining industries before the GFC and is expected to be a persistent one in the foreseeable future given the resources boom since late 2009. Helping create and protect employment for its citizens is one of the key responsibilities for any government in the world, and the Australian government is no exception.

Skilled labour shortage is often a major factor contributing to the inadequate capacity of the infrastructure and the delays in major project construction in Australia. The Australian resources sector is an important pillar of its national economy. However, given the cyclical nature of the demand of the global market for minerals, the demand for skilled labour also fluctuates. Such skilled labour demand creates a problem for the Australian minerals industry as the domestic skilled labour base is not big enough to meet such a demand, particularly during a resources boom period.

It is well-understood that importing skilled labour, even for a short period, is a very sensitive political issue in Australia. Currently, Australia's Department of Immigration and Citizenship has set several conditions for employer-sponsored workers, in particular: English proficiency, professional qualifications and minimal wages for imported labourers. A more balanced and flexible approach in granting temporary working visas to foreigners may be adopted to assist Australian miners to overcome their problems in recruiting skilled labour, particularly in the boom time, for enhancing the mining companies' productivity and improving foreign workers' living conditions, such as housing, on the fields.

## China's ODI-related policy issues

The Chinese government has played a significant role in encouraging, assisting and supporting its firms to invest in other countries, particularly since 2002 (Zhang, 2009). Judging from China's exports and ODI since 2003, such efforts by the Chinese government have been very effective in promoting export and outward investment. However, there are still several issues that the Chinese government may need to address to help improve Chinese investment in the Australian minerals industry.

### Government approval procedure

Most Chinese ODI is still subject to approvals by Chinese authorities, including the National Development and Reform Commission (NDRC), Ministry of Commerce (MOC) or its subcommittees at the provincial level and the State Administration of Foreign Exchange (SAFE). The NDRC was established in 2003 primarily through transforming the former State Development Planning Commission (State Planning Commission before 1998). The main functions of NDRC include formulating and implementing strategies of national economic and social development, coordinating, formulating policies for the development of national economy and directing and coordinating the restructuring of the economic system (National Development and Reform Commission, n.d). It is the most powerful Commission at the ministerial level in China.

The reasons Chinese authorities approve ODI include: protecting state-owned assets, coordinating Chinese outward investments and controlling the outflow of foreign currency. These approval procedures were developed in the 1980s when most Chinese enterprises were state-owned, and foreign currency was very short in China. Thus, the former State Planning Commission played the role of state owner and made investment decisions. Foreign currency control was necessary at that time as China was in need of it for critical imports during the 1980s. Nevertheless the privatisation of the Chinese SOEs over the past three decades has resulted in the substantial reduction in the number of SOEs, and the rapid increase of privately owned firms in China. China had amassed over $2.5 trillion in foreign currency reserves by the end of June 2010. Therefore, the existing government approval processes could be further simplified as some of the previous functions are no longer necessary. In their place, the State-owned Assets Supervision and Administration Commission (SASAC) should be engaged more, as it is the state agency that supervises the performance of Chinese SOEs.

The existing Chinese government approval procedures affect Chinese ODI in that they could generate uncertainty for Chinese investors and the foreign companies targeted as they are quite complex and often opaque, thereby retarding the investment process and creating a negative perception among foreigners about the Chinese government's direct intervention in the ODI of its domestic firms. Chinese firms are not only competing against themselves, but also other foreign rivals when proposing their ODI, particularly in Australia. For example, Japanese and Korean firms are very active in investing in the Australian resources sector: Korea's POSCO and LS-Nikko's investment in Sandfire Resources Limited; the Korea Gas Corporation taking a stake in Santos's gas assets; Japanese Mitsui's investment in the Honeymoon Uranium Project in WA; Mitsubishi's $150 million investment in Rio Tinto's Kintyre uranium venture; and the latter's acquisition of the Saraji coal mine in Central Queensland for A$2.45 billion through its BMA alliance with BHPB (Wallace, 2010). The investments made by Japanese and Korean firms are, to a lesser degree or not at all, subject to their governments' approval. Thus these approvals can be given much more quickly and with less uncertainty compared with those made by Chinese firms. The Chinese government approvals involve a long and complex process, which can only put Chinese firms at a disadvantage.

*Improving the regulatory environment for FDI in China*

Reciprocity is very important in international relations. It is widely acknowledged that China has substantially liberated its investment regulatory environment (WTO, 2010). However, it still has many restrictions on FDI even after its recently revised FDI guidelines, which classified its industries into three categories for FDI: encouraged, restricted and prohibited (National Development and Reform Commission, 2007).

As discussed in Chapter 3, the Australian government has clearly expressed an opinion that investment should be two-way (Crean, 2010). Since 2006, Chinese investment in Australia has increased rapidly, and its ODI stock had reached to $33.55 billion by the close of

2008 (Ministry of Commerce, 2009), accounting for 1.82 per cent of Australia's total FDI stock (UNCTAD, 2010). Australia's FDI stock in China was A$6.33 billion at the same time and only accounted for 0.56 per cent of its total FDI stock (ABS, 2010).

While decisions to invest in a foreign country could be affected by many factors, including the host country's market potential, its growth rate, cheapness of labour, legal and regulatory environment and investors' preferences, Australian politicians and business communities are concerned about the restriction posed by the Chinese authorities on FDI and the opaqueness in enforcing FDI-related regulations (Larum, 2010). The relatively low level of Australia's FDI stock in China may be a reflection of Australian investors' preference for a similarity in market structure, legal system and culture.

The differences in FDI restrictions between Australia and China are outlined in a recent report by the OECD, which rated 43 countries' (all OECD members and other G-20 countries) restrictions on FDI using 4 aggregate measures in 14 industries (Kalinova, Palerm & Thomsen, 2010). Although the appropriateness of these 43 country groupings is questionable as China is a developing country, China was scored highest overall (the most restrictive) and also in the financial industries. Table 7.1 shows the FDI Restrictiveness Index of China and Australia in the four areas as reported by the OECD (Kalinova et al., 2010).

The FTA negotiations between Australia and China provide an important channel for both governments to discuss important issues on trade and investment. Between May 2005 and the end of June 2010, 15 rounds of FTA negotiations were conducted. In the latest rounds, there were still several sticking points for two countries. Australia requested China to open its domestic markets more, particularly in the financial and agricultural products sectors, while China stated that it would like the Australian government to have more transparent and fair processes in assessing Chinese ODI in Australia.

*Table 7.1*  FDI Index scores by country and type of measure

|  | Equity restrictions | Screening | Key personnel | Operational restrictions | Total FDI Index |
|---|---|---|---|---|---|
| Australia | 0.023 | 0.108 | 0.003 | 0.003 | 0.138 |
| China | 0.226 | 0.135 | 0.048 | 0.069 | 0.457 |
| All countries | 0.072 | 0.020 | 0.006 | 0.021 | 0.117 |

*Note*: 1 = closed, 0 = open.

Like most countries, the purpose for opening domestic industries for FDI is to serve the national interest. The Chinese government's priorities have been social, economic and political stabilities over the past decade, and these will remain so in the foreseeable future. On the one hand, China still needs FDI for its economic development, particularly those bringing in new technologies; on the other hand, the Chinese government is not likely to give in to foreign pressure to loosen its restrictions on FDI, given its huge economic and political power, coupled with its long-embedded social value of "face". Thus, it is understandable that China would be more likely to open its industries based on its own political, social and economic needs rather than external pressure, and in an incremental manner.

The Chinese agricultural and banking industries are very important to its national economy as they can affect China's social and economic stability. China has a population of 1.3 billion, with over 50 per cent living in rural areas. Thus, the performance of its agricultural industry is crucial to China's social stability. The banking industry has been regarded as the last "firewall" for protecting the Chinese economy from global influence. Therefore, a blanket and radical opening-up of Chinese agricultural and financial industries, including banking industries, is very unlikely to happen in the near future, as it does not serve the priorities of the Chinese government well.

Nevertheless China can open more of its industries for FDI. One of the concerns the Chinese government had regarding FDI was the need to protect domestic firms, particularly those operating in infancy industries. It was long acknowledged that the competitive capability of China's large firms was still weak in relation to the global giants in most sectors (Nolan, 2001). However, as the Chinese economy becomes more integrated into that of the world, and more Chinese domestic firms develop their competence enabling them to compete globally, more industries could be opened for FDI.

Other matters the Chinese governments can do to improve the regulatory framework include the clarification of FDI policies and regulations to make them more transparent and less complex to implement. These "grey areas" in the FDI policies and regulations impose many challenges for foreign business executives, including Australian, to invest and/or manage their investment projects in China (Larum, 2010). This situation could either deter or reduce foreign business investments in China because they do not want to carry their own risk, or they choose to operate at a lower risk range for their activities.

Finally, FDI policy and regulations could also consider the different needs of the various regions in China. China is a large, diverse country with varying degrees of economic development. While China's coastal areas have attracted the majority of FDI so far and are economically well-developed, more FDI could be lured to develop its western areas, which are still in critical need of investment to develop their economy.

# References

Albanese, T. (2009). *Rio Tinto presentation.* Paper presented at the Bank of America Merrill Lynch Global Metals and Mining Conference. Retrieved 15 November 2009 from http://www.riotinto.com/documents/RT_Merrill_Lynch_Tom_Albanese.PDF.

Anonymous. (2009a, 26 August). The China syndrome. *The Australian.* Retrieved from http://www.theaustralian.com.au/news/the-china-syndrome/story-e6frg72f-1111117299064.

Anonymous. (2009b, 6 November). Punting too far ahead is risky. *Australian Financial Review*, p. 58.

Anonymous. (2010, 27 January). (from BLOOMBERG), Iron prices tipped to soar as Chinese mills feel the pinch. *The Australian*, p. 34.

Ashby, I. (2010). *Delivering the iron ore growth program.* Retrieved 1 September 2010 from http://www.bhp.com.au/bbContentRepository/docs/ianAshbyPresentationMarch23.pdf.

ASX Corporate Governance Council. (2003). *Principles of good corporate governance and best practice recommendations.* Retrieved 1 July 2010, from http://asx.ice4.interactiveinvestor.com.au/ASX0301/Principles%20of%20Good%20Corporate%20Governance/EN/body.aspx?z=1&p=1&v=1&uid=#.

Australian Associated Press (AAP). (2009a, 10 July). China accuses Rio's exec of bribery during iron ore talks. *The Australian.* Retrieved 1 October 2009, from www.theaustralian.com.au/business/mining-energy/china-accuses-rio-exec-of-bribery-during-iron-ore-talks/story-e6frg9df-1225748212214.

Australian Associated Press (AAP). (2009b, 12 November). Stern Hu's imprisonment extended. *The Australian.* Retrieved from http://www.theaustralian.com.au/ news/world/china-to-keep- aussie-exec-spy-in-jail/ story-fn3dxix6-1225796986017.

Australian Associated Press (AAP). (2010a, 30 March). Government in damage control over Hu Case. *The Sydney Morning Herald.*

Australian Associated Press (AAP). (2010b). *Premier Colin Barnett wants MRRT magnetite exemption.* Retrieved 17 September 2010 from http://www.perthnow.com.au/business/news/premier-colin-barnett-wants-mrrt-magnetite-exemption/story-e6frg2qu-1225892257393.

Australian Bureau of Agricultural and Resource Economics (ABARE). (2010). *Australian commodities.* Retrieved 1 August 2010, from ABARE: http://www.abare.gov.au/publications_html/data/data/data.html.

Australian Bureau of Statistics (ABS). (2005). *1301.0 – Year book Australia, 2005: 100 years of change in Australian industry.* Retrieved 1 May 2010, from http://www.abs.gov.au/ausstats/abs@.nsf/Previousproducts/1301.0Feature%20Article212005?opendocument&tabname=Summary&prodno=1301.0&issue=2005&num=&view=.

Australian Bureau of Statistics (ABS). (2009a). *5220.0 – Australian national accounts: State accounts, 2008–09.* (Reissue). Canberra.

Australian Bureau of Statistics (ABS). (2009b). *5368.0 – International trade in goods and services.* Australia, November 2009. Retrieved 11 May 2010, from http://www.abs.gov.au/AUSSTATS/abs@.nsf/allprimarymainfeatures/635E0B33 88892065CA2576BE001166F4?opendocument.

Australian Bureau of Statistics (ABS). (2010a). *5206.0 – Australian national accounts: National income, expenditure and product,* June 2010. Retrieved 15 October 2010 from ABS: http://www.abs.gov.au/AUSSTATS/abs@.nsf/DetailsPage/ 5206.0Jun%202010?OpenDocument.

Australian Bureau of Statistics (ABS). (2010b). *5352.0 – International investment position, Australia: Supplementary statistics, Calendar year 2009.* Canberra.

Australian Bureau of Statistics (ABS). (2010). *5352.0 – International investment position, Australia: Supplementary statistics, Calendar year 2009.* Canberra.

Australian Foundation Investment Company (AFIC). (2009). *Chinalco–Rio deal may be conflict of interest: AFIC.* Retrieved 8 July 2010, from http://www.abc. net.au/news/stories/2009/03/16/2517728.htm.

Barnett, C. (2010a). *Committee for economic development of Australia.* Retrieved 8 October 2010, from http://www.premier.wa.gov.au/Ministers/Colin-Barnett/ documents/speeches/speechCBarnett_20100304.pdf.

Barrett, J. (2010b). WA to build new port for next boom. *The Australian Financial Review,* p. 25.

Baton, A. (2010, 8 February). China faces rising global backlash. *The Australian,* p. 25, 05 March 2010.

Behrmann, E. (2009, 26 May). Rio to consult ahead of any Chinalco deal changes. *Dowjones.* Retrieved from http://www.theaustralian.news.com.au/ business/story/0,,25540363-5017996,00.html.

Behrmann, E. (2010, 20 March). $200m profit for China's Minmetals. *The Australian.*

Berkovic, N. (2009, 18 March). Crean pressures China on trade. *The Australian.* Retrieved 1 October 2009, from www.theaustralian.com.au/politics/crean- pressure-china-on-trade/story-e6frgczf-1111119165155.

Buckley, P. J., & Casson, M. (1976). *The future of the multinational enterprises.* London: Macmillan.

Buckley, P. J., Clegg, J. L., Adam, R. C., Hinrich, V., Rhodes, M., & Zheng, P. (2008). Explaining China's outward FDI: An institutional perspective. In K. P. Sauvant (ed.), *The rise of transnational corproations from emerging markets: threat or opportunity?* (Chapter 7, pp. 107–157) Cheltenham: Edward Elgar.

Buckley, P. J., Clegg, L. J., Cross, A. R., Liu, X., Voss, H., & Zheng, P. (2007). The determinants of Chinese outward foreign direct investment. *Journal of International Business Studies, 38*(4), 499.

Buckley, P. J., Cross, A. R., Tan, H., Xin, L., & Voss, H. (2008). Historic and emergent trends in Chinese outward direct investment. *Management International Review, 48*(6), 715.

Burchell, D. (2010a, 22 March). Silence speaks volumes as Stern faces the music. *The Australian,* p. 16.

Burrell, A., Vaughan, M., & Krestser, A. D. (2009, 11–12 July). China spells out charges against Hu. *The Weekend Australian Financial Review.*

Business Council of Australia (2010). *A scorecard of state red tape reform.* Melbourne: Business Council of Australia.

Cadbury, A. (1992). *The financial aspects of corporate governance*. London: Gee and Co. Ltd.

Callick, R. (2009b, 14 March). China's leaders change their slogan. *The Australian*. Retrieved from http://www.theaustralian.com.au/business/news/china-hammers-new-theme/story-e6frg906-1111119128240.

Callick, R. (2009a, 2 March). Chinalco sponsors research in push to gain influence. *The Australian*.

Callick, R. (2009d, 2 April). We don't seek control: Beijing. *The Australian*.

Callick, R. (2009e, 26 November). China bubble puts recovery in doubt. *The Australian*, p. 21.

Callick, R. (2009c, 18 March). Pollies speak in Chinese whispers. *The Australian*. Retrieved from http://www.theaustralian.com.au/business/in-depth/pollies-chinese-whispers/story-e6frgah6-1111119163212.

Callick, R. (2010a, 2–3 January). China's century: On the march. *The Weekend Australian*.

Callick, R. (2010c, 26 February). Economists urges debate on China investment. *The Australian*, p. 28, from http://www.theaustralian.com.au/business/economist-urges-debate-on-china-investment/story-e6frg8zx-1225834506524.

Callick, R. (2010b, 15 February). Iron ore shake-up may improve relations. *The Australian*. Retrieved from http://www.theaustralian.com.au/business/opinion/iron-ore-shake-up-may-improve-relations/story-e6frg9if-1225830277043.

Callick, R. (2010d, 27–28 March). Truth, justice and the Chinese way of business. *The Weekend Australian*, p. 13.

Canning, S. (2009, 6 April). Chinese investors have local help. *The Australian*.

Caves, R. E., & Krause, L. B. (1984). *The Australian economy*. Sydney: George Allen & Unwin.

Chambers, M. (2009a, 2 May). Beijing cash "critical" to economic growth. *The Australian*.

Chambers, M. (2009b, 29 May). Chinalco reminds Rio of break fee to keep deal on track. *The Australian*.

Chambers, M. (2009c, 4 March). Investors warming to Chinalco: Rio. *The Australian*.

Chambers, M. (2009d, 17 March). Key shareholder concerned over China Inc influence – AFIC attacks Rio deal. *The Australian*.

Chambers, M. (2009e, 28 May). Patient du Plessis fends off Rio critics. *The Australian*. Retrieved from http://www.theaustralian.news.com.au/business/story/0,,25548168-5017996,00.html?from=marketwatch_rss.

Chambers, M. (2009f, 17 February). Rio fails to ease Chinalco doubts. *The Australian*.

Chambers, M. (2009g, 15 May). Rio plunges as Chinalco deal teeters. *The Australian*.

Chambers, M. (2009h, 18 February). Rio Tinto to Rudd government: Jobs are in danger. *The Australian*. Retrieved from http://www.theaustralian.com.au/business/news/rio-to-rudd-jobs-in-danger/story-e6frg90f-1111118882484.

Chambers, M. (2009i, 23 May). Time is short for deal on Chinalco. *The Australian*.

Chambers, M. (2009j, 5–6 December). BHP-Rio Pilbara deal on track. *The Weekend Australian*, p. 25.

Chambers, M. (2009k, 16 June). Combined mines, rail lines to save Rio, BHP $US10bn. *The Australian*. Retrieved 2 October 2009, from www.theaustralian.news.com.au/business/story/0,28124,25590989-643,00.html.

Chambers, M., & Berkovic, N. (2009, 13 February). Laws to change for $30bn Rio deal. *The Australian*.

Chambers, M., & Callick, R. (2009, 26 May). Chair en route for Rio's Chinese reckoning. *The Australian*.

Chambers, M., & Tasker, S.-J. (2009, 14 February). Rio Tinto facing hard sell – local investors not convinced by $30bn alliance with Chinalco. *The Australian*.

Chen, X., & Wang, J. (2010). The commercial models of Chinese firms' cross-boarder M&A. In X. Chen & Z. Li (eds), *Merger & acquisition and restructure of Chinese enterprises* (pp. 188–199). Beijing: China Development Press.

Chen, Z. (2010). *CITIC Pacific Mining's initial experience of love for Australian iron ore*. Retrieved 19 April 2010 http://magazine.caing.com/2010-04-18/100136268_1.html.

Child, J., & Rodrigues, S. B. (2005). The internationalization of Chinese firms: A case for theoretical extension? *Management and Organization Review, 1*(3), 381–410.

China Council for the Promotion of International Trade (2009). *Report on the survey of status and future intention of outward direct investment in Chinese firms*. Beijing.

China Mining Association (2009). *China may boost energy, mining aquisitions by half*. Retrieved 1 October 2010, from http://www.chinamining.org/Investment/2009-08-14/1250236621d28062.html.

Chong, F. (2009, 6 April). Rio chief's Chinalco sales pitch. *Dowjones*. Retrieved from http://www.theaustralian.news.com.au/business/story/0,28124,25293444-36418,00.html.

Clarke, T. (2009). Challenging the inevitability of the globalisation of corporate governance. In S. Young (ed.), *Comtemporary issues in international corporate governance* (pp. 207–224). Melbourne: Tilde University Press.

Coorey, P. (2009, 18 February). Costello challenges Rio deal. *The Sydney Morning Herald*. Retrieved from http://www.smh.com.au/national/costello-challenges-rio-deal-20090217-8aay.html.

Cornell, A. (2010, 26 March). A big Australian bows out, but he's not going quietly. *The Australian Financial Review*.

Costello, M., & Robertson, D. (2009, 20 February). Rio Tinto's independent directors test leading UK investors' appetite for rights issue. *The Times UK*. Retrieved from http://business.timesonline.co.uk/tol/business/industry_sectors/natural_resources/article5767048.ece.

Court, R. (2010, 28 May). States must stop Canberra stealing their wealth. *The Australian*, p. 16.

Crean, S. (2010). *Australia and China: Expanding our horizons*. Retrieved 15 October 2010 from http://www.trademinister.gov.au/speeches/2010/100621_australia_china.html.

Crean, S. (2010). *Australia and China: Expanding our horizons*. Retrieved 20 September 2010 from http://www.trademinister.gov.au/speeches/2010/100621_australia_china.html.

Cui, L., & Jiang, F. (2009). FDI entry mode choice of Chinese firms: A strategic behavior perspective. *Journal of World Business, 44*(4), 434.

Dampier Port Authority. (2009). *Annual report*. Perth Australia.

Deloitte. (2010). *Along path to corporate governance: 2010 China listed companies corporate governance survey*. Retrieved 17 September 2010 from http://www.deloitte.com.mx/documents/BoletinFactorChina/cn_cg_2010 ChinalistedcoCGsurvey_220410.pdf.

Deng, P. (2007). Investing for strategic resources and its rationale: The case of outward FDI from Chinese companies. *Business Horizons, 50*(1), 71.

Deng, P. (2009). Why do Chinese firms tend to acquire strategic assets in international expansion? *Journal of World Business, 44*(1), 74.

Department of Defence. (2009). The defence white paper: Australian Department of Defence.

Department of Foreign Affairs and Trade. (2009). *Australia's composition of trade 2008–09*. Retrieved 2 May 2010, from http://www.dfat.gov.au/geo/china/china_brief.html.

Department of Foreign Affairs and Trade. (2010). *People's Republic of China country brief*. Retrieved 19 September 2010, from http://www.dfat.gov.au/geo/china/china_brief.html.

Department of Immigration and Citizenship (DIAC). (2010). *Employer sponsored workers*. Retrieved 15 May 2010, from http://www.immi.gov.au/skilled/skilled-workers/.

Department of Innovation, Industry, Science and Research. (2010). *Australia's exports fact sheet*. Retrieved 21 September 2010, from www.innovation.gov.au/section/aboutdiisr/factsheets/pages/australia'sexportsfactsheet.aspx.

Department of Mines and Petroleum WA. (2010a). *Quick resource facts*. Retrieved 1 September 2010, from http://www.dmp.wa.gov.au/7846.aspx.

Department of Mines and Petroleum WA. (2010b). *Annual report*. Perth.

Department of Mines and Petroleum WA. (2010c). *Western Australia versus Australia versus world*. http://www.dmp.wa.gov.au/1521.aspx#1557.

Dobson, L. (2010, 15–16 May). The tug of war over tax: What was the government thinking. *The Weekend Australian Financial Review*, pp. 24–25.

Doggett, T. (2010). *U.S. aims to end China's rare earth metals monopoly*. Retrieved 13 October 2010, from http://www.reuters.com/article/idUSTRE68T68T20101001.

Drysdale, P., & Findlay, C. (2008). *Chinese foreign direct investment in Australia: Policy issues for the resource sector*. Retrieved 15 September 2009 from http://www.eastasiaforum.org/wp-content/uploads/2008/09/drysdale_and_findlay_chinese_fdi_300808.pdf.

Dunning, J. H. (2001). The eclectic (OLI) paradigm of international production: Past, present and future. *International Journal of the Economics of Business, 8*(2), 173–190.

Durie, J. (2009, 1 April). Sale puts rocket up Mac satellites. *The Australian*.

Dwyer, F. R., Schurr, P. H., & Oh, S. (1987). Developing buyer–seller relationships. *Journal of Marketing, 51*(2), 11–27.

Earl, G. (2007, October). Sing & tell. *The Australian Financial Review Magazine*, pp. 96–89, 91–92.

Editor. (2009, 18 December). Dithering over Chinese capitals. *The Australian Financial Review*, p. 50.

Environmental Protection Authority (EPA). (2009). *EPA Reports 1321 & 1322 – Karara & Mungada Mines in the Midwest*. Retrieved 5 January 2010, from http://www.epa.wa.gov.au/article.asp?ID=2934&area=News&CID=18&Category=Media+Statements.

Fitzgerald, B. (2009a, 6 June). Chinalco in the cold as Rio, BHP strike deal. *The Sydney Morning Herald*. Retrieved 2 October 2009, from http://business.smh.com.au/business/chinalco-in-the-cold-as-rio-bhp-strike-deal-20090605-byjb.html.

Fitzgerald, B. (2009b, 3 March). Chinalco and Rio chiefs fly in to sell $30bn China splurge. *The Sydney Morning Herald*. Retrieved from http://www.theage.com.au/business/chinalco-and-rio-chiefs-fly-in-to-sell-30bn-china-splurge-20090302-8mg3.html.

Fitzgerald, B., & Sharp, A. (2009, 16 October). Canberra accused over BHP lobbying. *The Australian*.

Fitzgerald, R. (2010, 22–23 May). Tax suggest we need a change of government. *The Weekend Australian*, p. 7.FMG Group (2009). *Investor update: London 9–10 June 2009*. Retrieved 1 September 2010, from http://www.fmgl.com.au/IRM/Company/ShowPage.aspx?CPID=1840.

Foreign Investment Policy Division. (2009). *Summary of Australia's foreign investment policy*. Retrieved 21 January 2010, from http://www.firb.gov.au/content/_downloads/Australia's_Foreign_Investment_Policy_September_2009_v2.pdf.

Foreign Investment Review Board (FIRB). (2008). *Annual Report 2006–07*. Canberra.

Foreign Investment Review Board (FIRB). (2009). *Annual Report 2007–08*. Canberra.

Foreign Investment Review Board (FIRB). (2010a). *Annual Report 2008–09*. Canberra.

Foreign Investment Review Board (FIRB). (2010b). *Foreign investment policy*. Retrieved 31 July 2010, from http://www.firb.gov.au/content/_downloads/Australia's_Foreign_Investment_Policy.pdf.

Fraedrich, J. P., & Bateman, C. R. (1996). Transfer pricing by multinational marketers: Risky business. *Business Horizons, 39*(Jan–Feb), 17–22.

Franklin, M., & Berkovic, N. (2009, 19 February). AWU claims Rio "blackmailing" Rudd on Chinalco. *The Australian*.

Freed, J. (2009, 5 June). Mining giant digs itself out of a hole after shareholder revolt. *The Sydney Morning Herald*. Retrieved 2 October 2009, from http://business.smh.com.au/business/mining-giant-digs-itself-out-of-a-hole-after-shareholder-revolt-20090605-bxde.html.

Freed, J., & Garnaut, J. (2009, 6 June). Exit the dragon. *The Sydney Morning Herald*. Retrieved from http://www.smh.com.au/business/exit-the-dragon-20090605-byk0.html.

Frith, B. (2009a, 4 February). Alcan blunder: Rio's deal with Chinalco will only compound earlier bungles. *The Australian*.

Frith, B. (2009b, 2 April). Fortescue decision has implications for Chinalco sphere of influence. *The Australian*.

Frith, B. (2009c, 17 July). Keep politics out of FIRB decisions. *The Australian*, p. 18.

Fuhrmann, K. (2010). *CITIC scraps power station contract*. Retrieved 18 October 2010, from http://www.wabusinessnews.com.au/en-story/1/84310/CITIC-scraps-power-station-contract.

Garnaut, J. (2009, 15 October). How BHP scuppered China Inc. *The Sydney Morning Herald*. Retrieved from http://www.smh.com.au/business/how-bhp-scuppered-china-inc-20091014-gxhs.html?autostart=1.

Geoff, D. (2009). The not so hidden hand of the state. *Financial Times*, p. 2. Retrieved from http://proquest.umi.com/pqdweb?did=1870089371&Fmt=7& clientId=20923&RQT=309&VName=PQD.

Geoscience Australia. (2007). *Sustaining the mineral resources industry – Overcoming the tyranny of depth*. Retrieved 15 September 2009 from http://www.abs. gov.au/ausstats/abs@.nsf/Latestproducts/1301.0Feature%20Article18012008? opendocument&tabname=Summary&prodno=1301.0&issue=2008&num=& view=.

Geoscience Australia. (2009). *Australia's identified mineral resources 2009*. Retrieved 17 March 2010, from http://www.ga.gov.au/image_cache/GA16013.pdf.

Geraldton Port Authority. (2009). *Annual report*. Perth Australia.

Globerman, S., & Shapiro, D. (2009). Economic and strategic considerations surrounding Chinese FDI in the United States. *Asia Pacific Journal of Management, 26*, 163–183.

Grant, R., Butler, B., Hung, H., & Orr, S. (2011). *Contemporary strategic management*. Singapore: John Wiley & Sons.

Guy, R. (2009, 13–14 June). The old booming story. *The Weekend Australian Financial Review*, pp. 22–23.

Håkansson, H. (1982). *International marketing and purchasing of industrial goods: An interaction approach*. Sydney: John Wiley & Sons, Ltd.

Hanson, D., Dowling, O. J., Hitt, M., Ireland, R. D., & Hoskisson, R. E. (2008). *Strategic management: Competitiveness & globalisation*. Melbourne: Cengage Learning.

He, W., & Lyles, M. A. (2008). China's outward foreign direct investment. *Business Horizons, 51*(6), 485.

Hewett, J. (2009a, 27 May). Chinalco limits "worthless". *The Australian*.

Hewett, J. (2009b, 6 June). Rudd will still take some flak over Chinalco. *The Australian*.

Hewett, J. (2009c, 21 February). Sorting out the miner kerfuffle. *The Australian*.

Hewett, J. (2009d, 14–15 November). China ambassador busy mending fences. *The Weekend Australian*, p. 34.

Hewitt, J. (2010, 31 March). Nervous companies to tread carefully. *The Australian*, p. 35.

Hewett, J., & Tasker, S.-J. (2010, 3–4 April). BHP treads softly on ore price revolution. *The Weekend Australian*, p. 21.

Hilmersson, M., & Jansson, H. (2009, 1–2 October). *Collective internationalisation process of small and medium sized enterprises from China*. Paper presented at the 3rd China Goes Global, Harvard University, Boston.

Hofstede, G. (1980). *Culture's consequences: International differences in work-related values*. Beverly Hills, CA: Sage Publications.

Huang, X., Austin, I., Zhang, Z., & Grainger, S. (2009, 30 September–2 October). *Chinese outward direct investment in the Australian resources sector: Benefits, concerns and policy implication*. Paper presented at China Goes Global, Harvard University, Boston.

International copper study group. (2009). *The world copper factbook 2009*. Retrieved 1 August 2010, from http://www.icsg.org/index.php?option=com_ content&task=view&id=22&Itemid=26.

International Energy Agency. (2010). *Key world energy statistics*. Retrieved 1 October 2010, from http://www.iea.org/textbase/nppdf/free/2010/key_stats_ 2010.pdf.

International Monetary Fund. (2010). World economic outlook database, April 2010. Retrieved 17 September 2010, from http://www.imf.org/external/data.htm.

Joint Ore Reserves Committee (JORC). (2004). *The JORC code: 2004 edition.* Retrieved 15 September 2009 from http://www.jorc.org/pdf/jorc2004web_v2.pdf.

Jury, A. (2009, 10 July). Rio enmeshed in Chinese puzzle. *The Australian Financial Review*, p. 60.

Kalinova, B., Palerm, A., & Thomsen, S. (2010). OECD's FDI Restrictiveness Index: 2010 Update OECD Working Papers on International Investment, No. 2010/3. Retrieved 1 September 2010from www.oecd.org/daf/investment.

Kang, T. G. (2010). Assessing China's approach to regional multilateral security. *Australian Journal of International Affairs, 64*(4), 381–405.

Keenan, R. (2009, 2 March). Chinalco says it doesn't want control of Rio Tinto Group. *Bloomberg.* Retrieved from http://www.bloomberg.com/apps/news?pid=20601089&refer=china&sid=a.RmIPbH3SDs.

Kehoe, J., Wyatt, S., & Ear, G. (2010, 21 May). WA mines $1bn resource windfall. *The Australian Financial Review*, pp. 1, 14.

Kelly, P. (2009, 15 July). Mixed messages on China leave Rudd exposed. *The Australian*, p. 12.

Kelly, P. (2010, 22–23 May). Trust lost in pivotal super tax stand-off. *The Weekend Australian*, p. 11.

Kerin, J. (2010, 19 March). All eyes on Hu trial: Rudd. *The Australian Financial Review*.

Kitney, G. (2010, 25 February). China offers vital funds, says Crean. *The Australian Financial Review*, p. 8.

Klinger, P. (2009, 13 February). China Inc move to send shudder though ore negotiators. *The West Australian*, p. 45.

Klinger, P. (2010). Axed contract sparks Sino chaos in Pilbara. *The West Australian*.

Korporaal, G. (2009, 13 November). China figures large for Aussie holding a loan. *The Australian*, p. 32.

Kretser, A. D., & Vaughan, M. (2009, 11–12 July). Rio's China nightmare. *The Weekend Australian Financial Review*, p. 22.

Krugman, P. (1980). Scale economies, product differentiation, and the pattern of trade. *The American Economic Review, 70*(5), 950.

Krugman, P. (2009). The increasing returns revolution in trade and geography. *The American Economic Review, 99*(3), 561.

Larum, J. (2010, 17 August). *Into the dragon's den: Australian investment into China.* Retrieved 15 Septemberfrom http://www.lowyinstitute.org/.

Lattemann, C. (2009). Corporate governance in Chinese firms. In S. Young (ed.), *Contemporary issues in international corporate governance* (pp. 184–203). Melbourne: Tilde University Press.

Lattermann, C. (2009). Corporate governance in Chinese firms. In S. Young (ed.), *Comtemporary issues in international corporate governance* (pp. 184–203). Melbourne: Tilde University Press.

Litterick, D. (2009, 13 May). Rio's Tom Albanese and BHP's Marius Kloppers at mining conference. *The Telegraph UK.* Retrieved from http://www.telegraph.co.uk/finance/newsbysector/energy/2789874/Rios-Tom-Albanese-and-BHPs-Marius-Kloppers-at-mining-conference.html.

Liu, J., & McDonald, T. (2010). *China: growth, unbanisation and mineral resource demand*. Retrieved 21 October 2010, from www.treasury.gov.au/.../05_China_-_growth_urbanisation_and_mineral_resource_demand.rtf.

Liu, J., & Tan, B. (2004). The competitive advantages of Chinese SMEs. *Overseas Investment, 12*, 75–77.

Lynas Corporation. (2009). *CNMC trabsaction update*. Retrieved 1 December 2009, from http://www.lynascorp.com/content/upload/files/Announcements/2009/FIRB_advice_announcement_240909_v5_765890.pdf.

Macdonald-Smith, A. (2010, 9 September). China demand buoys export returns. *The Australian Financial Review*, p. 7.

Maher, K., & Pulizzi, H. J. (2010, 1 January). US votes against cheap Chinese steel. *The Australian*, p. 24.

Maiden, M. (2009a, 16 October). Time for Australia to spell out consistent rules on China Inc. *The Sydney Morning Herald*. Retrieved from http://www.smh.com.au/business/time-for-australia-to-spell-out-consistent-rules-on-china-inc-20091015-gz77.html.

Maiden, M. (2009b, 23 April). With a fresh face, can BHP and Rio get close again? *The Age*. Retrieved from http://www.theage.com.au/business/with-a-fresh-face-can-bhp-and-rio-get-close-again-20090422-afhf.html.

Mathieson, C. (2009a, 5 June). $24.4bn Chinalco deal with Rio Tinto is dead. *The Australian*.

Mathieson, C. (2009b, 6 June). Times change, and now Chinalco can blame it on Rio. *The Australian*.

Mayne, S. (2007). *Time for Rio Tinto to call Australia home*. Retrieved 4 November 2009, from http://www.crikey.com.au/2007/09/28/time-for-rio-tinto-to-call-australia-home/.

McCrann, T. (2009, 13–14 June). Chinalco snub sets new agenda. *The Weekend Australian*, p. 35.

Mercer, P. (2010, 25 September). *Australia, China conduct live-fire naval exercise in yellow sea*. Retieved from http://www.voanews.com/english/news/Australia-China-Conduct-Live-Fire-Naval-Exercise-in-Yellow-Sea-103780194.html.

Meredith, D., & Dyster, B. (1999). *Australia in the global economy: Continuity and change*. Cambridge, UK: Cambridge University Press.

Metzle, J. F. (2010, 9 April). China must do more as a big power. *The Australian*, p. 12.

Meyer, K. E., Estrin, S., Bhaumik, S. K., & Peng, M. W. (2009). Institutions, resources, and entry strategies in emerging economies. *Strategic Management Journal, 30*, 61–80.

Miles, M. B., & Huberman, A. M. (1994). *Qualitative Data Analysis: An Expanded Sourcebook*. Thousand Oaks, CA: Sage Publications, Inc.

Miller, J. W., & Walker, M. (2010, 7 January). China overtakes Germany as world's top goods exporter, *The Australian*, p. 18.

Mills, M. (2010). *WA Govt. gives Anketell deepwater port the green light*. Retrieved 1 September 2010, from http://www.miningaustralia.com.au/news/wa-govt-gives-anketell-deepwater-port-the-green-li.

Milne, G. (2009, 2 March). PM must decide whether he is for or against free trade. *The Australian*.

Ministry of Commerce (Producer). (2008). *2007 Statistical bulletin of China's outward foreign direct investment*. Retrieved 1 September 2009 from http://fec.mofcom.gov.cn/tjzl/jwtz/39067.shtml.

Ministry of Commerce (MOC). (2009). *2008 Statistical bulletin of China's outward foreign direct investment.*

Ministry of Commerce (MOC). (2009). *2008 Statistical bulletin of China's outward foreign direct investment.*

Ministry of Commerce (MOC). (2010). *2009 Statistical bulletin of China's outward foreign direct investment.*

Ministry of Commerce (MOC). (2010). *2009 Statistical bulletin of China's outward foreign direct investment.*

Mitchell, A. (2010, 15–16 May). China's leaders running to keep ahead. *The Weekend Australian Financial Review*, p. 46.

Molinski, D., & Lyons, J. (2010, 20 April). China lends $22bn to Venezuela. *The Australian*, p. 26.

Moncrief, M. (2008, 18 February). Swan gives foreign governments a peek at FIRB guidelines. *The Age*. Retrieved from http://www.theage.com.au/business/swan-gives-foreign-governments-a-peek-at-firb-guidelines-20080217-1snl.html.

Murdoch, S. (2009, 1 June). Rio chairman cuts short his Chinalco round. *The Australian*.

Murphy, M. (2009). Rio's London rights issue brings in $14.5bn. *The Sydney Morning Herald*. Retrieved from http://www.smh.com.au/business/rios-london-rights-issue-brings-in-145b-20090702-d6mi.html.

National Bureau of Statistics of China. (2009). *Second national economic census*. Retrieved 1 August 2010, from http://www.stats.gov.cn/tjfx/fxbg/t20091225_402610155.htm.

National Bureau of Statistics of China. (2010). *Statistical yearbook of China*. Retrieved 5 August 2010 from http://www.stats.gov.cn/tjshujia/jptj/t20090921_402588672.htm.

National Bureau of Statistics of China. (2011). *Statistical Communiqué of the People's Republic of China on the 2010 National Economic and Social Development*. Retrieved 30 March 2011, from http://www.stats.gov.cn/tjgb/ndtjgb/qgndtjgb/t20110228_402705692.htm.

National Development and Reform Commission. (2007). *Catalogue of Industries for Guiding Foreign Investment (Revised 2007). No.57*. Retrieved 1 May 2010, from www.china-tax.net/.

National Development and Reform Commission. (n.d). *Main Functions of the NDRC*. Retrieved 1 August 2010, from http://en.ndrc.gov.cn/mfndrc/default.htm.

Needham, K. (2010, 30 March). Confidence in China shaken by Hu's "tough" jail sentence. *Sydney Morning Herald*.

Nolan, P. (2001). *China and the global economy*. Basingstoke, UK: Palgrave.

Nolan, P. (2002). China and the global business revolution. *Cambridge Journal of Economics, 26*(1), 119–137.

O'Brien, A. (2009, 8 December). Huge projects start moving. *The Australian*, p. 20.

O'Malley, S. (2009, 26 May). China, Rio move to assure Australia over Chinalco deal. *AAP*. Retrieved from http://www.perthnow.com.au/business/china-rio-move-to-assure-australia-over-chinalco-deal/story-e6frg2qc-1225716618649.

Onselen, P. V. (2010, 24 March). National interest must prevail over capital desires. *The Australian*, p. 40.

Onstad, E. (2008). *Vale to spend $4.4 bln on iron ore expansion in '08*. Retrieved 1 July 2010, from http://www.reuters.com/article/idUSL1358106720080513.

Organisation for Economic Co-operation and Development (OECD) (2004). *OECD Principles of corporate governance.* Retrieved 15 September 2009 from http://www.oecd.org/dataoecd/32/18/31557724.pdf.

Oster, S., & Carew, R. (2009b, 17 April). *The Wall Street Journal* published in *The Australian.* p. 20.

Parnell, S. (2009, 19 February). We can't control job cuts. *The Australian.* Retrieved from http://www.theaustralian.com.au/news/nation/we-cant-control-job-cuts-says-bligh/story-e6frg6oo-1111118896126.

Peng, M. W., Wang, D. Y., & Jiang, Y. (2008). An institution-based view of international business strategy: A focus on emerging economies. *Journal of International Business Studies, 39*, 920–936.

Perlmutter, H. V. (1969). The tortuous evolution of the multinational corporation. *Columbia Journal of World Business*, (4), 9–18.

Poon, T. (2010, 11 March). Chinese exports soar. *The Australian*, p. 19.

Port Hedland Port Authority (2009). *Annual report.*

Rabinovitch, S. (2009, 26 May). *Chinalco to consider changes to Rio deal.* Retrieved 23 October 2009, from http://www.reuters.com/article/innovationNews/idUSTRE54P0IZ20090526?pageNumber=1&virtualBrandChannel=0.

Restall, H. (2010, 31 March). Broken trust put steel in China's laws. *The Australian*, p. 9.

Richardson, C. (2010, 6 August). China ties still contain risks as well as rewards. *The Australian Financial Review*, p. 59.

Rio dumps Chinalco for BHP tie-up (2009, 5 June). *The Sydney Morning Herald.* Retrieved 2 October 2009, from http://business.smh.com.au/business/rio-dumps-chinalco-for-bhp-tieup-20090605-bxw9.html.

Rio Tinto (2007). *Rio Tinto welcomes Put up or Shut up deadline.* Retrieved 15 May, 2010, from http://www.riotinto.com/media/18435_media_releases_6975.asp.

Rio Tinto. (2009a). *Rio Tinto announces pioneering strategic partnership with Chinalco.* Rio Tinto.

Rio Tinto. (2009b). *Expanded ports will keep pace with output.* Retrieved 1 September 2010 from http://www.riotinto.com/whoweare/who_we_are_features_6105.asp.

Rio Tinto. (2010a). *Rio Tinto and Chinalco subsidiary Chalco sign binding agreement for Simandou iron ore project joint venture.* Retrieved 1 September 2010, from http://www.riotinto.com/media/18435_media_releases_19491.asp.

Rio Tinto. (2010b). *Rio Tinto to invest US$230 million to expand Pilbara iron ore capacity to 230 Mt/a.* Retrieved 1 September 2010, from http://www.riotinto.com/media/18435_media_releases_19600.asp.

Robertson, D., & Power, H. (2009, 12 February). BHP Billiton to gatecrash Chinalco's Rio Tinto bailout. *The Times UK.* Retrieved from http://business.timesonline.co.uk/tol/business/industry_sectors/natural_resources/article5712389.ece.

Ryan, C. (2009, 13–14 June). Can China's recovery hold?. *The Weekend Australian Financial Review* pp. 30–31.

Sainsbury, M. (2009a, 23 March). Minister flock to cement China ties. *The Australian.*

Sainsbury, M. (2009b, 4–5 April). Step up uranium export: Ferguson. *The Weekend Australian*, p. 35.

Sainsbury, M. (2009c, 8 April). Stern Hu will not appeal guilty verdict. *The Australian*. Retrieved 8 October 2010, from http://www.theaustralian. com.au/news/nation/stern-hu-will-not-appeal-guilty-verdict/story-e6frg6nf-1225851548205.

Sainsbury, M. (2009d, 23 April). Rio's China deal will save jobs, says Chinalco. *The Australian*. Retrieved from http://www.theaustralian.com.au/business/news/rio-deal-to-save-jobs/story-e6frg906-1225702004339.

Sainsbury, M. (2009e, 8 June). Foreign investment review board methods cause confusion. *The Australian*. Retrieved 2 October 2009, from www.theaustralian. news.com.au/story/0,25197,25601327-5014019,00.html.

Sainsbury, M. (2009f, 12 June). Chinalco sweet as buy-in goes sour. *The Australian*.

Sainsbury, M. (2009g, 18–19 July). China's crackdown with fist of steel. *The Weekend Australian*, p. 28.

Sainsbury, M. (2009h, 4 November). Beijing wants to invest more in Australia. *The Australian*, p. 44. Retrieved 5 November 2009, from www. theaustralia.com.au/business/news/beijing-wants-to-invest-more-in-australia/story-e6frg90f-1225794082525.

Sainsbury, M. (2009i, 14 December). Home consumption key to China expansion. *The Australian*, p. 26.

Sainsbury, M. (2010a, 9–10 January). Spot market may sink contracts. *The Weekend Australian*, p. 22.

Sainsbury, M. (2010b, 22 January). Beijing tightens rein on growth surge. *The Australian*, p. 19.

Sainsbury, M. (2010c, 29 January). Rio Tinto execs await "rule of law". *The Australian*. Retrieved 8 October 2010, from http://www. theaustralian.com.au/business/legal-affairs/rio-tinto-execs-await-rule-of-law/story-e6frg97x-1225824477440.

Sainsbury, M. (2010d, 17 March). Chinese tariff threat in iron price war. *The Australian*, p. 35.

Sainsbury, M. (2010e, 18 March). China to tackle Pilbara merger. *The Australian*, p. 19.

Sainsbury, M. (2010f, 20 August). Global role for Minmetals arm: Chinalco. *The Australian*.

Sainsbury, M., & Tasker, S.-J. (2009, 6 February). Labor link to Chinalco lobbyist. *The Australian*. Retrieved from http://www.hawkerbritton.com/hawker-britton-media/media-2009/labor-ink-chinalco-lobbyists.htm.

Sauvant, K. (2005). New sources of FDI: The BRICs. Outward FDI from Brazil, Russia, India and China. *Journal of World Investment and Trade*, 6, 639–709.

Schwab, K. (2009). *The global competitiveness report 2009–2010*. Geneva, Switzerland: World Economic Forum.

Shaw Research. (2009). *Iron Ore: Price Hike in 2010*. Retrieved 1 July 2010, from www.shawstock.com.au.

Sheridan, G. (2009a, 26 March). China's iron-fisted PR. *The Australian*.

Sheridan, G. (2009b, 26 February). Say no to Chinalco. *The Australian*.

Sheridan, G. (2009c, 10 July). Big risk in nasty business. *The Australian*. Retrieved 1 October 2009, from www.theaustralian.news.com.au/stry/0,25197,25759154-5013460,00.html.

Sheridan, G. (2010, 1 April). Appeasement gets use nowhere with bellicose Beijing. *The Australian*, p. 12.

Smith, B. (1978). The Japanese connection. In P. Hastings & A. Farran (eds), *Australia's resources future*. Melbourne: Nelson.

Smith, S. (2009). *Australia-China relations: A long-term view*. Retrieved 1 March 2010, from http://www.foreignminister.gov.au/speeches/2009/091026_aus_china.html.

Stevens, M. (2009a, 26 March). ACCC lobs grenade as Chinalco gets nod. *The Australian*.

Stevens, M. (2009b, 3 February). Albanese for best of worst outcome. *The Australian*.

Stevens, M. (2009c, 27 March). BHP's mystery dash for cash. *The Australian*.

Stevens, M. (2009d, 3 November). China rejected Pilbara invite. *The Australian*. Retrieved from http://www.theaustralian.news.com.au/business/story/0,,26296395-30538,00.html.

Stevens, M. (2009e, 1 April). Michelmore on verge of reverse in fortunes. *The Australian*.

Stevens, M. (2009f, 13 February). Miner's abacus could be faulty. *The Australian*.

Stevens, M. (2010a, 30–31 January). Miners see red as Rudd mulls over rent tax. *The Weekend Australian*, p. 25.

Stevens, M. (2010b, 24 March). Secret Rio probe cleared company left Hu in doubt. *The Australian*, p. 1.

Stutchbury, M. (2010a, 8–9 May). Mine the boom, share the loot. *The Weekend Australian*, p. 12.

Stutchbury, M. (2010b, 9 February). West Struggles to Adjust to China's Rapid Growth. *The Australian*, p. 12.

Stutchbury, M. (2010c, 10 November). Deficit masked by coal iron ore. *The Australian*, pp. 1, 5.

Swan, W. (2008a, 21 September). *Foreign investment approval: Sinosteel's interests in Murchison Metals Ltd*. Retrieved 1 October 2009, from http://www.treasurer.gov.au/DisplayDocs.aspx?doc=pressreleases/2008/100. htm& pageID=003&min=wms&Year=2008&DocType=0.

Swan, W. (2008b, 4 July). *Australia, China and this Asian century*. Speech to the Australia–China Business Council, Melbourne. Retrieved from http://ministers.treasury.gov.au/DisplayDocs.aspx?doc=speeches/2009/017.htm&pageID=005&min=wms&Year=2009&DocType=1.

Swan, W. (2009a, 10 December). *Address to the global foundation*. Retrieved from http://ministers.treasury.gov.au/DisplayDocs.aspx?doc=speeches/2009/017.htm&pageID=005&min=wms&Year=2009&DocType=1.

Swan, W. (2009b, 14 July). *Australia, China and the global recession*. Address to the ANU China Update Conference. Retrieved from http://ministers.treasury.gov.au/DisplayDocs.aspx?doc=speeches/2009/017.htm&pageID=005&min=wms&Year=2009&DocType=1.

Swan, W. (2009c, 12 Febuary). *Amendments to foreign acquisition and takeovers act*. Retrieved 23 October 2009, from http://ministers.treasury.gov.au/DisplayDocs.aspx?doc=pressreleases/2009/017.htm&pageID=003&min=wms&Year=&DocType=.

Tasker, S.-J. (2009a, 4 April). Albanese flies in to shore up Chinalco deal. *The Australian*.

Tasker, S.-J. (2009b, 24 March). BHP fears China's price power. *The Australian*.

Tasker, S.-J. (2009c, 2 April). Crisis forced Rio Tinto into China deal: CEO. *The Australian.*

Tasker, S.-J. (2009d, 27 March). Rio has plan B if China bid falls. *The Australian.*

Tasker, S.-J. (2009e, 15 April). Rio Tinto fixed bond issue draws investors. *The Australian.* Retrieved from http://www.theaustralian.news.com.au/business/story/0,28124,25337296-5005200,00.html.

Tasker, S.-J. (2009f, 24 April). Swan rubber-stamps China's OZ takeover. *The Australian.*

Tasker, S.-J. (2009g, 13 February). BHP battles to block interloper. *The Australian,* p. 18.

Tasker, S.-J. (2009h, 16 December). Higher demand for iron ore expected. *The Australian,* p. 20.

Tasker, S.-J. (2010a, 26 March). ACCC widens BHP–Rio probe with fears of price collusion. *The Australian.* Retrieved 22 October 2010, from http://www.theaustralian.com.au/business/accc-widens-bhp-rio-probe-with-fears-of-price-collusion/story-e6frg8zx-1225845525361.

Tasker, S.-J. (2010b, 30 March 30). Rio reviews its systems after Hu sentenced. *The Australian,* p. 19.

Tasker, S.-J. (2010c, 19 March). OZ saviour Minmetals back on the acquisition trail. *The Australian.*

Tasker, S.-J., & Mathieson, C. (2009, 1 April). Chinalco secures cut-price loans. *The Australian.*

Taylor, L. (2009a, 7 April). Majority back push to block Chinalco bid. *The Australian.*

Taylor, L. (2009b, 28–29 March). China mine bid fails security test. *The Weekend Australian,* p. 12. Retrieved from http://www.theaustralian.com.au/news/china-mine-bid-for-oz-minerals-fails-security-test/story-fn2py0vz-1225715380125.

Taylor, L., & Sainsbury, M. (2009, 1 April). Fortescue nod paves way for Chinalco. *The Australian.*

Thompson, P., & Macklin, R. (2009). *The big fella: The rise and rise of BHP Billtion.* South Australia: William Heinmaan.

Tingle, L. (2009, 13–14 June). Canberra wary of Beijing, Tokyo ire. *The Weekend Australian Financial Review,* p. 3.

Treadgold, T. (2010a, 8 July). Iron ore the odd one out in new tax regime. *WA Business News.*

Treadgold, T. (2010b, 22 July). Tax bogeyman may end magnetite dream. *WA Business News.*

The Treasury of Australian Government. (n.d). *Foreign investment policy in Australia – A brief history and recent developments.* Retrieved 1 May 2010, from http://www.treasury.gov.au/documents/195/pdf/round5.pdf.

Turnbull, M. (2009). *Block Chinalco's Rio deal,* Turnbull says. Retrieved 7 July 2010, from http://www.smh.com.au/business/block-chinalcos-rio-deal-turnbull-says-20090501-aq35.html.

United Nations (2010). *World urbanization prospects: The 2009 revision population database.* Retrieved 25 October 2010 from http://esa.un.org/wup2009/unup/index.asp?panel=1.

United Nations Conference on Trade and Development (UNCTAD). (2010a). *Interactive database: Division on Invetsment and Enterprise.* Retrieved 17 September 2010, from http://www.unctad.org/Templates/Page.asp?intItemID=3199&lang=1.

United Nations Conference on Trade and Development (UNCTAD). (2010b, 1 July). *World investment report*. New York and Geneva: UN.

Uren, D. (2009a, 10 December). Trade balance deteriorates as China cuts mineral imports. *The Australian*, p. 2.

Uren, D. (2009b, 23 February). Bars on foreign deals too clumsy. *The Australian*.

Uren, D. (2010, 10 November). Inflation fear in "full" economy. *The Australian*, pp. 1, 4.

Uren, D., & Sainsbury, M. (2009, 16 March). Crean warns China to let market determine the outcome of iron ore price negotiations. *The Australian*, pp. 19–20.

U.S. Geological Survey (2004). *U.S. GEOLOGICAL SURVEY MINERALS YEARBOOK—2004. Retrieved May 1, 2010, from http://minerals.usgs.gov/minerals/pubs/country/2004/chmyb04.pdf* United Nations Conference on Trade and Development (UNCTAD) (2010a). *Interactive database: Division on investment and enterprise.* Retrieved 17 September 2010, from http://www.unctad.org/Templates/Page.asp?intItemID=3199&lang=1.

Vaughan, M., Krestser, A. D., & Crowe, D. (2009, 10 July). China says Rio executive is guilty. *The Australian Financial Review*, p. 1.

Vivoda, V. (2009). China challenges global capitalism. *Australian Journal of International Affairs, 63*(1), 22–40.

Wallace, R. (2010, 8 April). Japanese investment in Australia slips under the radar. *The Australian*.

Wang, K. Y., Zhang, X., & Goodfellow, R. (2003). *China business culture: Strategies for success.* Singapore: Talisman Publishing PTE LTD.

White, H. (2010, 4–5 September). Our role in Asia's superpower shuffle. *The Australian*, p. 5.

Wighton, D. (2009, 24 March). Out, but BHP will still be counting. *The Times UK*. Retrieved from http://business.timesonline.co.uk/tol/business/columnists/article5963254.ece.

Wilkins, T. (2010). The new "Pacific Century" and the rise of China: An international relations perspective. *Australian Journal of International Affairs, 64*(4), 381–405.

Williams, F. (2009a, 1 June). Rio boss rushes home. *The Herald Sun*. Retrieved from http://www.heraldsun.com.au/business/rio-boss-rushes-home/story-e6frfh4f-1225719171447.

Williams, F. (2009b, 26 May). Rio Tinti rethinks Chinalco deal. *The Courier Mail*. Retrieved from http://www.news.com.au/couriermail/story/0,,25543077-3122,00.html.

Williamson, O. E. (1991). Strategizing, economizing, and economic organization. *Strategic Management Journal, 12* (special issue), 75–94.

Wilson, A. (2009). BHP sees unprecedented industry growth due to China, India demand. *The Australian*. Retrieved 22 October 2009, from www.theaustralian.news.com.au/business/news/bhp-sees-unprecedented-industry-growth-due-to-china-india-demand/story-e6frg90f-1225789943998.

Wilson, P. (2009, 6 June). Bitter rivals were talking since April. *The Australian*.

World Steel Association (2010). Crude steel statistics total 2009. Retrieved 15 July 2010, from http://www.worldsteel.org/?action=stats&type=steel&period=latest&month=13&year=2009.

The World Bank. (2010). *China quarterly update*, June 2010. Retrieved 1 August 2010, from http://web.worldbank.org/WBSITE/EXTERNAL/COUNTRIES/EAST ASIAPACIFICEXT/CHINAEXTN/0,,contentMDK:22502137~pagePK:1497618~ piPK:217854~theSitePK:318950,00.html.

World Trade Organisation (WTO). (2010). *Trade policy review: China revision.* WTO Trade Policy Review Body.

Wyatt, S. (2009a, 13–14 June). Beijing's rage will need to be assuaged. *The Weekend Australian Financial Review*, p. 23.

Wyatt, S. (2009b, 22 October). China's growth to keep demand on the boil. *The Australian Financial Review*, p. 30.

Yahoo Finance. (2010). *Rio Tinto Limited – Historical Prices* (Publication). Retrieved 1 October 2010 from http://au.finance.yahoo.com/q/hp?s=RIO.AX&a=00&b= 1&c=2008&d=11&e=31&f=2009&g=d.

Yeates, C. (2009, 5 June). Govt talks up Chinese investments. *The Sydney Morning Herald*. Retrieved 3 October 2009, from http://business.smh.com.au/business/ govt-talks-up-chinese-investments-20090605-bxz3.html.

Young, S., & Thyil, V. (2009). Anglo-based governance – rules versus flexibility: A continual debate. In S. Young (ed.), *Contemporary issues in international corporate governance* (pp. 11–23). Melbourne: Tilde University Press.

Yuan, C. (2010). Streamlining administrative systems for outward investment and supporting for Chinese firms' outward investment and M&A. In X. Chen & Z. Li (eds), *Merger & acquisition and restructure of Chinese enterprises* (pp. 200–213). Beijing: China Development Press.

Zhang, G. (2009). On the development and evolution of Chinese fundamental policies on outward direct investment. Retrieved 7 September 2009, from http://www.caitec.org.cn/c/cn/news/2009-08/10/news_1554.html.

Zhang, J. (2009, 2 April). Chinese seek to invest, not dominate. *The Australian.* Retrieved 1 October 2009, from www.theaustralian.news.com.au/story/0, 25197,25276296-7583,00.html.

Zhang, W. (2010). Chinese firms' cross-boarder merger and acquisitions: Status, overall evaluation and policy discussion. In X. Chen & Z. Li (eds), *Merger & acquisition and restructure of Chinese enterprises* (pp. 172–187). Beijing: China Development Press.

Zappone, C. (2009, 5 June). Iron ore behemoth bad news for China. *The Sydney Morning Herald*. Retrieved 2 October 2009, from http://business.smh.com.au/ business/iron-ore-behemoth-bad-news-for-china-20090605-by01.html.

# Index